ISBN 978-1-390-98419-4
PIBN 11188596

1 MONTH OF
FREE
READING

at
www.ForgottenBooks.com

By purchasing this book you are eligible for one month membership to ForgottenBooks.com, giving you unlimited access to our entire collection of over 1,000,000 titles via our web site and mobile apps.

To claim your free month visit: www.forgottenbooks.com/free1188596

English
Français
Deutsche
Italiano
Español
Português

www.forgottenbooks.com

Mythology Photography **Fiction**
Fishing Christianity **Art** Cooking
Essays Buddhism Freemasonry
Medicine **Biology** Music **Ancient
Egypt** Evolution Carpentry Physics
Dance Geology **Mathematics** Fitness
Shakespeare **Folklore** Yoga Marketing
Confidence Immortality Biographies
Poetry **Psychology** Witchcraft
Electronics Chemistry History **Law**
Accounting **Philosophy** Anthropology
Alchemy Drama Quantum Mechanics
Atheism Sexual Health **Ancient History**
Entrepreneurship Languages Sport
Paleontology Needlework Islam
Metaphysics Investment Archaeology
Parenting Statistics Criminology
Motivational

THE

P·HILOSOPHY

OF

SLEEP.

BY

ROBERT MACNISH,

AUTHOR OF "THE ANATOMY OF DRUNKENNESS," AND MEMBER OF THE FACULTY OF PHYSICIANS
AND SURGEONS OF GLASGOW.

HARTFORD:

WILLIAM ANDRUS.

1842.

PREFACE TO THE SECOND EDITION.

The present edition of THE PHILOSOPHY OF SLEEP is so different from its predecessor, that it may almost be regarded as a new treatise. The work has been, in a great measure, re-written, the arrangement altered, and a great accession made to the number of facts and cases : the latter, many of which are now published for the first time, will, I hope, add much to its value. Some of them have occurred in my own practice ; and for others, I am indebted to the kindness of several ingenious friends. Notwithstanding every care, the work is far from being what it ought to be, and what I could have wished ; but, imperfect as it is, it may, perhaps, stimulate some other inquirer to investigate the subject more deeply, and thus give rise to an abler disquisition. So far as I know, this is the only treatise in which an attempt is made to give a complete account of Sleep. The subject is not an easy one ; and, in the present state of our knowledge, moderate success is probably all that can be looked for.

In the first edition Dr Gall's theory, that the brain is composed of a plurality of organs, each organ being the seat of a particular mental faculty, was had recourse to for the purpose of explaining the different phenomena of Sleep ; in the present edition, this doctrine is more prominently brought forward. The great objection to the prevailing metaphysical systems is, that none of their positions can be proved ; and that scarcely two writers, agree upon any particular point. The disciples of Gall, on the one hand, assume that his system, having ascertainable facts to illustrate it, is at all times susceptible of demonstration—that nothing is taken for granted ; and that the inquirer has only to make an appeal to nature to ascertain its fallacy or its truth. The science is entirely one of observation : by that it must stand or fall, and by that alone ought it to be tested. The phrenological system appears to me the only one capable of affording a rational and easy explanation of all the phenomena of mind. It is impossible to account for dreaming, idiocy, spectral illusions, monomania, and partial genius in any other way. For these reasons, and for the much stronger one, that having studied the science for several years with a mind rather hostile than otherwise to its doctrines, and found that nature invariably vindicated their truth, I could come to no other conclusion than that of adopting them as a matter of belief, and employing them for the explanation of phenomena which they alone seem calculated to elucidate satisfactorily. The system of Gall is gaining ground rapidly among scientific men, both in Europe and America. Some of the ablest physiologists in both quarters of the globe have admitted its accordance with nature ; and, at this moment, it boasts a greater number of proselytes than at any previous period of its career. The prejudices still existing against it, result from ignorance of its real character. As people get better acquainted with the science, and the formidable evidence by which it is supported, they will think differently.

Many persons who deny the possibility of estimating individual character, with any thing like accuracy, by the shape of the head, admit the great phrenological principle that the brain is composed of a plurality of organs. To them, as well as to those who go a step farther, the doctrine laid down in the present work will appear satisfactory. An admission that the brain is the material apparatus by which the mind manifests itself, and that each mental faculty is displayed through the medium of a particular part of the brain, is all that is demanded in considering the philosophy of the science. These points are only to be ascertained by an appeal to nature. No man can wisely reject phrenology without making such an appeal.

PHILOSOPHY OF SLEEP.

CHAP. I.

INTRODUCTION.

Sleep is the intermediate state between wakefulness and death : wakefulness being regarded as the active state of all the animal and intellectual functions, and death as that of their total suspension.

Sleep exists in two states ; in the complete and the incomplete. The former is characterized by a torpor of the various organs which compose the brain, and by that of the external senses and voluntary motion. Incomplete sleep, or dreaming, is the active state of one or more of the cerebral organs while the remainder are in repose : the senses and the volition being either suspended or in action according to the circumstances of the case. Complete sleep is a temporary metaphysical death, though not an organic one—the heart and lungs performing their offices with their accustomed regularity under the control of the involuntary muscles.

Sleep is variously modified, as we shall fully explain hereafter, by health and disease. The sleep of health is full of tranquillity. In such a state we remain for hours at a time in unbroken repose, nature banqueting on its sweets, renewing its lost energies, and laying in a fresh store for the succeeding day. This accomplished, slumber vanishes like a vapour before the rising sun ; languor has been succeeded by strength ; and all the faculties, mental and corporeal, are recruited. In this delightful state, man assimilates most with that in which Adam sprang from his Creator's hands, fresh, buoyant, and vigourous ; rejoicing as a racer to run his course, with all his appetencies of enjoyment on edge, and all his feelings and faculties prepared for exertion.

Reverse the picture, and we have the sleep of disease. It is short, feverish, and unrefreshing, disturbed by frightful or melancholy dreams. The pulse is agitated, and, from nervous excitation, there are frequent startings and twitchings of the muscles. Nightmare presses like an incarnation of misery upon the frame—imagination, distempered by its connexion with physical disorder, ranging along the gloomy confines of terror, holding communication with hell and the grave, and throwing a discolouring shade over human life.

Night is the time for sleep ; and assuredly the hush of darkness as naturally courts to repose as meridian splendour flashes on us the necessity of our being up at our labour. In fact, there exists a strange, but certain sympathy between the periods of day and night, and the performance of particular functions during these periods. That this is not the mere effect of custom, might be readily demonstrated. All nature awakes with the rising sun. The birds begin to sing ; the bees to fly about with murmurous delight. The flowers which shut under the embrace of darkness, unfold themselves to the light. The cattle arise to crop the dewy herbage ; and ' man goeth forth to his labour until the evening.' At close of day, the reverse of all this activity and motion is observed. The songs of the woodland choir, one after another, become hushed, till at length

twilight is left to silence, with her own star and her falling dews. Action is succeeded by listlessness, energy by languor, the desire of exertion by the inclination for repose. Sleep, which shuns the light, embraces darkness, and they lie down together under the sceptre of midnight.

From the position of man in society, toil or employment of some kind or other is an almost necessary concomitant of his nature—being essential to healthy sleep, and consequently to the renovation of our bodily organs and mental faculties. But as no general rule can be laid down as to the quality and quantity of labour best adapted to particular temperaments, so neither can it be positively said how many hours of sleep are necessary for the animal frame. When the body is in a state of increase, as in the advance from infancy to boyhood, so much sleep is required, that the greater portion of existence may be fairly stated to be absorbed in this way. It is not mere repose from action that is capable of recruiting the wasted powers, or restoring the nervous energy., Along with this is required that oblivion of feeling and imagination which is essential to, and which in a great measure constitutes, sleep. But if in mature years the body is adding to its bulk by the accumulation of adipose matter, a greater tendency to somnolency occurs than when the powers of the absorbents and exhalents are so balanced as to prevent such accession of bulk. It is during the complete equipoise of these animal functions that health is enjoyed in greatest perfection ; for such a state presupposes exercise, temperance, and the tone of the stomach quite equal to the process of digestion.

Sleep and stupor have been frequently treated of by physiological writers as if the two states were synonymous. This is not the case. In both there is insensibility ; but it is easy to awake the person from sleep, and difficult, if not impossible, to arouse him from stupor. The former is a necessary law of the animal economy ; the latter is the result of diseased action.

Birth and death are the Alpha and Omega of existence ; and life, to use the language of Shakspeare, ' is rounded by a sleep.'

When we contemplate the human frame in a state of vigour, an impression is made on the mind that it is calculated to last forever. One set of organs is laying down particles and another taking them up, with such exquisite nicety, that for the continual momentary waste there is continual momentary repair ; and this is capable of going on with the strictest equality for a half a century.

What is life ? Those bodies are called living in which an appropriation of foreign matter is going on ; death is where this process is at an end. When we find blood in motion, the process of appropriation is going on. The circulation is the surest sign of life. Muscles retain irritability for an hour or two after circulation ceases, but irritability is not life. Death is owing to the absence of this process of appropriation.

Bichat has divided life into two varieties, the *organic* and the *animal*. The first is common to both vegetables and animals, the last is peculiar to animals alone. Organie life applies to the functions which nourish and sustain the object—animal life to those which make it a sentient being ; which give it thought, feeling, and motion, and bring it into communication with the surrounding world. The processes of assimilation and excretion exist both in animals and vegetables : the other vital processes are restricted solely to animals. The digestive organs, the kidneys, the heart, and the lungs, are the apparatus which carry into effect the organic life of animals. Those which manifest animal life are the brain, the organs of the senses, and the voluntary powers. Sleep is the suspension of animal life ; and during its continuance the creature is under the influence of organic life alone.

Notwithstanding the renovating influence of sleep, which apparently brings up the lost vigour of the frame to a particular standard, there is a power in animal life which leads it almost imperceptibly on from infancy to second childhood, or that of old age. This power, sleep, however, healthy, is incapable of counteracting. The skin wrinkles, and everywhere shows marks of the ploughshare of Saturn ; the adipose structure dissolves ; the bones become brittle ; the teeth decay or drop out ; the eye loses its exquisite sensibility to sight ; the ear to sound ; and the hair is bleached to whiteness. These are accompanied with a general decay of the intellectual faculties ; there is a loss of memory, and less sensibility to emotion ; the iris hues of fancy subside to twilight ; and the sphere of thought and action is narrowed. The principle of decay is implanted in our nature, and cannot be counteracted. Few people, however, die of mere decay, for death is generally accelerated by disease. From sleep we awake to exertion—from death not at all, at least on this side of time. Methuselah in ancient, and Thomas Parr in modern times, ate well, digested well, and slept well ; but at length they each died. Death is omnivorous. The worm which crawls on the highway and the monarch on his couch of state, are alike subjected to the same stern and inexorable law ; they alike become the victims of the universal tyrant.

CHAPTER II.

SLEEP IN GENERAL.

Every animal passes some portion of its time in sleep. This is a rule to which there is no exception ; although the kind of slumber and the degree of profoundness in which it exists in the different classes are extremely various. Some physiologists lay it down as a general rule, that the larger the brain of an animal the greater is the necessity for a considerable proportion of sleep. This, however, I suspect is not borne out by facts. Man, for instance, and some birds, such as the sparrow, have the largest brains in proportion to their size, and yet it is probable that they do not sleep so much as some other animals with much smaller brains. The serpent tribe, unless when stimulated by hunger, (in which case they will remain awake for days at a time waiting for their prey,) sleep much more than men or birds, and yet their brain are proportionally greatly inferior in size : the boa, after dining on a stag or goat, will continue in profound sleep for several days. Fishes,* indeed, whose brains are small, require little sleep ; but the same remark applies to birds,† which have

* As a proof that fishes sleep, Aristotle, who seems to have paid more attention to their habits than any modern author, states, that while in this condition they remain motionless, with the exception of a gentle movement of the tail—that they may then be readily taken by the hand, and that, if suddenly touched, they instantly start. The tunny, he adds, are surprised and surrounded by nets while asleep, which is known by their showing the white of their eyes.
† The sleep of some birds is amazingly light. Such is the

large brains, and whose slumber is neither profound nor of long continuance. The assertion, therefore, that the quantum of sleep has any reference to the size of the brain may be safely looked upon as unfounded. That it has reference to the quality of the brain is more likely, for we find that carnivorous animals sleep more than such as are herbivorous ; and it is probable that the texture, as well as form, of the brains of these two classes is materially different. This remark, with regard to the causes of the various proportions of sleep required by the carnivorous and herbivorous tribes, I throw out not as as a matter of certainty, but merely as surmise which seems to have considerable foundation in truth.

In proportion as man exceeds all other animals in the excellency of his physical organization, and an intellectual capability, we shall find that in him the various phenomena of sleep are exhibited in greater regularity and perfection. Sleep seems more indispensably requisite to man than to any other creature, if there can be supposed to exist any difference where its indispensability is universal, and where every animal must, in some degree or other, partake of it ; but, as regards, man, it is certain that he sustains any violation of the law ordaining regular periods of repose with less indifference than the lower grades of creation—that a certain proportion of sleep is more essential to his existence than theirs—that he has less power of enduring protracted wakefulness, or continuing in protracted sleep—and that he is more refreshed by repose and more exhausted by the want of it than they. The sleep of man, therefore, becomes a subject of deeper interest and curiosity than that of any other animal, both on account of the more diversified manner in which it displays itself, and the superior opportunity which exists of ascertaining the various phenomena which in the inferior animals can only be conjectured or darkly guessed at.

Sleep, being a natural process, takes place in general without any very apparent cause. It becomes, as it were, a habit, into which we insensibly fall at stated periods, as we fall into other natural or acquired habits. But it differs from the latter in this, that it cannot in any case be entirely dispensed with, although by custom we may bring ourselves to do with a much smaller portion than we are usually in the practice of indulging in. In this respect it bears a strong analogy to the appetite for food or drink. It has a natural tendency to recur every twenty-four hours, and the periods of its accession coincide with the return of night.

But though sleep becomes a habit into which we would naturally drop without any obvious, or very easily discovered cause, still we can often trace the origin of our slumbers ; and we are all acquainted with many circumstances which either produce or heighten them. I shall mention a few of these causes.

Heat has a strong tendency to produce sleep. We often witness this in the summer season ; sometimes in the open air, but more frequently at home, and above all in a crowded meeting. In the latter case the soporific tendency is greatly increased by the impurity of the air. A vitiated atmosphere is strongly narcotic, and when combined with heat and monotony, is apt to induce slumber, not less remarkable for the rapidity of its accession than its overpowering character. In such a situation, the mind in a few minutes ceases to act, and sinks into a state of overpowering oblivion. The slumber, however, not being a natural one, and seldom occurring at the usual period, is generally short : it rarely exceeds an hour ; and when the person awakes from it, so far from being refreshed, he is unusually dull, thirsty, and feverish, and finds more than common. case with the goose which is disturbed by the slightest noise, and more useful than any watch-dog for giving warning of danger. It was the cackling of the sacred geese that saved the capitol of Rome from the soldiers of Brennus, when the watch-dogs failed to discover the approach of an enemy.

mon difficulty in getting his mental powers into their usual state of activity.

A heated church and a dull sermon are almost sure to provoke sleep. There are few men whose powers are equal to the task of opposing the joint operation of two such potent influences. They act on the spirit like narcotics, and the person seems as if involved in a cloud of aconite or belladonna. The heat of the church might be resisted, but the sermon is irresistable. Its monotony falls in leaden accents upon the ear, and soon subdues the most powerful attention. Variety, whether of sight or sound, prevents sleep, while monotony of all kinds is apt to induce it. The murmuring of a river, the sound of a Eolian harp, the echo of a distant cascade, the ticking of a clock, the hum of bees under a burning sun, and the pealing of a remote bell, all exercise the same influence. So conscious was Boerhaave of the power of monotony, that in order to procure sleep for a patient, he directed water to be placed in such a situation as to drop continually on a brass pan. When there is no excitement, sleep is sure to follow. We are all kept awake by some mental or bodily stimulus, and when that is removed our wakefulness is at an end. Want of stimulus, especially in a heated atmosphere, produces powerful effects; but where sufficient stimulus exists, we overcome the effects of the heat, and keep awake in spite of it. Thus, in a crowded church, where a dull, inanimate preacher would throw the congregation into a deep slumber, such a man as Massilon, or Chalmers, would keep them in a state of keen excitement. He would arrest their attention, and counteract whatever tendency to sleep would otherwise have existed. In like manner, a prosing, monotonous, long-winded acquaintance is apt to make us doze, while another of a lively, energetic conversation keeps us brisk and awake. It will generally be found that the reasoning faculties are those which are soonest prostrated by slumber, and the imaginative the least so. A person would more readily fall asleep if listening to a profound piece of argumentation, than to a humorous or fanciful story; and probably more have slumbered over the pages of Bacon and Locke, than over those of Shakspeare and Milton.

Cold produces sleep as well as heat, but to do so a very low temperature is necessary, particularly with regard to the human race; for, when cold is not excessive, it prevents, instead of occasioning slumber: in illustration of which, I may mention the case of several unfortunate women, who lived thirty-four days in a small room overwhelmed with the snow, and who scarcely slept during the whole of that period. In very northern and southern latitudes, persons often lose their lives by lying down in a state of drowsiness, occasioned by intense cold. The winter sleep, or hybernation of animals, arises from cold; but as this species of slumber is of a very peculiar description; I have discussed it separately in another part of the work.

The finished gratification of all ardent desires has the effect of inducing slumber; hence, after any keen excitement, the mind becomes exhausted, and speedily relapses into this state. Attention to a single sensation has the same effect. This has been exemplified in the case of all kinds of monotony, where there is a want of variety to stimulate the ideas, and keep them on the alert. 'If the mind,' says Cullen, 'is attached to a single sensation, it is brought very nearly to the state of the total absence of impression;' or, in other words, to the state most closely bordering upon sleep. Remove those stimuli which keep it employed, and sleep ensues at any time.

Any thing which mechanically determines the blood to the brain, acts in a similar manner, such as whirling round for a great length of time, ascending a lofty mountain, or swinging to and fro. The first and last of these actions give rise to much giddiness, followed by intense slumber, and at last by death, if they be

continued very long. By lying flat upon a millstone while performing its evolutions, sleep is soon produced, and death, without pain, would be the result, if the experiment were greatly protracted. Apoplexy, which consists of a turgid state of the cerebral vessels, produces perhaps the most complete sleep that is known, in so far that, while it continues it is utterly impossible to waken the individual: no stimulus, however powerful, has any influence in arousing his dormant faculties. When the circulating mass in the brain is diminished beyond a certain extent, it has the same effect on the opposite state; whence excessive loss of blood excites sleep.

Opium, hyoscyamus, aconite, belladonna, and the whole tribe of narcotics, induce sleep, partly by a specific power which they exert on the nerves of the stomach, and partly by inducing an apoplectic state of the brain. The former effect is occasioned by a moderate—the latter by an over dose.

A heavy meal, especially if the stomach is at the same time weak, is apt to induce sleep. In ordinary circumstances, the nervous energy or sensorial power of this viscus is sufficient to carry on its functions; but when an excess of food is thrown upon it, it is then unable to furnish, from its own resources, the powers requisite for digestion. In such a case it draws upon the whole body—upon the chest, the limbs, &c., from whence it is supplied with the sensorial power of which it is deficient; and is thus enabled to perform that which by its own unassisted means it never could have accomplished. But mark the consequences of such accommodation! Those parts, by communicating vigor to the stomach, become themselves debilitated in a corresponding ratio, and get into a state analogous to that from which they had extricated this viscus. The extremities become cold, the respiration heavy and stertorous, and the brain torpid. In consequence of the torpor of the brain, sleep ensues. It had parted with that portion of sensorial energy which kept it awake, and by supplying another organ is itself thrown into the state of sleep. It is a curious fact, that the feeling of sleep is most strong while the food remains on the stomach, shortly after the accession of the digestive process, and before that operation which converts the nourishment into chyle has taken place.

When, therefore, the sensorial power is sufficiently exhausted, we naturally fall asleep. As this exhaustion, however, is a gradual process, so is that of slumber. Previous to its accession, a feeling of universal lassitude prevails, and exhibits itself in yawning,[*] peevishness, heaviness, and weakness of the eyes; indifference to surrounding objects, and all the characteristics of fatigue. If the person be seated, his head nods and droops; the muscles become relaxed; and, when circumstances admit of it, the limbs are thrown into the recumbent position, or that most favorable for complete inaction. The senses then become unconscious of impressions, and, one after the other, part with sensation; the sight first, then taste, smell, hearing, and touch, all in regular order. The brain does not all at once glide into repose: its different organs being successively thrown into this state; one dropping asleep, then another, then a third, till the whole are locked up in the fetters of slumber. This gradual process of intellectual obliteration is a sort of confused dream—a mild delirium which always precedes sleep. The ideas have no resting-place, but float about in the con-

* We yawn before falling asleep and when we wake; yawning, therefore, precedes and follows sleep. It seems an effort of nature to restore the just equilibrium between the flexor and extensor muscles. The former have a natural predominancy in the system; and on their being fatigued, we, by an effort of the will, or rather by a species of instinct, put the latter into action for the purpose of redressing the balance, and poising the respective muscular powers. We do the same thing on awaking, or even on getting up from a recumbent posture—the flexors in such circumstances having prevailed over the extensors, which were in a great measure inert.

fused tabernacle of the mind, giving rise to images of the most perplexing description. In this state they continue for some time, until, as sleep becomes more profound, the brain is left to thorough repose, and they disappear altogether.

Sleep produces other important changes in the system. The rapidity of the circulation is diminished, and, as a natural consequence, that of respiration : the force of neither function, however, is impaired ; but, on the contrary, rather increased. Vascular action is diminished in the brain and organs of volition, while digestion and absorption . shall proceed with increased energy. The truth of most of these propositions it is not difficult to establish.

The diminished quickness of the circulation is shown in the pulse, which is slower and fuller than in the waking state ; that of respiration in the more deliberate breathing which accompanies sleep. Diminished action of the brain is evident from the abolition of its functions, as well as direct evidence. A case is related by Blumenbach, of a person who had been trepanned, and whose brain was observed to sink when he was asleep, and swell out when he was awake. As for the lessened vascular action in the voluntary powers, this is rendered obvious by the lower temperature on the surface which takes place during the slumbering state. Moreover, in low typhus, cynanche maligna, and other affections attended with a putrid diathesis, the petechiæ usually appear during sleep when the general circulation is least vigorous, while the paroxysms of reaction or delirium take place, for the most part, in the morning when it is in greater strength and activity.

In some individuals the stronger and more laborious respiration of sleep is made manifest by that stertorous sound commonly denominated snoring. Stout apoplectic people—those who snuff much or sleep with their mouths open, are most given to this habit. It seems to arise principally from the force with which the air is drawn into the lungs in sleep. The respiratory muscles being less easily excited during this state do not act so readily, and the air is consequently admitted into the chest with some degree of effort. This, combined with the relaxed state of the fauces, gives rise to the stertorous noise. Snuffing, by obstructing the nasal passages and thus rendering breathing more difficult, has the same effect ; consequently snuffers are very often great snorers. The less rapidly the blood is propelled through the lungs, the slower is the respiration, and the louder the stertor becomes. Apoplexy, by impairing the sensibility of the respiratory organs, and thus reducing the frequency of breathing, produces snoring to a great extent ; and all cerebral congestions have, to a greater or less degree, the same effect.

That sleep increases absorption is shown in the disappearance or diminution of many swellings, especially œdema of the extremities, which often disappears in the night and recurs in the daytime, even when the patient keeps his bed, a proof that its disappearance does not not always depend on the position of the body :. that it increases digestion, and, as a natural consequence, nutrition, is rendered probable by many circumstances : hence it is the period in which the regeneration of the body chiefly takes place. Were there even no augmentation given to the assimilative function, as is maintained by Broussais and some other physiologists, it is clear that the body would be more thoroughly nourished than when awake, for all those actions which exhaust it in the latter condition are quiescent, and it remains in a state of rest, silently accumulating power, without expending any.

Sleep lessens all the secretions, with one exception— that of the skin. The urinary, salivary, and bronchial discharges, the secretions from the nose, eyes, and ears, are all formed less copiously than in the waking state. The same rule holds with regard to other secretions—

hence diarrhœa, menorrhagia, &c., are checked during the intervals of slumber.

From the diminished vascular action going on upon the surface, we would be apt to expect a decrease of perspiration, but the reverse is the case. Sleep relaxes the cutaneous vessels, and they secrete more copiously than in the waking state. According to Sanctorius, a person sleeping some hours undisturbed, will perspire insensibly twice as much as one awake. This tendency of sleep to produce perspiration is strikingly exhibited in diseases of debility ; whence the nocturnal sweats so prevailing and so destructive in all cachectic affections. Sanctorius farther states, that the insensible perspiration is not only more abundant, but less acrimonious during sleep than in the waking state ; that, if diminished during the day, the succeeding sleep is disturbed and broken, and that the diminution in consequence of too short a sleep, disposes to fever, unless the equilibrium is established, on the following day, by a more copious perspiration.

Sleep produces peculiar effects upon the organs of vision. A priori, we might expect that, during this state, the pupil would be largely dilated in consequence of the light being shut out. On opening the eyelids cautiously it is seen to be contracted ; it then quivers with an irregular motion, as if disposed to dilate, but at length ceases to move, and remains in a contracted state till the person awakes. This fact I have often verified by inspecting the eyes of children. Sleep also communicates to these organs a great accession of sensibility, so much so, that they are extremely dazzled by a clear light. This, it is true, happens on coming out of a dark into a light room, or opening our eyes upon the sunshine even when we are awake, but the effect is much stronger when we have previously been in deep slumber.

Sleep may be natural or diseased—the former arising from such causes as exhaust the sensorial power, such as fatigue, pain, or protracted anxiety of mind ; the latter from cerebral congestion, such as apoplexy or plethora. The great distinction between these varieties is, that the one can be broken by moderate stimuli, while the other requires either excessive stimuli, or the removal of the particular cause which gave rise to it.

During complete sleep no sensation whatever is experienced by the individual : he neither feels pain, hunger, thirst, nor the ordinary desires of nature. He may be awakened to a sense of such feelings, but during perfect repose he has no consciousness whatever of their existence—if they can indeed be said to exist where they are not felt. For the same reason, we may touch him without his feeling it ; neither is he sensible to sounds, to light, or to odours. When, however, the slumber is not very profound, he may hear music or conversation, and have a sense of pain, hunger, and thirst ; and, although not awakened by such circumstances, may recollect them afterwards. These impressions, caught by the senses, often give rise to the most extraordinary mental combinations, and form the groundwork of the most elaborate dreams.

I am of opinion that we rarely pass the whole of any one night in a state of perfect slumber. My reason for this supposition is, that we very seldom remain during the whole of that period in the position in which we fall asleep. This change of posture must have been occasioned by some emotion, however obscure, affecting the mind, and through it the organs of volition, whereas in complete sleep we experience no emotion whatever.

The position usually assumed in sleep has been mentioned ; but sleep may ensue in any posture of the body ; persons fall asleep on horseback, and continue riding in this state for a long time without being awakened. Horses sometimes sleep for hours in the standing posture ; and the circumstance of somnambulism shows that the same thing may occur in the human race.

Some animals, such as the hare, sleep with their eyes open; and I have known similar instances in the human subject. But the organ is dead to the ordinary stimulus of light, and sees no more than if completely shut.

Animals which prey by night, such as the cat, hyena, &c., pass the greater part of their time in sleep; while those that do not, continue longer awake than asleep. The latter slumber part of the night and continue awake so long as the sun continues above the horizon. The propensity of the former to sleep in the day time seems to proceed from the structure of their eyes; as they see much better in darkness than in light, and consequently pass in slumber that period in which their vision is of least avail to them. It is a very curious fact, however, that these animals, when kept in captivity, reverse the order of their nature, and remain awake by day while they sleep by night. This fact has been ascertained in the menagerie at Paris.' In such cases I apprehend that some corresponding change must take place in the structure of the eyes, assimilating them to those animals which naturally sleep by night.

M. Castel observes,* that the greater part of animals sleep longer in winter than in summer. It is precisely on account of perspiration that in the first of these seasons sleep is more necessary than in the second. In winter, the want of perspiration during the day is furnished in sleep; in summer, the diurnal sweat supplies that of the night, and renders' much sleep less uecessary. In other words, during summer the perspiration is so much excited by atmospheric temperature, that a shorter time is sufficient to give issue to the fluids which have to be expelled by this means. For the same reason, the inhabitants of very cold climates sleep more than those who live in the warmer latitudes.

The profoundness of sleep differs greatly in different individuals. The repose of some is extremely deep; that of others quite the reverse. One will scarcely obey the roar of cannon; another will start at the chirping of a cricket or the faintest dazzling of the moonbeams. Heavy-minded, phlegmatic people generally belong to the former class; the irritable, the nervous, and the hypochondriac to the latter, although we shall at times find the cases reversed with regard to the nature of sleep enjoyed by these different temperaments. Man is almost the only animal in whom much variety is to be found in this respect. The lower grades are distinguished by a certain character, so far as their slumber is concerned, and this character runs through the whole race; thus, all hares, cats, &c., are light sleepers; all bears, turtles, badgers, &c., are the reverse. In man, the varieties are infinite. Much of this depends upon the age and temperament of the individual, and much upon custom.

The profoundness of sleep differs also during the same night. For the first four or five hours, the slumber is much heavier than towards morning. The cause of such difference is obvious; for we go to bed exhausted by previous fatigue, and consequently enjoy sound repose, but, in the course of a few hours, the necessity for this gradually abates, and the slumber naturally becomes lighter.

That sleep from which we are easily roused is the healthiest: very profound slumber partakes of the nature of apoplexy.

On being suddenly awakened from a profound sleep our ideas are exceedingly confused; and it is sometime before we can be made to comprehend what is said to us. For some moments, we neither see, nor hear, nor think without our usual distinctness, and are, in fact, in a state of temporary reverie.

When there is a necessity for our getting up at a cer-

* 'Journal Complémentaire.'

tain hour, the anxiety of mind thus produced not only prevents the sleep from being very profound, but retards its accession; and even after it does take place, we very seldom oversleep ourselves, and are almost sure to be awake at, or before, the stipulated time.

Shortly after falling asleep, we often awake with a sudden start, having the mind filled with painful impressions; although we often find it impossible to say to what subject they refer. Some persons do this regularly every night, and there can be no doubt that it proceeds from the mind being tortured by some distressing vision; which, however, has faded away without leaving behind it any feeling, save one of undefinable melancholy. There are some persons who are sure to be aroused in this startling and painful manner if they happen to fall asleep in the position in which they at first lay down, who nevertheless escape if they turn themselves once or twice before falling into repose. This fact we must take as we find it: any explanation as to its proximate cause seems quite impracticable.

Disease exercises a powerful influence upon sleep. All affections attended with acute pain prevent it, in consequence of the undue accumulation of sensorial power, which they occasion. This is especially the case where there is much *active* determination of blood to the head, as in phrenetic affections, and fevers in general.

Sleep is always much disturbed in hydrothorax; and almost every disease affects it, more or less; some preventing it altogether, some limiting the natural proportion, some inducing fearful dreams, and all acting with a power proportioned to the direct or indirect influence which they exercise upon the sensorium.

From the increased irritability of the frame and relaxed state of the cutaneous vessels during sleep, the system at that time is peculiarly apt to be acted upon by all impressions, especially of cold; and those who fall asleep exposed to a current of air are far more apt to feel the consequences thereof than if they were broad awake. By a law of nature the sensibility of the system is increased by any suspension of the mental or voluntary powers, for the same reason that it is diminished, while these powers resume their action. In drunkenness, for instance, where the mind is vehemently excited, we are far less susceptible of cold than in a state of sobriety.

Sleep is much modified by habit. Thus, an old artillery-man often enjoys tranquil repose, while the cannon are thundering around him; an engineer has been known to fall asleep within a boiler, while his fellows were beating it on the outside with their ponderous hammers; and the repose of a miller is nowise incommoded by the noise of his mill. Sound ceases to be a stimulus to such men, and what would have proved an inexpressible annoyance to others, is by them altogether unheeded. It is common for carriers to sleep on horseback, and coachman on their coaches. During the battle of the Nile, some boys were so exhausted, that they fell asleep on the deck amid the deafening thunder of that dreadful engagement. Nay, silence itself may become a stimulus, while sound ceases to be so. Thus, a miller being very ill, his mill was stopped that he might not be disturbed by its noise; but this so far from inducing sleep, prevented it altogether; and it did not take place till the mill was set a-going again. For the same reason, the manager of some vast iron-work who, slept close to them amid the incessant din of hammers forges, and blast furnaces, would awake if there was any cessation of the noise during the night. To carry the illustration still farther, it has been noticed, that a person who falls asleep near a church, the bell of which is ringing, may hear the sound during the whole of his slumber, and be nevertheless aroused by its sudden cessation. Here the sleep must have been imperfect, otherwise he would have been insensible to the sound: the noise of the bell was no stimulus; it was its cessation which, by breaking the monotony, became so, and caused the sleeper to awake.

The effects of habit may be illustrated in various ways. 'If a person, for instance, is accustomed to go to rest exactly at nine o'clock in the evening, and to rise again at six in the morning, though the time of going to sleep be occasionally protracted till twelve, he will yet awake at his usual hour of six ; or, if his sleep be continued by darkness, quietude or other causes, till the day be farther advanced, the desire for sleep will return in the evening at nine.'

Persons who are much in the habit of having their repose broken, seldom sleep either long or profoundly, however much they may be left undisturbed. This is shown in the cases of soldiers and seamen, nurses, mothers, and keepers.

Seamen and soldiers on duty can, from habit, sleep when they will, and wake when they will. The Emperor Napoleon was a striking instance of this fact. Captain Barclay, when performing his extraordinary feat in walking a mile an hour for a thousand successive hours, obtained at last such a mastery over himself, that he fell asleep the instant he lay down. Some persons cannot sleep from home, or on a different bed from their usual one : some cannot sleep on a hard, others on a soft bed. A low pillow prevents sleep in some, a high one in others. The faculty of remaining asleep for a great length of time, is possessed by some individuals. Such was the case with Quin, the celebrated player, who could slumber for twenty-four hours successively—with Elizabeth Orvin, who spent three-fourths of her life in sleep—with Elizabeth Perkins, who slept for a week or a fortnight at a time—with Mary Lyall, who did the same for six successive weeks—and with many others, more or less remarkable. In Bowyer's life of Beattie, a curious anecdote is related of Dr Reid, viz., that he could take as much food and immediately afterwards as much sleep as were sufficient for two days.

A phenomenon of an opposite character is also sometimes observed, for there are individuals who can subsist upon a surprisingly small portion of sleep. The celebrated General Elliot was an instance of this kind : he never slept more than four hours out of the twenty-four. In all other respects he was strikingly abstinent ; his food consisting wholly of bread, water, and vegetables. In a letter communicated to Sir John Sinclair, by John Gordon, Esq. of Swiney, Caithness, mention is made of a person named James Mackay, of Skerray, who died in Strathnaver in the year 1797, aged ninety-one : he only slept, on an average, four hours in the twenty-four, and was a remarkably robust and healthy man. Frederick the Great, of Prussia, and the illustrious surgeon, John Hunter, only slept five hours in the same period ; and the sleep of the active-minded is always much less than that of the listless and indolent. The celebrated French General Pichegru, informed Sir Gilbert Blane, that, during a whole year's campaigns, he had not above one hour's sleep in the twenty-four. I know a lady who never sleeps above half an hour at a time, and the whole period of whose sleep does not exceed three or four hours in the twenty-four ; and yet she is in the enjoyment of excellent health. Gooch gives an instance of a man who slept only for fifteen minutes out of the twenty-four hours, and even this was only a kind of dozing, and not a perfect sleep: notwithstanding which, he enjoyed good health, and reached his seventy-third year. I strongly suspect there must be some mistake in this case, for it is not conceivable that human nature could subsist upon such a limited portion of repose. Instances have been related of persons who *never slept* ; but these must be regarded as purely fabulous.

The period of life modifies sleep materially. When a man is about his grand climacteric, or a few years beyond it, he slumbers less than at any former period of life ; but very young children always sleep away the most of their time. At this early period, the nerves being extremely sensitive and unaccustomed to impressions, become easily fatigued. As the children get older, the brain besides becoming habituated to impressions, acquires an accession of sensorial power, which tends to keep it longer awake. For the first two or three years, children sleep more than once in the twenty-four hours. The state of the fœtus has been denominated, by some writers, a continued sleep, but the propriety of this definition may be doubted ; for the mind having never yet manifested itself, and the voluntary organs never having been exercised, can hardly be said to exist in slumber, a condition which supposes a previous waking state of the functions. Middle-aged persons who lead an active life, seldom sleep above eight or nine hours in the twenty-four, however much longer they may lie in bed ; while a rich, lazy, and gormandizing citizen will sleep twelve or thirteen hours at a time.

Sleep is greatly modified in old people. They usually slumber little, and not at all profoundly. Sometimes, however, when they get into a state of dotage, in consequence of extreme old age, the phenomena of childhood once more appear, and they pass the greater part of their time in sleep. The repose of the aged is most apt to take place immediately after taking food, while they often solicit it in vain at that period at which, during the former years of their lives, they had been accustomed to enjoy it. The celebrated de Moivre slept twenty hours out of the twenty-four, and Thomas Parr latterly slept away by far the greater part of his existence.

Those who eat heartily, and have strong digestive powers, usually sleep much. The great portion of sleep required by infants is owing, in part, to the prodigious activity of their digestive powers. The majority of animals sleep after eating, and man has a strong tendency to do the same thing, especially when oppressed with heat. In the summer season, a strong inclination is often felt, to sleep after dinner, when the weather is very warm.

A heavy meal, which produces no uneasy feeling while the person, will often do so if he fall asleep. According to Dr. Darwin, this proceeds from the sensorial actions being increased, when the volition is suspended. The digestion from this circumstance goes on with increased rapidity. 'Heat is produced in the system faster than it is expended ; and, operating on the sensitive actions, carries them beyond the limitations of pleasure, producing, as is common in such cases, increased frequency of pulse.' In this case, incomplete sleep is supposed, for. when the slumber is perfect, no sensation whatever, either painful or the reverse, can be experienced.

In recovering from long protracted illness, accompanied with great want of rest, we generally sleep much—far more, indeed, than during the most perfect health. This seems to be a provision of nature for restoring the vigour which had been lost during disease, and bringing back the body to its former state. So completely does this appear to be the case, that as soon as a thorough restoration to health takes place, the portion of sleep diminishes till it is brought to the standard at which it originally stood before the accession of illness.

After continuing a certain time asleep, we awake, stretch ourselves, open our eyes, rub them, and yawn several times. At the moment of awaking, there is some confusion of ideas, but this immediately wears away. The mental faculties from being in utter torpor, begin to act one after the other ;[*] the senses do the

[*] 'In the gradual progress from intense sleep, when there can be no dream, to the moment of perfect vigilance, see what occurs. The first cerebral organ that awakes enters into the train of thinking connected with its faculty : some kind of *dream* is the result ; as organ after organ awakes, the dream becomes more vivid ; and as the number of active organs increases, so

same. At last, the mind, the senses, and the locomotion being completely restored, what are our sensations? Instead of the listlessness, lassitude, and general fatigue experienced on lying down, we feel vigorous and refreshed. The body is stronger, the thoughts clearer and more composed; we think coolly, clearly, rationally, and can often comprehend with ease what baffled us on the previous night.

One or two other points remain to be noticed. On awaking, the eyes are painfully affected by the light, but this shortly wears away, and we then feel them stronger than when we went to bed. The muscular power, also, for a few seconds, is affected. We totter when we get up; and if we lay hold of any thing, the hand lacks its wonted strength. This, however, as the current of nervous energy is restored throughout the muscles, immediately disappears; and we straightway possess redoubled vigour. On examining the urine, we find that it is higher in its colour than when we lay down. The saliva is more viscid, the phlegm harder and tougher, the eyes glutinous, and the nostrils dry. If we betake ourselves to the scale, we find that our weight has diminished in consequence of the nocturnal perspirations; while, by subjecting our stature to measurement, we shall see that we are taller by nearly an inch than on the preceding night. This fact was correctly ascertained in a great variety of instances, by Mr. Wasse, Rector of Aynho in Northumberland; and is sufficiently accounted for by the intervertebral cartilages recovering their elasticity, in consequence of the bodily weight being taken off them during the recumbent posture of sleep.

Such are the leading phenomena of sleep. With regard to the purposes which it serves in the economy, these are too obvious to require much detail. Its main object is to restore the strength expended during wakefulness; to recruit the body by promoting nutrition and giving rest to the muscles; and to renovate the mind by the repose which it affords the brain. Action is necessarily followed by exhaustion; sleep by checking the one restrains the other, and keeps the animal machine in due vigour. Mr Carmichael supposes sleep to be the period when assimilation goes on in the brain. In this respect, I believe that the brain is not differently situated from the rest of the body. There, as elsewhere, the assimilative process proceeds both in the slumbering and in the waking state; but that it is only at work in the brain during sleep analogy forbids us to admit. So long as circulation continues, a deposition of matter is going on; and circulation, we all know, is at work in the brain as in other organs, whether we be asleep or awake. According to Richerand, one of the great purposes, served by sleep, is to diminish the activity of the circulation, which a state of wakefulness has the invariable effect of increasing. 'The exciting causes' he observes, 'to which our organs are subject during the day, tend progressively to increase their action. The throbbings of the heart, for instance, are more frequent at night than in the morning; and this action, gradually, accelerated, would soon be carried to such a degree of activity as to be inconsistent with life, if its velocity were not moderated at intervals by the recurrence of sleep.'

To detail the beneficent purposes served by sleep in the cure of diseases, as well as in health, would be a work of supererogation. They are felt and recognised by mankind as so indispensable to strength, to happiness, and to life itself, that he who dispenses with that portion of repose required by the wants of nature, is in reality curtailing the duration of its own existence.

does the complication of dreams; and if all the internal organs are awake, the man is still asleep until his awakening senses bring him into direct communication with the world.'

Carmichael's Memoir of Spurzheim, p. 92.

CHAPTER III.

DREAMING.

In perfect sleep, as we have elsewhere stated, there is a quiescence of all the organs which compose the brain; but when, in consequence of some inward excitement, one organ or more continues awake, while the remainder are in repose, a state of incomplete sleep is the result, and we have the phenomena of dreaming. If, for instance, any irritation, such as pain, fever, drunkenness, or a heavy meal, should throw the perceptive organs into a state of action while the reflecting ones continue asleep, we have a consciousness of objects, colors, or sounds being presented to us, just as if the former organs were actually stimulated by having such impressions communicated to them by the external senses;* while in consequence of the repose of the reflecting organs, we are unable to rectify the illusions, and conceive that the scenes passing before us, or the sounds that we hear, have a real existence. This want of mutual co-operation between the different organs of the brain accounts for the disjointed nature, the absurdities, and incoherencies of dreams.

Many other doctrines have been started by philosophers, but I am not aware of any which can lay claim even to plausibility; some, indeed, are so chimerical, and so totally unsupported by evidence, that it is difficult to conceive how they ever entered into the imaginations of their founders. Baxter, for instance, in his 'Treatise on the Immortality of the Soul,' endeavours to show that dreams are produced by the agency of some spiritual beings, who either amuse, or employ themselves seriously, in engaging mankind in all those imaginary transaction with which they are employed in dreaming. The theory of Democritus and Lucretius is equally whimsical. They accounted for dreams by supposing that spectres, and simulacra of corporeal things constantly emitted from them, and floating up and down in the air, come and assault the soul in sleep. The most prevailing doctrine is that of the Cartesians, who supposed that the mind was continually active in sleep; in other words, that during this state we were always dreaming. Hazlitt, in his 'Round Table,' has taken the same view of the subject, and alleges, that if a person is awakened at any given time and asked what he has been dreaming about, he will at once be recalled to a train of associations with which his mind has been busied previously. Unfortunately for this theory it is not sustained by facts; experiments made on purpose having shown that, though in some few instances, the individual had such a consciousness of dreaming as is described, yet in the great majority he had no consciousness of any thing of the kind. The doctrine, therefore, so far as direct evidence is concerned must fall to the ground; and yet, unsupported as it is either by proof or analogy, this is the fashionable hypothesis of the schools, and the one most in vogue among our best metaphysical writers.

There is a strong analogy between dreaming and insanity. Dr. Abercrombie defines the difference between the two states to be, that in the latter the erroneous impression, being permanent, affects the conduct; whereas in dreaming, no influence on the conduct is produced, because the vision is dissipated on awaking. This definition is nearly, but not wholly correct; for in somnambulism and sleep-talking, the conduct is influenced by the prevailing dream. Dr. Rush has, with great shrewdness, remarked, that a dream may be considered as a transient paroxysm of delirium, and delirium as a permanent dream.

Man is not the only animal subject to dreaming. We have every reason to believe that many of the lower

* This internal stimulation of particular organs without the concurrence of outward impressions by the senses, is more fully stated under the head of Spectral Illusions.

animals do the same. Horses neigh and rear, and dogs bark and growl in their sleep. Probably, at such times, the remembrance of the chase or the combat was passing through the minds of these creatures; and they also not unfrequently manifest signs of fear, joy, playfulness, and almost every other passion.* Ruminating animals, such as the sheep and cow, dream less; but even they are sometimes so affected, especially at the period of rearing their young. The parrot is said to dream, and I should suppose some other birds do the same. Indeed the more intellectual the animal is, the more likely it is to be subject to dreaming. Whether fishes dream it is impossible to conjecture : nor can it be guessed, with any thing like certainty, at what point in the scale of animal intellect, the capability of dreaming ceases, although it is very certain there is such a point. I apprehend that dreaming is a much more general law than is commonly supposed, and that many animals dream which are never suspected of doing so.

Some men are said never to dream, and others only when their health is disordered : Dr. Beattie mentions a case of the latter description. For many years before his death, Dr. Reid had no consciousness of ever having dreamed ; and Mr. Locke takes notice of a person who never did so till his twenty-sixth year, when he began to dream in consequence of having had a fever. It is not impossible, however, but that, in these cases, the individuals may have had dreams from the same age as other people, and under the same circumstances, although probably they were of so vague a nature, as to have soon faded away from the memory.

Dreams occur more frequently in the morning than in the early part of the night ; a proof that the sleep is much more profound in the latter period than in the former. Towards morning, the faculties, being refreshed by sleep, are more disposed to enter into activity ; and this explains why, as we approach the hours of waking, our dreams are more fresh and vivid. Owing to the comparatively active state of the faculties, morning dreams are more rational—whence the old adage, that such dreams are true.

Children dream almost from their birth ; and if we may judge from what, on many occasions, they endure during sleep, we must suppose that the visions which haunt their young minds are often of a very frightful kind. Children, from many causes, are more apt to have dreams of terror than adults. In the first place, they are peculiarly subject to various diseases, such as teething, convulsions, and bowel complaints, those fertile sources of mental terror in sleep; and, in the second place, their minds are exceedingly susceptible of dread in all forms, and prone to be acted on by it, whatever shape it assume. Many of the dreams experienced at this early period, leave au indelible impression upon the mind. They are remembered in after-years with feelings of pain ; and, blending with the more delightful reminiscences of childhood, demonstrate that this era, which we are apt to consider one varied scene of sunshine and happiness, had, as well as future life, its shadows of melancholy, and was not untinged with hues of sorrow and care. The sleep of infancy, therefore, is far from being that ideal state of felicity which is commonly supposed. It is haunted with its own terrors, even more than that of adults ; and, if many of the visions which people it are equally delightful, there can be little doubt that it is also tortured by dreams of a more painful character than often fall to the share of after-life.

In health, when the mind is at ease, we seldom dream ; and when we do so our visions are generally of a pleasing character. In disease, especially of the

brain, liver, and stomach, dreams are both common and of a very distressing kind.

Some writers imagine, that as we grow older, our dreams become less absurd and inconsistent, but this is extremely doubtful. Probably, as we advance in life, we are less troubled with these phenomena than at the period of youth, when imagination is full of activity, and the mind peculiarly liable to impressions of every kind ; but when they do take place, we shall find them equally preposterous, unphilosophical, and crude, with those which haunted our early years. Old people dream more, however, than the middle-aged, owing doubtless to the more broken and disturbed nature of their repose.

I believe that dreams are uniformly the resuscitation or re-embodiment of thoughts which have formerly, in some shape or other, occupied the mind. They are old ideas revived either in an entire state, or heterogeneously mingled together. I doubt if it be possible for a person to have, in a dream, any idea whose elements did not, in some form, strike him at a previous period. If these break loose from their connecting chain, and become jumbled together incoherently, as is often the case, they give rise to absurd combinations; but the elements still subsist, and only manifest themselves in a new and unconnected shape. As this is an important point, and one which has never been properly insisted upon, I shall illustrate it by an example. I lately dreamed that I walked upon the banks of the great canal in the neighbourhood of Glasgow. On the side opposite to that on which I was, and within a few feet of the water, stood the splendid portico of the Royal Exchange. A gentleman, whom I knew, was standing upon one of the steps, and we spoke to each other. I then lifted a large stone, and poised it in my hand, when he said that he was certain I could not throw it to a certain spot which he pointed out. I made the attempt, and fell short of the mark. At this moment, a well known friend came up, whom I knew to excel at *putting* the stone ; but, strange to say, he had lost both his legs, and walked upon wooden substitutes. This struck me as exceedingly curious ; for my impression was that he had only lost one leg, and had but a single wooden one. At my desire he took up the stone, and, without difficulty, threw it beyond the point indicated by the gentleman upon the opposite side of the canal. The absurdity of this dream is extremely glaring ; and yet, on strictly analyzing it, I find it to be wholly composed of ideas which passed through my mind on the previous day, assuming a new and ridiculous arrangement. I can compare it to nothing but to cross readings in the newspapers, or to that well known amusement which consists in putting a number of sentences, each written on a separate piece of paper, into a hat, shaking the whole, then taking them out one by one as they come, and seeing what kind of medley the heterogeneous compound will make, when thus fortuitously put together. For instance, I had, on the above day, taken a walk to the canal, along with a friend. On returning from it, I pointed out to him a spot where a new road was forming, and where, a few days before, one of the workmen had been overwhelmed by a quantity of rubbish falling upon him, which fairly chopped off one of his legs, and so much damaged the other that it was feared amputation would be necessary. Near this very spot there is a park, in which, about a month previously, I practised throwing the stone. On passing the Exchange on my way home, I expressed regret at the lowness of its situation, and remarked what a fine effect the portico would have were it placed upon more elevated ground. Such were the previous circumstances, and let us see how they bear upon the dream. In the first place, the canal appeared before me. 2. Its situation is an elevated one. 3. The portico of the exchange, occurring to my mind as being placed too low, became associated with the elevation of the canal,

* 'The stag-hounds, weary with the chase,
　Lay stretched upon the rushy floor,
　　And urged in dreams the forest race
From Teviot-stone to Eskdale moor.'
　　　　　　　Lay of the last Minstrel.

and I placed it close by on a similar altitude. 4. The gentleman I had been walking with, was the same whom, in the dream, I saw standing upon the steps of the portico. 5. Having related to him the story of the man who lost one limb, and had a chance of losing another, this idea brings before me a friend with a brace of wooden legs, who, moreover, appears in connexion with putting the stone, as I know him to excel at that exercise. There is only one other element in the dream which the preceding events will not account for, and that is, the surprise at the individual referred to having more than one wooden leg. But why should he have even one, seeing that in reality he is limbed like other people? This also, I can account for. Some years ago he slightly injured his knee while leaping a ditch, and I remember of jocularly advising him to get it cut off. I am particular in illustrating this point with regard to dreams, for I hold, that if it were possible to analyze them all, they would invariably be found to stand in the same relation to the waking state as the above specimen. The more diversified and incongruous the character of a dream, and the more remote from the period of its occurrence the circumstances which suggest it, the more difficult does its analysis become; and, in point of fact, this process may be impossible, so totally are the elements of the dream often dissevered from their original source, and so ludicrously huddled together. This subject shall be more fully demonstrated in speaking of the remote causes of dreams.

Dreams generally arise without any assignable cause, but sometimes we can very readily discover their origin. Whatever has much interested us during the day, is apt to resolve itself into a dream; and this will generally be pleasurable, or the reverse, according to the nature of the exciting cause. If, for instance, our reading or conversation be of horrible subjects, such as spectres, murders, or conflagrations, they will appear before us magnified and heightened in our dreams. Or if we have been previously sailing upon a rough sea, we are apt to suppose ourselves undergoing the perils of shipwreck. Pleasurable sensations during the day are also apt to assume a still more pleasurable aspect in dreams. In like manner, if we have a longing for any thing, we are apt to suppose that we possess it. Even objects altogether unattainable are placed within our reach: we achieve impossibilities, and triumph with ease over the invincible laws of nature.

A disordered state of the stomach and liver will often produce dreams. Persons of bad digestion, especially hypochondriacs, are harassed with visions of the most frightful nature. This fact was well known to the celebrated Mrs Radcliffe, who, for the purpose of filling her sleep with those phantoms of horror which she has so forcibly embodied in the 'Mysteries of Udolpho,' and 'Romance of the Forest,' is said to have supped upon the most indigestible substances; while Dryden and Fuseli, with the opposite view of obtaining splendid dreams, are reported to have eaten raw flesh. Diseases of the chest, where the breathing is impeded, also give rise to horrible visions, and constitute the frequent causes of that most frightful modification of dreaming—nightmare.

The usual intoxicating agents have all the power of exciting dreams. The most exquisite visions, as well as the most frightful, are perhaps those occasioned by narcotics. These differences depend on the dose and the particular state of the system at the time of taking it. Dreams also may arise from the deprivation of customary stimuli, such as spirits, or supper before going to bed. More frequently, however, they originate from indulging in such excitations.

A change of bed will sometimes induce dreams; and, generally speaking, they are more apt to occur in a strange bed than in the one to which we are accustomed.

Dreams often arise from the impressions made upon the senses during sleep. Dr Beattie speaks of a man

O

on whom any kind of dream could be induced, by his friends gently speaking in his presence upon the particular subject which they wished him to dream about. I have often tried this experiment upon persons asleep, and more than once with a like result. I apprehend, that when this takes place, the slumber must have been very imperfect. With regard to the possibility of dreams being produced by bodily impressions, Dr Gregory relates that having occasion to apply a bottle of hot water to his feet when he went to bed, he dreamed that he was making a journey to the top of Mount Etna, and that he found the heat of the ground almost insufferable. Another person having a blister applied to his head, imagined that he was scalped by a party of Indians; while a friend of mine happening to sleep in damp sheets, dreamed that he was dragged through a stream. A paroxysm of gout during sleep, has given rise to the persons supposing himself under the power of the Inquisition, and undergoing the torments of the rack. The bladder is sometimes emptied during sleep, from the dreaming idea being directed (in consequence of the unpleasant fullness of the viscus) to this particular want of nature. These results are not uniform, but such is the path in which particular bodily states are apt to lead the imagination; and dreams, occurring in these states, will more frequently possess a character analogous to them than to any other modified, of course, by the strength of the individual cause, and fertility of the fancy.

Some curious experiments in regard to this point, were made by M. Giron de Buzareingues, which seems to establish the practicability of a person determining at will the nature of his dreams. By leaving his knees uncovered, he dreamed that he travelled during night in in a diligence: travellers, he observes, being aware that in a coach it is the knees that get cold during the night. On another occasion, having left the posterior part of his head uncovered, he dreamed that he was present at a religious ceremony performed in the open air. It was the custom of the country in which he lived to have the head constantly covered, except on particular occasions, such as the above. On awaking, he felt the back of his neck cold, as he had often experienced during the real scenes, the representation of which had been conjured up by his fancy. Having repeated this experiment at the end of several days, to assure himself that the result was not the effect of chance, the second vision turned out precisely the same as the first. Even without making experiments, we have frequent evidence of similar facts; thus, if the clothes chance to fall off us, we are liable to suppose that we are parading the streets in a state of nakedness, and feel all the shame and inconvenience which such a condition would in reality produce. We see crowds of people following after us and mocking our nudity; and we wander from place to place, seeking a refuge under this ideal misfortune. Fancy, in truth, heightens every circumstance, and inspires us with greater vexation than we would feel if actually labouring under such an annoyance. The streets in which we wander are depicted with the force of reality; we see their windings, their avenues, their dwelling-places, with intense truth. Even the inhabitants who follow us are exposed to view in all their various dresses and endless diversities of countenance. Sometimes we behold our intimate friends gazing upon us with indifference, or torturing with annoying impertinence. Sometimes we see multitudes whom we never beheld before; and each individual is exposed so vividly, that we could describe or even paint his aspect.

In like manner, if we lie awry, or if our feet slip over the side of the bed, we often imagine ourselves standing upon the brink of a fearful precipice, or falling from its beetling summit into the abyss beneath.[*] If the

* Dr Currie, in allusion to the visions of the hypochondriac observes, that if he dream of falling into the sea, he awakes just as

rain or hail patter against our windows, we have often the idea of a hundred cataracts pouring from the rocks; if the wind howl without, we are suddenly wrapt up in a thunderstorm, with all its terrible associations; if the head happen to slip under the pillow, a huge rock is hanging over us, and ready to crush us beneath its ponderous bulk. Should the heat of the body chance to be increased by febrile irritation or the temperature of the room, we may suppose ourselves basking under the fiery sun of Africa; or if, from any circumstance, we labour under a chill, we may then be careering and foundering among the icebergs of the pole, while the morse and the famished bear are prowling around us, and claiming us for their prey. Dr Beattie informs us, that once, after riding thirty miles in a high wind, he passed the night in visions terrible beyond description. The extent, in short, to which the mind is capable of being carried in such cases, is almost incredible. Stupendous events arise from the most insignificant causes —so completely does sleep magnify and distort every thing placed within its influence. The province of dreams is one of intense exaggeration—exaggeration beyond even the wildest conceptions of Oriental romance.

A smoky chamber, for instance, has given rise to the idea of a city in flames. The conflagrations of Rome and Moscow may then pass in terrific splendor before the dreamer's fancy. He may see Nero standing afar off, surrounded by his lictors and guards, gazing upon the imperial city wrapt in flames; or the sanguinary fight of Borodino, followed by the burning of the ancient capital of Russia, may be presented before him with all the intenseness of reality. Under these circumstances, his whole being may undergo a change. He is no longer a denizen of his native country, but of that land to which his visions have transported him. All the events of his own existence fade away; and he becomes a native of Rome or Russia, gazing upon the appalling spectacle.

On the other hand, the mind may be filled with imagery equally exaggerated, but of a more pleasing character. The sound of a flute in the neighborhood may invoke a thousand beautiful and delightful associations. The air is, perhaps, filled with the tones of harps, and all other varieties of music—nay, the performers themselves are visible; and while the cause of this strange scene is one trivial instrument, we may be regaled with a rich and melodious concert. For the same reason a flower being applied to the nostrils may, by affecting the sense of the smell, excite powerfully the imagination, and give the dreamer the idea of walking in a garden.

There is one fact connected with dreams which is highly remarkable. When we are suddenly awaked from a profound slumber by a loud knock at, or by the rapid opening of the door, a train of actions which it would take hours, or days, or even weeks to accomplish, sometimes passes through the mind. Time, in fact, seems to be in a great measure annihilated. An extensive period is reduced, as it were, to a single point, or rather a single point is made to embrace an extensive period. In one instant, we pass through many adventures, see many strange sights, and hear many strange sounds. If we are awaked by a loud knock, we have perhaps the idea of a tumult passing before us, and know all the characters engaged in it— their aspects, and even their very names. If the door open violently, the flood-gates of a canal may appear to be expanding, and we may see the individuals employed in the process, and hear their conversation, which may seem an hour in length. If a light be brought into the room, the notion of the house being in flames perhaps invades us, and we are witnesses to the waters close over him, and is sensible of the precise gurgling sound which those experience who actually sink under water. In falling from heights, during dreams, we always awake before reaching the ground.

the whole conflagration from its commencement till it be finally extinguished. The thoughts which arise in such situations are endless, and assume an infinite variety of aspects. The whole, indeed, constitutes one of the strangest phenomena of the human mind, and calls to recollection the story of the Eastern monarch, who, on dipping his head into the magician's water pail, fancied he had travelled for years in various nations, although he was only immersed for a single instant. This curious psychological fact, though occurring under somewhat different circumstances, has not escaped the notice of Mr De Quincey, better known as the 'English Opium-Eater.' 'The sense of space,' says he, 'and, in the end, the *sense of time* were both powerfully affected. Buildings, landscapes, &c., were exhibited in proportions so vast as the bodily eye is not fitted to receive. Space swelled, and was amplified to an extent of unutterable infinity. This, however, did not disturb me so much as the expansion of time. I sometimes seemed to have lived for seventy or a hundred years in one night; nay, sometimes had feelings representative of a millennium passed in that time, or however, of a duration beyond the limits of any human experience.' It is more easy to state the fact of this apparent expansion of time in dreams than to give any theory which will satisfactorily account for it. I believe that, whenever it occurs, the dream has abounded in events and circumstances which, had they occurred in reality, would have required a long period for their accomplishment. For instance, I lately dreamed that I made a voyage to India—remained some days in Calcutta—then took ship for Egypt, where I visited the cataracts of the Nile, and the pyramids : and, to crown the whole, had the honor of an interview with Mehemit Ali, Cleopatra, and the Sultan Saladin. All this was the work of a single night, probably of a single hour, or even a few minutes; and yet it appeared to occupy many months.

I must also mention another circumstance of a somewhat similar kind, which though it occur in the waking condition, is produced by the peculiar effect of previous sleep upon the mind. Thus, when we awake in a melancholy mood, the result probably of some distressing dream, the remembrance of all our former actions, especially those of an evil character, often rushes upon us as from a dark and troubled sea.* They do not appear individually, one by one, but come linked together in a close phalanx, as if to take the conscience by storm, and crush it beneath their imposing front. The whole span of our existence, from childhood downwards, sends them on; oblivion opens its gulphs and impels them forwards; and the mind is robed in a cloud of wretchedness, without one ray of hope to brighten up its gloom. In common circumstances, we possess no such power of grouping so instantaneously the most distant and proximate events of life ; the spell of memory is invoked to call them successively from the past ; and they glide before us like shadows, more or less distinct according to their remoteness, or the force of their impress upon the mind. But in the case of which I speak, they start abruptly forth from the bosom of time, and overwhelm the spirit with a crowd of most sad and appalling reminiscences. In the crucible of our distorted imagination, every thing is exaggerated and invested with a blacker gloom than belongs to it ; we see, at one glance, down the whole vista of time ; and each event of our life is written there in gloomy and distressing characters. Hence the mental depression occurring under these circumstances, and even the remorse which falls, like bitter and unrefreshing dews, upon the heart.

We have seldom any idea of past events in dreams ; if such are called forth, they generally seem to be pre-

* Something similar occurs in drowning. Persons recovered from this state have mentioned that, in the course of a single minute, almost every event of their life has been brought to their recollection.

sent and in the process of actual occurrence. We may dream of Alexander the Great, but it is as of a person who is co-existent with ourselves.

Dreams being produced by the active state of such organs as are dissociated from, or have not sympathised in, the general slumber, partake of the character of those whose powers are in greatest vigour, or farthest removed from the somnolent state. A person's natural character, therefore, or his pursuits in life, by strengthening one faculty, make it less susceptible, than such as are weaker, of being overcome, by complete sleep ; or, if it be overcome, it awakes more rapidly from its dormant state, and exhibits its proper characteristics in dreams. Thus, the miser dreams of wealth, the lover of his mistress, the musician of melody, the philosopher of science, the merchant of trade, and the debtor of duns and bailiffs. In like manner, a choleric man is often passionate in his sleep ; a vicious man's mind is filled with wicked actions ; a virtuous man's with deeds of benevolence ; a humorist's with ludicrous ideas. Pugnacious people often fight on such occasions, and do themselves serious injury by striking against the posts of the bed ; while persons addicted to lying, frequently dream of exercising their favourite vocation.

For such reasons persons who have a strong passion for music often dream of singing and composing melodies ; and the ideas of some of our finest pieces are said to have been communicated to the musician in his sleep. Tartini, a celebrated violin player, is said to have composed his famous *Devil's Sonata* from the inspiration of a dream, in which the Devil appeared to him and challenged him to a trial of skill upon his own fiddle. A mathematician, in like manner, is often engaged in the solution of problems, and has his brain full of Newton, Euler, Euclid, and Laplace ; while a poet is occupied in writing verses, or in deliberating upon the strains of such bards as are most familiar to his spirit ; it was thus in a dream that Mr Coleridge composed his splendid fragment of Kubla Khan.* To speak phrenologically : if the organ of *size* be large, then material images more than sounds or abstractions possess the mind, and every thing may be magnified to unnatural dimensions ; if *color* be fully developed, whatever is presented to the mental eye is brilliant and gaudy, and the person has probably the idea of rich paintings, shining flowers, or varied landscapes : should *locality* predominate, he is carried away to distant lands, and beholds more extraordinary sights than Cook, Ross, or Franklin ever described. An excess of *cautiousness* will inspire him with terror ; an excess of *self-esteem* cause him to be placed in dignified situations ; while *imitation* may render him a mimic or a

* The following is the account he himself gives of the circumstance :—'In the summer of the year 1797, the author, then in ill-health, had retired to a lonely farm-house between Porlock and Linton, on the Exmoor confines of Somerset and Devonshire. In consequence of a slight indisposition, an anodyne had been prescribed, from the effects of which he fell asleep in his chair at the moment that he was reading the following sentence, or words of the same substance, in 'Purchas's Pilgrimage:— 'Here the Khan Kubla commanded a palace to be built, and a stately garden thereunto. And thus ten miles of fertile ground were enclosed with a wall.' The author continued for about three hours in a profound sleep, at least of the external senses, during which time he had the most vivid confidence, that he could have composed not less than from two to three hundred lines; if that indeed can be called composition in which all the images rose up before him as *things*, with a parallel production of the correspondent expressions, without any sensation or consciousness of effort. On awaking, he appeared to himself to have a distinct recollection of the whole : and taking his pen, ink, and paper instantly and eagerly wrote down the lines that are here preserved. At this moment he was unfortunately called out by a person on business from Porlock, and detained by him above an hour ; and on his return to his room, found, to his no small surprise and mortification, that though he still retained some vague and dim recollection of the general purport of the vision ; yet, with the exception of some eight, or ten scattered lines and images, all the rest had passed away like the images on the surface of a stream into which a stone had been cast, but alas ! without the after restoration of the latter.'

player ; *language*, a wrangler or philologist ; *secretiveness*, a deceiver ; *acquisitiveness*, a thief. Occasionally, indeed, the reverse is the case, and those trains of thoughts in which we mostly indulge are seldom or never the subjects of our dreams. Some authors even assert that when the mind has been strongly impressed with any peculiar ideas, such are less likely to occur in dreams than their opposites ; but this is taking the exception for the general rule, and is directly at variance with both experience and analogy. In fact, whatever propensities or talents are strongest in the mind of the individual, will, in most cases, manifest themselves with greatest readiness and force in dreams ; and where a faculty is very weak it will scarcely manifest itself at all. Thus, one person who has large *tune* and small *casuality* will indulge in music, but seldom in ascertaining the nature of cause and effect ; while another, with a contrary disposition of organs, may attempt to reason upon abstract truths, while music will rarely intrude into the temple of his thoughts. It is but fair to state, however, that the compositions, the reasonings, and the poems which we concoct in sleep, though occasionally superior to those of our waking hours,* are generally of a very absurd description ; and, how admirable soever they have appeared, their futility is abundantly evident when we awake. To use the words of Dr Parr, ' In dreams we seem to reason, to argue, to compose ; and in all these circumstances, during sleep, we are highly gratified, and think that we excel. If, however, we remember our dreams, our reasonings we find to be weak, our arguments we find to be inconclusive, and our compositions trifling and absurd.' The truth of these remarks is undeniable : but the very circumstance of a man's dreams turning habitually upon a particular subject—however ridiculously he may meditate thereupon—is a strong presumption that that subject is the one which most frequently engrosses his faculties in the waking state ; in a word, that the power-er most energetic in the latter condition is that also most active in dreams.

Dreams are sometimes useful in affording prognostics of the probable termination of several diseases. Violent and impetuous dreams occurring in fevers generally indicate approaching delirium ; those of a gloomy, terrific nature give strong grounds to apprehend danger ; while dreams of a pleasant cast may be looked upon as harbingers of approaching recovery. The visions, indeed, which occur in a state of fever are highly distressing : the mind is vehemently hurried on from one train of ideas to another, and participates in the painful activity of the system. Those generated by hypochondria or indigestion are equally afflicting, but more confined to one unpleasant idea—the intellect being overpowered, as it were, under the pressure of a ponderous load, from which it experiences an utter incapacity to relieve itself. The febrile dream has a fiery, volatile, fugitive character : the other partakes of the nature of nightmare, in which the faculties seem frozen to torpor, by the presence of a loathsome and indolent fiend.

Other diseases and feelings besides fever give a character to dreams. The dropsical subject often has the idea of fountains, and rivers, and seas, in his sleep ; jaundice tinges the objects beheld with its own yellow and sickly hue ; hunger induces dreams of eating agreeable food ; an attack of inflammation disposes us to see all things of the colour of blood ; excessive thirst presents us with visions of dried up streams, burning sand-plains, and immitigable heat ; a bad taste in the mouth, with every thing bitter and nauseous in the vegetable world.

* Such was the case with Cabanis, who often, during dreams, saw clearly into the bearings of political events which had baffled him when awake ; and with Condorcet, who, when, engaged in some deep and complicated calculations, was frequently obliged to leave them in an unfinished state, and retire to rest, when the results to which they led were at once unfolded in his dreams.

If, from any cause, we chance to be relieved from the physical suffering occasioning such dreams, the dreams themselves also wear away, or are succeeded by others of a more pleasing description. Thus, if perspiration succeed to feverish heat, the person who, during the continuance of the latter, fancied himself on the brink of a volcano, or broiled beneath an African sun, is transported to some refreshing stream, and enjoys precisely the pleasure which such a transition would produce did it actually take place.

Some authors imagine that we never dream of objects which we have not seen; but the absurdity of this notion is so glaring as to carry its own refutation along with it. I have a thousand times dreamed of such objects.

When a person has a strong desire to see any place or object which he has never seen before, he is apt to dream about it ; while, as soon as his desire is gratified, he often ceases so to dream. I remember of hearing a great deal of the beauty of Rouen Cathedral, and in one form or other it was constantly presented before my imagination in dreams; but having at last seen the cathedral I never again dreamed about it. This is not the invariable result of a gratified wish; but it happens so often that it may be considered a general rule.

Sometimes we awake from dreams in a pleasing, at other times in a melancholy mood, without being able to recollect them. They leave a pleasurable or disagreeable impression upon the mind, according doubtless to their nature; and yet we cannot properly remember what we were dreaming about. Sometimes, though baffled at the time, we can recall them afterwards, but this seldom happens.

It often happens that the dreamer, under the influence of a frightful vision, leaps from his bed and calls aloud in a paroxysm of terror. This is very frequently the case with children and persons of weak nerves ; but it may happen even with the strongest minded. There is something peculiarly horrible and paralyzing in the terror of sleep. It lays the energies of the soul prostrate before it, crushes them to the earth as beneath the weight of an enormous vampyre, and equalizes for a time the courage of the hero and the child. No firmness of mind can at all times withstand the influence of these deadly terrors. The person awakes panic-struck from some hideous vision ; and even after reason returns and convinces him of the unreal nature of his apprehensions, the panic for some time continues, his heart throbs violently, he is covered with cold perspiration, and hides his head beneath the bed-clothes, afraid to look around him, lest some dreadful object of alarm should start up before his affrighted vision. Courage and philosophy are frequently opposed in vain to these appalling terrors. The latter dreads what it disbelieves ; and spectral forms, sepulchral voices, and all the other horrid superstitions of sleep arise to vindicate their power over that mind, which, under the fancied protection of reason and science, conceived itself shielded from all such attacks, but which, in the hour of trial, often sinks beneath their influence as completely as the ignorant and unreflecting mind, who never employed a thought as to the real nature of these fantastic and illusive sources of terror. The alarm of a frightful dream is sometimes so overpowering, that persons under the impression thus generated, of being pursued by some imminent danger, have actually leaped out of the window to the great danger and even loss of their lives. In the 9th volume of the ' Philosophical Transactions of the Royal Society of London,' a curious case is given by Archdeacon Squire, of a person who, after having been dumb for years, recovered the use of his speech by means of a dream of this description : ' One day, in the year 1741, he got very much in liquor, so much so, that on his return at home at night to the Devizes, he fell from his horse three or four times, and was at last taken up by a neighbour, and put to bed in

a house on the road. He soon fell asleep ; when, dreaming that he was falling into a furnace of boiling wort, it put him into so great an agony of fright, that, struggling with all his might to call out for help, he actually did call out aloud, and recovered the use of his tongue that moment, as effectually as ever he had it in his life, without the least hoarseness or alteration in the old sound of his voice.'

There have been instances where the terror of a frightful dream has been so great as even to produce insanity. Many years ago, a woman in the West Highlands, in consequence of a dream of this kind, after being newly brought to bed, became deranged, and soon after made her escape to the mountains, where for seven years, she herded with the deer, and became so fleet that the shepherds and others, by whom she was occasionally seen, could never arrest her. At the end of this term, a very severe storm brought her and her associates to the valley, when she was surrounded, caught, and conveyed to her husband, by whom she was cordially received and treated with the utmost kindness. In the course of three months, she regained her reason, and had afterwards several children. When caught, her body is said to have been covered with hair, thus giving a colour to the story of Orson and other wild men of the wood.

Instances have not been wanting where, under the panic of a frightful vision, persons have actually committed murder. They awake from such a dream— they see some person standing in the room, whom they mistake for an assassin, or dreadful apparition; driven to desperation by terror, they seize the first weapon that occurs, and inflict a fatal wound upon the object of their alarm. Hoffbauer, in his Treatise on Legal Medicine, relates a case of this kind. Although he does not state that the circumstances which occasioned the panic was a previous dream of terror, I do not doubt that such, in reality, must have been the case. ' A report,' says he, ' of the murder committed by Bernard Schidmaizig was made by the Criminal College of Silesia. Schidmaizig awoke suddenly at midnight : at the moment of awaking, he beheld a frightful phantom (at least his imagination so depicted it) standing near him, (in consequence of the heat of the weather he slept in an open coach-house.) Fear, and the obscurity of the night, prevented him from recognizing any thing distinctly, and the object which struck his vision appeared to him an actual spectre. In a tremulous tone, he twice called out, 'who goes there ?—he received no answer, and imagined that the apparition was approaching him. Frightened out of his judgment, he sprung from his bed, seized a hatchet which he generally kept close by him, and with this weapon assaulted the imaginary spectre. To see the apparition, to call out who goes there? and to seize the hatchet where the work of a moment : he had not an instant for reflection, and with one blow the phantom was felled to the ground. Schidmaizig uttered a deep groan. This, and the noise occasioned by the fall of the phantom, completely restored him to his senses ; and all at once the idea flashed across his mind that he must have struck down his wife, who slept in the same coach-house. Falling instantly upon his knees, he raised the head of the wounded person, saw the wound which he had made, and the blood that flowed from it ; and in a voice full of anguish exclaimed Susannah, Susannah, come to yourself! He then called his eldest daughter, aged eight years, ordered her to see if her mother was recovering, and to inform her grandmother that he had killed her. In fact, it was his unhappy wife who received the blow, and she died the next day.'*

* This case is highly important in a legal point of view ; and to punish a man for acting similarly in such a state would be as unjust as to inflict punishment for deeds committed under the influence of insanity or somnambulism. ' This man,' as Hoffbauer properly remarks, 'did not enjoy the free use of his senses : he knew not what he saw : he believed that he was repulsing an unlooked for attack. He soon recognised the place where he usually slept ; it was natural that he should seize the hatchet

The passion of horror is more frequently felt in dreams than at any other period. Horror is intense dread, produced by some unknown or superlatively disgusting object. The visions of sleep, therefore, being frequently undefined, and of the most revolting description, are apt to produce this emotion, as they are to occasion simple fear. Under its influence, we may suppose that fiends are lowering upon us; that dismal voices, as from the bottomless pit, or from the tomb, are floating around us; that we are haunted by apparitions; or that serpents, scorpions and demons are our bed-fellows. Such sensations are strongly akin to those of nightmare; but between this complaint and a mere dream of terror, there is a considerable difference. In incubus, the individual feels as if his powers of volition were totally paralyzed; and as if he were altogether unable to move a limb in his own behalf, or utter a cry expressive of his agony. When these feelings exist, we may consider the case to be one of nightmare: when they do not, and when notwithstanding his terror, he seems to himself to possess unrestrained muscular motion, to run with ease, breathe freely, and enjoy the full capability of exertion, it must be regarded as a simple dream.

Dr Elliotson has remarked, with great acuteness, that dreams, in which the perceptive faculties alone are concerned, are more incoherent, and subject to more rapid transitions than those in which one or more of the organs of the feelings are also in a state of activity. ' Thus, in our dreams, we may walk on the brink of a precipice, or see ourselves doomed to immediate destruction by the weapon of a foe, or the fury of a tempestuous sea, and yet feel not the slightest emotion of fear, though, during the perfect activity of the brain, we may be naturally disposed to the strong manifestation of this feeling; again we may see the most extraordinary object or event without surprise, perform the most ruthless crime without compunction, and see what, in our waking hours, would cause us unmitigated grief, without the smallest feeling of sorrow.'

Persons are to be found, who, when they speak much during sleep, are unable to remember their dreams on awaking, yet recollect them perfectly if they do not speak. This fact is not very easily accounted for. Probably when we are silent, the mind is more directed upon the subject of the dream, and not so likely to be distracted from it. There is perhaps another explanation. When we dream of speaking, or actually speak, the necessity of using language infers the exercise of some degree of reason; and, thus the incongruities of the dream being diminished, its nature becomes less striking, and consequently less likely to be remembered. Though we often dream of performing impossibilities, we seldom imagine that we are relating them to others.

When we dream of visible objects, the sensibility of the eyes is diminished in a most remarkable manner; and on opening them, they are much less dazzled by the light than if we awoke from a slumber altogether unvisited by such dreams. A fact equally curious is noticed by Dr. Darwin, in his 'Zoonomia,'—' If we sleep in the day time, and endeavor to see some object in dreams, the light is exceedingly painful to our eyes; and, after repeated struggles, we lament in our sleep that we cannot see it. In this case, I apprehend, the eyelid is in some measure opened by the vehemence of our sensations; and the iris being dilated, shows as great, or greater sensibility than in our waking hours.'

There are some persons to whom the objects of their dreams are always represented in a soft, mellow lustre, similar to twilight. They never seem to behold any thing in the broad glare of sunshine; and, in general, the atmosphere of our vision is less brilliant than that through which we are accustomed to see things while awake.

since he had taken the precaution to place it beside him; but the idea of his wife and the possibility of killing her were the last things that occurred to him.'

The most vivid dreams are certainly those which have reference to sight. With regard to hearing, they are less distinctly impressed upon the mind, and still more feebly as regards smell, or taste. Indeed, some authors are of opinion that we never dream of sounds, unless when a sound takes place to provoke a dream: and the same with regard to smell and taste; but this doctrine is against analogy, and unsupported by proof. There are, beyond doubt, certain parts of the brain which take cognizance of taste, odors, and sounds, for the same reason that there are others which recognise forms, dimensions, and colors. As the organs of the three latter sensations are capable of inward excitement, without any communication, by means of the senses, with the external world, it is no more than analogical to infer that, with the three former, the same thing may take place. In fever, although the individual is ever so well protected against the excitement of external sounds, the internal organ is often violently stimulated, and he is harassed with tumultuous noises. For such reasons, it is evident that there may be in dreams a consciousness of sounds, of tastes, and of odors, where such have no real existence from without.

Dreams are sometimes exceedingly obscure, and float like faint clouds over the spirit. We can then resolve them into nothing like shape or consistence, but have an idea of our minds being filled with dim, impalpable imagery, which is so feebly impressed upon the tablet of memory, that we are unable to embody it in language, or communicate its likeness to others.

At other times, the objects of sleep are stamped with almost supernatural energy. The dead, or the absent, whose appearance to our waking faculties had become faint and obscure, are depicted with intense truth and reality; and even their voices, which had become like the echo of a forgotten song, are recalled from the depths of oblivion, and speak to us as in former times. Dreams therefore, have the power of brightening up the dim regions of the past, and presenting them with a force which the mere effects of unassisted remembrance could never have accomplished our waking hours.

This property of reviving past images, is one of the most remarkable possessed by sleep. It even goes the length, in some cases, of recalling circumstances which had been entirely forgotten, and presenting them to the mind with more than the force of their original impression. This I conceive to depend upon a particular part of the brain—that, for instance, which refers to the memory of the event—being preternaturally excited; hence forgotten tongues are sometimes brought back to the memory in dreams, owing doubtless to some peculiar excitement of the organ of *Language*. The dreamer sometimes converses in a language of which he has no knowledge whatever when he awakes, but with which he must at one period have been acquainted. Phenomena of a similar kind occasionally occur in madness, delirium, or intoxication, all of which states have an analogy to dreaming. It is not uncommon, for instance, to witness in the insane an unexpected and astonishing resuscitation of knowledge—an intimacy with events and languages of which they were entirely ignorant in the sound state of their minds. In like manner, in the delirium attendant upon fevers, people sometimes speak in a tongue* they know nothing of in

* A girl was seized with a dangerous fever, and, in the delirious paroxysm accompanying it, was observed to speak in a strange language which, for some time, no one could understand. At last it was ascertained to be Welsh—a tongue she was wholly ignorant of at the time she was taken ill, and of which she could not speak a single syllable after her recovery. For some time the circumstance was unaccountable, till, on inquiry, it was found she was a native of Wales, and had been familiar with the language of that country in her childhood, but had wholly forgotten it afterwards. During the delirium of fever, the obliterated impressions of infancy were brought to her mind, and continued to operate there so long as she remained under the mental excitation occasioned by the disease, but no longer,

health; and in drunkenness events are brought to the memory which desert it in a state of sobriety.* Analogous peculiarties occur in dreams. Forgotten facts are restored to the mind. Sometimes those adhere to it and are remembered when we awake : at other times—as can be proved in cases of sleep-talking—they vanish with the dream which called them into existence, and are recollected no more.

I believe that the dreams of the aged, like their memory, relate chiefly to the events of early life, and less to those of more recent occurrence. My friend, Dr Cumin, has mentioned to me the case of one of his patients, a middle-aged man, whose visions assumed this character in consequence of severe mental anxiety. Owing to misfortunes in trade, his mind had been greatly depressed : he lost his appetite, became restless, nervous, and dejected; such sleep as he had was filled with incessant dreams, which at first were entirely of events connected with the earliest period of his life, so far as he recollected it, and never by any chance of late events. In proportion as he recovered from this state, the dreams changed their character, and referred to circumstances farther on in life; and so regular was the progression, that, with the march of his recovery, so was the onward march of his dreams. During the worst period of his illness, he dreamed of occurrences which happened in boyhood : no sooner was convalescence established than his visions had reference to manhood ; and on complete recovery they were of those recent circumstances which had thrown him into bad health. In this curious case, one lateral half of the head was much warmer than the other. This was so remarkable as to attract the notice of the barber who shaved it.

One of the most remarkable phenomena of dreams is the absence of surprise. This, indeed, is not invariable, as every one must occasionally have felt the sensation of surprise, and been not a little puzzled in his visions to account for the phenomena which present themselves ; but, as a general rule, its absence is so exceedingly common, that, when surprise does occur, it is looked upon as an event out of the common order, and remarked accordingly. Scarcely any event, however incredible, impossible, or absurd, gives rise to this sensation. We see circumstance at utter variance with the laws of nature, and yet their discordancy, impracticability, and oddness, seldom strike us as at all out of the usual course of things. This is one of the strongest proofs that can be alleged in support of the dormant condition of the reflecting faculties. Had these powers been awake, and in full activity, they would have pointed out the erroneous nature of the impressions conjured into existence by fancy : and shown us truly that the visions passing before us were merely the chimeras of excited imagination—the airy phantoms of imperfect sleep.

In visions of the dead, we have a striking instance of the absence of surprise. We almost never wonder at beholding individuals whom we yet know, in our dreams, to have even been buried for years. We see them among us, and hear them talk, and associate with them on the footing of fond companionship. Still the circumstance seldom strikes us with wonder, nor do we attempt to account for it. They still seem alive as when they were on earth, only all their qualities, whether good or bad, are exaggerated by sleep. If we hated them while in life, our animosity is now exaggerated to a double degree. If we loved them, our affection becomes more passionate and intense than ever. Under

for so soon as the state of mind which recalled these impressions was removed, they also disappeared, as she was as ignorant of Welsh as before she was taken ill.
* Mr Combe mentions the case of an Irish porter to a warehouse, who, in one of his drunken fits, left a parcel at the wrong house, and when sober could not recollect what he had done with it ; but the next time he got drunk, he recollected where he had left it, and went and recovered it.

these circumstances, many scenes of most exquisite pleasure often take place. The slumberer supposes himself enjoying the communionship of those who were dearer to him than life, and has far more intense delight than he could have experienced, had these individuals been in reality alive, and at his side.

'I hear thy voice in dreams
　Upon me softly call;
Like echo of the mountain streams
　In sportive waterfall :
I see thy form, as when
　Thou wert a living thing,
And blossomed in the eyes of men
　Like any flower of spring.'

Nor is the passion of love, when experienced in dreams, less vivid than any other emotion, or the sensation to which it gives rise less pleasurable. I do not here allude to the passion in its physical sense, but to that more moral and intellectual feeling, the result of deep sensibility and attachment. Men who never loved before, have conceived a deep affection to some particular woman in their dreams, which, continuing to operate upon them after they awoke, has actually terminated in a sincere and lasting fondness for the object of their visionary love. Men, again, who actually are in love, dream more frequently of this subject than of any thing else—fancying themselves in the society of their mistresses, and enjoying a happiness more exquisite than is compatible with the waking state—a happiness, in short, little removed from celestial. Such feelings are not confined to men ; they pervade the female breast with equal intensity ; and the young maiden, stretched upon the couch of sleep, may have her spirit filled with the image of her lover, while her whole being swims in the ecstacies of impassioned, yet virtuous attachment. At other times, this pure passion may, in both sexes, be blended with one of a grosser character ; which also may acquire an increase of pleasurable sensation : to such an extent is every circumstance, whether of delight or suffering, exaggerated by sleep.

For the same reason that the lover dreams of love, does the newly married woman dream of children. They, especially if she have a natural fondness for them—if she herself be pregnant, or possess an ardent longing for offspring—are often the subject of her sleeping thoughts ; and she conceives herself to be encircled by them, and experiencing intense pleasure in their innocent society. Men who are very fond of children often experience the same sensations ; and both men and women who are naturally indifferent in this respect, seldom dream about them, and never with any feelings of peculiar delight.

During the actual process of any particular dream, we are never conscious that we are really dreaming : but it sometimes happens that a second dream takes place, during which we have a consciousness, or a suspicion, that the events which took place in the first dream were merely visionary, and not real. People, for instance, sometimes fancy in sleep, that they have acquired wealth : this may be called the first dream ; and during its progress they never for a moment doubt the reality of their impressions ; but a second one supervenes upon this, and they then begin to wonder whether their riches be real or imaginary—in other words, they try to ascertain whether they had been previously dreaming or not. But even in the second dream we are unconscious of dreaming. We still seem to ourselves to be broad awake—a proof that in dreams we are never aware of being asleep. This unconsciousness of being asleep during the dreaming state, is referable to the quiescent condition of the reasoning powers. The mind is wholly subject to the sceptre of other faculties; and whatever emotions or images they invoke seem to be real, for want of a controlling power to point out their true character.

' You stood before me like a thought,
A dream remembered in a dream.'

Those troubled with deafness do not hear distinctly
such sounds as they conceive to be uttered during
sleep. Dr. Darwin speaks of a gentleman who, for
thirty years, had entirely lost his hearing, and who in
his dreams never seemed to converse with any person
except by the fingers or in writing : he never had the
impression of hearing them speak. In like manner, a
blind man seldom dreams of visible objects, and never
if he has been blind from his birth. Dr Blacklock, indeed, who became blind in early infancy, may seem an
exception to this rule. While asleep, he was conscious
of a sense which he did not possess in the waking state,
and which bears some analogy to sight. He imagined
that he was united to objects by a sort of distant contact, which was effected by threads or strings passing
from their bodies to his own.

The illusion of dreams is much more complete than
that of the most exquisite plays. We pass, in a second
of time, from one country to another ; and persons who
lived in the most different ages of the world are brought
together in strange and incongruous confusion. It is
not uncommon to see, at the same moment, Robert the
Bruce, Julius Cæsar, and Marlborough in close conversation. Nothing, in short, however monstrous, incredible, or impossible, seems absurd. Equally striking
examples of illusion occur when the person awakes
from a dream, and imagines that he hears voices or beholds persons in the room beside him. In the first
cases we are convinced, on awaking, of the deceptive
nature of our visions, from the utter impossibility of
their occurrence; they are at variance with natural
laws; and a single effort of reason is sufficient to point
out their absolute futility. But when the circumstances
which seem to take place are not in themselves conceived impossible, however unlikely they may be, it is
often a matter of the utmost difficulty for us so to be convinced of their real character. On awaking, we are
seldom aware that, when they took place, we laboured
under a dream. Such is their deceptive nature, and
such the vividness with which they appear to strike our
senses, that we imagine them real ; and accordingly
often start up in a paroxysm of terror, having the idea
that our chamber is invaded by thieves, that strange
voices are calling upon us, or that we are haunted by
the dead. When there is no way of confuting these
impressions, they often remain ineradicably fixed in the
mind, and are regarded as actual events, instead of the
mere chimeras of sleep. This is particularly the case
with the weak-minded and superstitious, whose feelings
are always stronger than their judgments ; hence the
thousand stories of ghosts and warnings with which the
imaginations of those persons are haunted—hence the
frequent occurrence of nocturnal screaming and terror
in children, whose reflecting faculties are naturally too
weak to correct the impressions of dreams, and point
out their true nature—hence the painful illusions occurring even to persons of strong intellect, when they are
debilitated by watchfulness, long-continued mental suffering, or protracted disease. These impressions often
arise without any apparent cause : at other times, the
most trivial circumstances will produce them. A voice,
for instance, in a neighbouring street, may seem to proceed from our own apartment, and may assume a character of the most appalling description ; while the tread
of footsteps, or the knocking of a hammer over-head,
may resolve itself into a frightful figure stalking before us.

' I know,' says Mr Waller, ' a gentleman who is
living at this moment a needless slave to terror, which
arises from a circumstance which admits easily of explanation. He was lying in his bed with his wife, and,
as he supposed, quite awake, when he felt distinctly the
impression of some person's hand upon his right shoulder. which created such a degree of alarm that he dared

not to move himself in bed, and indeed could not, if he
had possessed the courage. It was some time before
he had it in his power to awake his wife. and communicate to her the subject of his terror. The shoulder
which had felt the impression of the hand, continued
to feel benumbed and uncomfortable for some time.
It had been uncovered, and most probably, the *cold*
to which it was exposed was the cause of the phenomenon.'*

An attack of dreaming illusion, not, however, accompanied with any unpleasant feeling, occurred to myself
lately. I had fallen accidentally asleep upon an arm-
chair, and was suddenly awaked by hearing, as I supposed, two of my brothers talking and laughing at the
door of the room, which stood wide open. The impressions were so forcible, that I could not believe
them fallacious, yet I ascertained that they were so entirely ; for my brothers had gone to the country an
hour before, and did not return for a couple of hours
afterwards.

There are few dreams involving many circumstances,
which are, from beginning to end, perfectly philosophical and harmonious : there is usually some absurd
violation of the laws of consistency, a want of congrui-
ty, a deficiency in the due relation of cause and effect,
and a string of conclusions altogether unwarranted by
the premises. Mr Hood, in his ' Whims and Oddities,'
gives a curious illustration of the above facts. ' It occurred,' says he, ' when I was on the eve of marriage,
a season when, if lovers sleep sparingly, they dream
profusely. A very brief slumber sufficed to carry me,
in the night coach, to Bogner, It had been concerted
between Honoria and myself that we should pass the
honeymoon at some such place upon the coast. The
purpose of my solitary journey was to procure an appropriate dwelling, and which, we had agreed upon,
should be a little pleasant house, with an indispensable
look-out upon the sea. I chose one accordingly, a
pretty villa, with bow windows, and a prospect delightfully marine. The ocean murmur sounded incessantly
from the beach. A decent elderly body, in decayed
sables, undertook on her part to promote the comfort of
the occupants by every suitable attention, and, as she
assured me, at a very reasonable rate. So far the nocturnal faculty had served me truly : a day dream could
not have proceeded more orderly : but alas ! just here,
when the dwelling was selected, the sea-view was secured, the rent agreed upon, when every thing was
plausible, consistent, and rational, the incoherent fancy
crept in, and confounded all—by marrying me to the
old woman of the house !'

There are no limits to the extravagancies of those
visions sometimes called into birth by the vivid exercise
of the imagination. Contrasted with them, the wildest
fictions of Rabelais, Ariosto, or Dante, sink into absolute probabilities. I remember of dreaming on one occasion that I possessed ubiquity, twenty resemblances
of myself appearing in as many different places, in the
same room ; and each being so thoroughly possessed
by my own mind, that I could not ascertain which of
them was myself, and which my double, &c. On this
occasion, fancy so far travelled into the regions of absurdity, that I conceived myself riding upon my own
back—one of the resemblances being mounted upon
another, and both animated with the soul appertaining
to myself. in such a manner that I knew not whether I
was the *carrier* or the *carried*. At another time, I
dreamed that I was converted into a mighty pillar of
stone, which reared its head in the midst of a desert,
where it stood for ages, till generation after generation
melted away before it. Even in this state, though unconscious for possessing any organs of sense, or being
else than a mass of lifeless stone, I saw every object
around—the mountains growing bald with age—the
forest trees drooping in decay ; and I heard whatever

* Waller's ' Treatise on the Incubus or Nightmare.'

sounds nature is in the custom of producing such as the thunder-peal breaking over my naked head, the winds howling past me, or the ceaseless murmur of streams. At last I also waxed old, and began to crumble into dust, while the moss and ivy accumulated, upon me, and stamped me with the aspect of hoar antiquity. The first of these visions may have arisen from reading Hoffman's 'Devil's Elixir,' where there is an account of a man who supposed he had a double, or, in other words, was both himself and not himself; and the second had perhaps its origin in the Heathen Mythology, a subject to which I am extremely partial, and which abounds in stories of metamorphosis.

Such dreams as occur in a state of drunkenness are remarkable for their extravagance. Exaggeration beyond limits is a very general attendant upon them; and they are usually of a more airy and fugitive character than those proceeding from almost any other source. The person seems as if he possessed unusual lightness, and could mount into the air, or float upon the clouds, while every object around him reels and staggers with emotion. But of all dreams, there are none which, for unlimited wildness, equal those produced by narcotics. An eminent artist, under the influence of opium, fancied the ghastly figures in Holbein's 'Dance of Death' to become vivified—each grim skeleton being endowed with life and motion, and dancing and grinning with an aspect with hideous reality. The 'English Opium Eater,' in his 'Confessions,' has given a great variety of eloquent and appalling descriptions of the effects produced by this drug upon the imagination during sleep. Listen to one of them :—

'Southern Asia is, and has been for thousands of years, the part of the earth most swarming with human life; the great *officina gentium*. Man is a weed in those regions. The vast empires, also, into which the enormous population of Asia has always been cast, give a farther sublimity to the feelings associated with all Oriental names or images. In China, over and above what it has in common with the rest of Southern Asia, I am terrified by the modes of life, by the manners, and the barrier of utter abhorrence and want of sympathy placed between us by feelings deeper than I can analyze. I could sooner live with lunatics or brute animals. All this, and much more than I can say, or have time to say the reader must enter into before he can comprehend the unimaginable horror which these dreams of Oriental imagery and mythological tortures impressed upon me. Under the connecting feeling of tropical heat and vertical sunlights, I brought together all creatures, birds, beasts, reptiles, all trees 'and plants, usages and appearances, that are found in all tropical regions, and assembled them together in China or Indostan. From kindred feelings I soon brought Egypt and all her gods under the same law. I was stared at, hooted at, grinned at, chattered at, by monkeys, by paroquets, and cockatoos. I ran into pagodas: and was fixed for centuries at the summit, or in the secret rooms; I was the idol; I was the priest; I was worshipped; I was sacrificed. I fled from the wrath of Brama through all the forests of Asia: Vishnu hated me: Seeva laid in wait for me. I came suddenly upon Isis and Osiris: I had done a deed, they said, which the ibis and the crocodile trembled at. I was buried for a thousand years, in stone coffins, with mummies and sphinxs, in narrow chambers, at the heart of eternal pyramids. I was kissed, with cancerous kisses, by crocodiles, and laid confounded with all unutterable slimy things, amongst reeds and Nilotic mud.'

Again; 'Hitherto the human face had mixed often in my dreams, but not so despotically, nor with any special power of tormenting. But now that which I have called the tyranny of the human face began to unfold itself. Perhaps some part of my London life might be answerable for this. Be that as it may, now it was that upon the rocking waters of the ocean, the human face began to appear; the sea appeared paved with innumerable faces, upturned to the heavens: faces imploring, wrathful, despairing, surged upwards by thousands, by myriads, by generations, by centuries : —my agitation was infinite—my mind tossed and surged with the ocean.'

I have already spoken of the analogy subsisting between dreaming and insanity, and shall now mention a circumstance which occurs in both states, and points out a very marked similitude of mental condition. The same thing also occasionally, or rather frequently, takes place in drunkenness, which is, to all intents and purposes, a temporary paroxysm of madness. It often happens, for instance, that such objects or persons as we have seen before and are familiar with, become utterly changed in dreams, and bear not the slightest resemblance to their *real* aspect. It might be thought that such a circumstance would so completely annihilate their identity as to prevent us from believing them to be what, by us, they are conceived; but such is not the case. We never doubt that the particular object or person presented to our eyes appears in its true character. In illustration of this fact, I may mention, that I lately visited the magnificent palace of Versailles in a dream, but that deserted abode of kings stood not before me as when I have gazed upon it broad awake; it was not only magnified beyond even its stupendous dimensions, and its countless splendors immeasurably increased, but the very aspect itself of the mighty pile was changed; and instead of stretching its huge Corinthian front along the entire breadth of an elaborate and richly fantastic garden, adorned to profusion with alcoves, fountains, waterfalls, statues, and terraces, it stood alone in a boundless wilderness—an immense architectural creation of the Gothic ages, with a hundred spires and ten thousand minarets sprouting up, and piercing with their pointed pinnacles the sky. The whole was as different as possible from the reality, but this never once occurred to my mind ; and, while gazing upon the visionary fabric, I never doubted for an instant that it then appeared as it had ever done, and was in no degree different from what I had often previously beheld.

Another dream I shall relate in illustration of this point. It was related to me by a young lady, and, independent of its illustrative value, is well worthy of being preserved as a specimen of fine imagination. 'I dreamed,' said she, 'that I stood alone upon the brink of a dreadful precipice, at the bottom of which rolled a great river. While gazing awe-struck upon the gulph below, some one from behind laid a hand upon my shoulder, and, on looking back, I saw a tall, venerable figure with a long, flowing, silvery beard, and clothed in white garments, whom I at once knew to be the Saviour of the world. "Do you see," he inquired, "the great river that washes the foundation of the rock upon which you now stand? I shall dry it up, so that not a drop of its waters shall remain, and all the fishes that are in it shall perish." He then waved his hand, and the river was instantly dried up; and I saw the fishes gasping and writhing in the channel, where they all straightway died. "Now," said he, "the river is dried up and the fishes are dead ; but to give you a farther testimony of my power, I shall bring back the flood, and every creature that was wont to inhabit it shall live again." And he waved his hand a second time, and the river was instantly restored, its dry bed filled with volumes of water, and all the dead fishes brought back unto life. On looking round to express to him my astonishment at those extraordinary miracles, and to fall down and worship him, he was gone ; and I stood by myself upon the precipice, gazing with astonishment at the river which rolled a thousand feet beneath me.' In this fine vision, the difference between the aspect of Christ as he appeared in it, and as be is represented in the sacred writings, as well as in paintings, did not suggest itself to the mind of the dreamer. He came in the guise of an aged man, which is diametrically opposite to our habitual impressions of his aspect. If it be asked what produces such differences between the reality and the representation, I apprehend we must refer it to some sudden second dream or flash of thought breaking in upon the first, and confusing its character. For instance, I have a dream of an immense Gothic pile, when something about Versailles, somehow, occurs to my mind, and this I immediately associate with the object before me. The lady has the idea of an old man in her dream, and the thought of Christ happening to come across her at the instant, she identifies it involuntarily with the object of her vision. There is yet another explanation of the latter. The old man has the power of working a great miracle ; so had Christ, and she is thus led to confound the two together. She, it is true, imagines she knows the old man at once to be the Saviour, without any previous intimation of his miraculous gifts ; but, this, very possibly, may be a mistake ; and the knowledge which she only acquires after witnessing his power, she may, by the confusion attendant on dreams, suppose to have occurred to her in the first instance. These facts, combined with the dormant state of the reflecting faculties, which do not rectify the erroneous impressions, render the explanation of such dreams sufficiently easy, however puzzling, and unaccountable at first sight.

In some cases, the illusion is not merely confined to sleep, but extends itself to the waking state. To illustrate this I may state the following circumstance : Some years ago, my impressions concerning the aspect and localities of Inverness, were strangely confused by a dream which I had of that town, taking so strong a bold upon my fancy as to be mistaken for a reality. I had been there before, and was perfectly familiar with the appearance of the town, but this was presented in so different a light, and with so much force by the dream, that I, at last, became unable to say which of the two aspects was the real one. Indeed, the visionary panorama exhibited to my mind, took the strongest bold upon it ; and I rather felt inclined to believe that this was the veritable appearance of the town, and that the one which I had actually beheld, was merely the illusion of the dream. This uncertainty continued for several years, till, being again in that quarter, I satisfied myself on the real state of the case. On this occasion, the dream must have occurred to my mind some time after it had happened, and taken such a firm bold upon it as to dethrone the reality, and taken its place. I remember distinctly of fancying that the little woody hill of Tomnachurich was in the centre of the town, although it stands at some distance from it ; that the principle steeple was on the opposite side of the street to that on which it stands ; and that the great mountain of Ben-Wevis, many miles off, was in the immediate neighborhood.

The power of imagination is perhaps never so vividly displayed, as in those dreams which haunt the guilty mind. When any crime of an infamous character has been perpetrated, and when the person is not so utterly hardened as to be insensible of his iniquity, the wide storehouse of retributive vengeance is opened up, and its appalling horrors poured upon him. In vain does he endeavor to expel the dreadful remembrance of his deeds, and bury them in forgetfulness ; from the abyss of slumber they start forth, as the vampyres start from their sepulchres, and hover around him like the furies that pursued the footsteps of Orestes ; while the voice of conscience stuns his ears with murmurs of judgment and eternity. Such is the punishment reserved for the guilty in sleep. During the busy stir of active existence, they may contrive to evade the memory of their wickedness—to silence the whispers of the ' still small voice' within them, and cheat themselves with a

semblance of happiness ; but when their heads are laid upon the pillow, the flimsy veil which bung between them and crime, melts away like an illusive cloud, and displays the latter in naked and horrid deformity. Then, in the silence of night, the ' still small voice' is heard like an echo from the tomb ; then, a crowd of doleful remembrances rush in upon the criminal, no longer to be debarred from visiting the depths of his spirit ; and when dreams succeed to such broken and miserable repose, it is only to aggravate his previous horrors, and present them in a character of still more overwhelming dread.*

"Though thy slumber may be deep,
Yet thy spirit shall not sleep;
There are shades which will not vanish,
There are thoughts thou canst not banish ;
By a power to thee unknown,
Thou canst never be alone ;
Thou art wrapt as with a shroud,
Thou art gathered in a cloud ;
And forever shalt thou dwell
In the spirit of this spell."

Such are the principal phenomena of dreams ; and from them it will naturally be deduced, that dreaming may occur under a great variety of circumstances ; that it may result from the actual state of the body or mind, previous to falling asleep ; or exist as a train of emotions which can be referred to no apparent external cause. The forms it assumes are also as various as the causes giving rise to it, and much more striking in their nature. In dreams, imagination unfolds, most gorgeously, the ample stores of its richly decorated empire ; and in proportion to the splendor of that faculty in any individual, are the visions which pass before him in sleep. But even the most dull and passionless, while under the dreaming influence, frequently enjoy a temporary inspiration : their torpid faculties are aroused from the benumbing spell which hung over them in the waking state, and lighted up with the Promethean fire of genius and romance ; the prose of their frigid spirits is converted into magnificent poetry ; the atmosphere around them peopled with new and unheard-of imagery ; and they walk in a region to which the proudest flights of their limited energies could never otherwise have attained.

I shall conclude this chapter with a few words on the management of dreams.

When dreams are of a pleasing character, no one cares any thing about their removal : it is only when they get distressing and threaten to injure the health of the individual, by frequent recurrence, that this becomes an important object. When dreams assume the character of nightmare, they must be managed according to the methods laid down for the cure of that affection. In all cases, the condition of the digestive organs must be attended to, as any disordered state of these parts is

* ' No fiction of romance presents so awful a picture of the ideal tyrant as that of Caligula by Suetonius. His palace—radiant with purple and gold, but murder every where lurking beneath flowers ; his smiles and echoing laughter- masking (yet hardly meant to mask) his foul treachery of heart ; his hideous and tumultuous dreams ; his baffled sleep, and his sleepless nights, compose the picture of an Æschylus. What a master's sketch lies in those few lines :—' Incitabatur insomnio maxime ; neque enim plus tribus horis nocturnis quiescebat ; ac ne his placida quiete, at pavida miris rerum imaginibus ; ut qui inter ceteras pelagi quondam speciem colloquentem secum videre visus sit. Ideoque magna parte noctis, vigiliæ cubandique tædio, nunc toro residens, nunc per longissimas porticus vagus, invocare identidem atque expectare lucem consueverat ;'—i. e. But above all, he was tormented with nervous irritation, by sleeplesness ; for he enjoyed not more than three hours of nocturnal repose : nor even these in pure, untroubled rest, but agitated by phantasmata of portentous augury ; as, for example, upon one occasion he fancied he saw the sea, under some definite impersonation, conversing with himself. Hence it was, that from this incapacity of sleeping, and from weariness of lying awake, that he had fallen into habits of ranging all the night long through the palace, sometimes throwing himself on a couch, sometimes wandering along the vast corridors—watching for the earliest dawn, and anxiously invoking its approach.'—Blackwood's Magazine, vol. xxxiii. p. 59.

apt to induce visions of a very painful character. For this purpose, mild laxatives may become useful ; and if the person is subject to heartburn, he should use a little magnesia, chalk, or carbonate of soda, occasionally. Attention, also, must be paid to the diet ; and as suppers, with some people, have a tendency to generate dreams of all kinds, these meals should, in such cases, be carefully avoided. At the same time, great care should be taken not to brood over any subject upon lying down, but to dispel, as soon as possible, all intrusive ideas, especially if they are of a painful nature. If there is any unpleasant circumstances, such as hardness, irregularity, &c., connected with the bed, which tends to affect sleep, and thus induce dreams, it must be removed. Late reading, the use of tea or coffee shortly before going to rest, or any thing which may stimulate the brain, ought likewise to be avoided.

If dreaming seems to arise from any fulness of the system, blooding and low diet will sometimes effect a cure. Mr Stewart, the celebrated pedestrian traveller, states that he never dreamed when he lived exclusively upon vegetable food. This, however, may not hold true with every one. ' When dreams arise from a diminution of customary stimuli, a light supper, a draught of porter, a glass of wine, or a dose of opium, generally prevent them. ' Habitual noises, when suspended should be restored.'*

In speaking of dreams representative of danger, I may mention that there are instances of persons, who, having determined to remember that the perils seen in them are fallacious, have actually succeeded in doing so, while asleep; and have thus escaped the terrors which those imaginary dangers could otherwise have produced. Haller relates a case of this kind ; and Mr Dugald Stewart mentions that the plan was successfully adopted by Dr Reid to get rid of the distress of those fearful visions by which he was frequently annoyed. Whenever, in a dream, the Doctor supposed himself on the brink of a precipice, or any other dangerous situation, it was his custom to throw himself over, and thus destroy the illusion. Dr Beattie also relates, that at one time he found himself in a dangerous situation upon the parapet of a bridge. Reflecting that he was not subject to pranks of this nature, he began to fancy that it might be a dream, and determined to pitch himself over, with the conviction that this would restore him to his senses, which accordingly took place.† I could never manage to carry this system into effect in an ordinary dream of terror, but I have sometimes succeeded in doing so during an attack of nightmare ; and have thus very materially mitigated the alarm produced by that distressing sensation. This intellectual operation may also be successfuly employed to dispel the lowness of spirits under which we often awake from unpleasant visions by teaching us that the depression we experience is merely the result of some unnatural excitement in the brain. Indeed, all kinds of melancholy, not based upon some obvious foundation, might be mitigated or dispelled altogether, could we only oppose our feelings with the weapons of reason, and see things as they really are, and not as they only seem to be.

CHAPTER IV.

PROPHETIC POWER OF DREAMS.

Dreams have been looked upon by some, as the occasional means of giving us an insight into futurity,

* Rush's Medical Inquiries.

† These facts do not controvert what is elsewhere stated of a person never being aware during the actual process of a dream, that he was dreaming. While the above dreams were in progress, the individuals never doubted that they were dreaming: the doubt, and the actions consequent upon it, were after-operations.

This opinion is so singularly unphilosophical, that I would not have noticed it, were it not advocated even by persons of good sense and education. In ancient times, it was so common as to obtain universal belief ; and the greatest men placed as implicit faith in it as in any fact of which their own senses afforded them cognizance. That it is wholly erroneous, however, cannot be doubted ; and any person who examines the nature of the human mind, and the manner in which it operates in dreams, must be convinced, that under no circumstances, except those of a miracle. in which the ordinary laws of nature are triumphed over, can such an event ever take place. The sacred writings testify that miracles were common in former times ; but I believe no man of sane mind will contend that they ever occur in the present state of the world. In judging of things as now constituted, we must discard supernatural influence altogether, and estimate events according to the general laws which the great ruler of nature has appointed for the guidance of the universe. If, in the present day, it were possible to conceive a suspension of these laws, it must, as in former ages, be in reference to some great event, and to serve some mighty purpose connected with the general interests of the human race ; but if faith is to be placed in modern miracles, we must suppose that God suspended the above laws for the most trivial and useless of purposes —as, for instance, to intimate to a man that his grandmother will die on a particular day, that a favourite mare has broke her neck, that he has received a present of a brace of game, or that a certain friend will step in and take pot-luck with him on the morrow.

At the same time, there can be no doubt that many circumstances occurring in our dreams have been actually verified ; but this must be regarded as altogether the effect of chance ; and for one dream which turns out to be true, at least a thousand are false. In fact, it is only when they are of the former description, that we take any notice of them ; the latter are looked upon as mere idle vagaries, and speedily forgotten. If a man, for instance, dreams that he has gained a law-suit in which he is engaged, and if this circumstance actually takes place, there is nothing at all extraordinary in the coincidence : his mind was full of the subject, and, in sleep, naturally resolved itself into that train of ideas in which it was most deeply interested. Or if we have a friend engaged in war, our fears for his safety will lead us to dream of death or captivity, and we may see him pent up in a hostile prison-house, or lying dead upon the battle plain. And should these melancholy catastrophies ensue we call our vision to memory ; and, in the excited state of mind into which we are thrown, are apt to consider it as a prophetic warning, indicative of disaster. The following is a very good illustration of this particular point.

Miss M——, a young lady, a native of Ross-shire, was deeply in love with an officer who accompanied Sir John Moore in the peninsular war. The constant danger to which he was exposed, had an evident effect upon her spirits. She became pale and melancholy in perpetually brooding over his fortunes ; and, in spite of all that reason could do, felt a certain conviction, that when she last parted with her lover, she had parted with him for ever. In vain was every scheme tried to dispel from her mind the awful idea ; in vain were all the sights which opulence could command, unfolded before her eyes. In the midst of pomp and gaiety, when music and laughter echoed around her, she walked as a pensive phantom, over whose head some dreadful and mysterious influence hung. She was brought by her affectionate parents to Edinburgh, and introduced into all the gaiety of that metropolis, but nothing could restore her, or banish from her mind the insupportable load which oppressed it. The song and the dance were tried in vain : they only aggravated her distress, and made the bitterness of despair more poignant. In a surprisingly short period, her graceful form declined into all the appalling characteristics of a fatal illness ; and she seemed rapidly hastening to the grave, when a dream confirmed the horrors she had long anticipated, and gave the finishing stroke to ner sorrows. One night, after falling asleep, she imagined she saw her lover, pale, bloody, and wounded in the breast, enter her apartment. He drew aside the curtains of the bed, and with a look of the utmost mildness, informed her that he had been slain in battle, desiring her, at the same time, to comfort herself, and not take his death too seriously to heart. It is needless to say what influence this vision had upon a mind so replete with woe. It withered it entirely, and the unfortunate girl died a few days thereafter, but not without desiring her parents to note down the day of the month on which it happened, and see if it would be confirmed, as she confidently declared it would. Her anticipation was correct, for accounts were shortly after received that the young man was slain at the battle of Corunna, which was fought on the very day, on the night of which his mistress had beheld the vision.

This relation, which may be confidently relied upon, is one of the most striking examples of identity between the dream and the real circumstances with which I am acquainted, but it must be looked upon as merely accidental. The lady's mind was deeply interested in the fate of her lover, and full of that event which she most deeply dreaded—his death. The time of this occurrence, as coinciding with her dream, is certainly curious ; but still there is nothing in it which can justify us in referring it to any other origin than chance. The following events, which occurred to myself, in August 1821, are almost equally remarkable, and are imputable to the same fortuitous cause.

I was then in Caithness, when I dreamed that a near relation of my own, residing three hundred miles off, had suddenly died : and immediately thereafter awoke in a state of inconceivable terror, similar to that produced by a paroxysm of nightmare. The same day, happening to be writing home, I mentioned the circumstance in a half-jesting, half-earnest way. To tell the truth, I was afraid to be serious, lest I should be laughed at for putting any faith in dreams. However, in the interval between writing and receiving an answer, I remained in a state of most unpleasant suspense. I felt a presentiment that something dreadful had happened, or would happen ; and although I could not help blaming myself for a childish weakness in so feeling, I was unable to get rid of the painful idea which had taken such rooted possession of my mind. Three days after sending away the letter, what was my astonishment when I received one written the day subsequent to mine, and stating that the relative of whom I had dreamed, had been struck with a fatal shock of palsy the day before—viz. the very day on the morning of which I had beheld the appearance in my dream ! My friends received my letter two days after sending their own away, and were naturally astonished at the circumstance. I may state that my relation was in perfect health before the fatal event took place. It came upon him like a thunderbolt, at a period when no one could have the slightest anticipation of danger.

The following case will interest the reader, both on its own account, and from the remarkable coincidence between the dream and the succeeding calamity ; but, like all other instances of the kind, this also must be referred to chance.

'Being in company the other day, when the conversation turned upon dreams, I related one, which as it happened to my own father, I can answer for the perfect truth of it. About the year 1731, my father, Mr D. of K——, in the County of Cumberland, came to Edinburgh to attend the classes, having the advantage of an uncle in the regiment then in the Castle, and re-

mained under the protection of his uncle and aunt, Major and Mrs Griffiths, during the winter. When spring arrived, Mr D. and three or four young gentlemen from England, (his intimates,) made parties to visit all the neighboring places about Edinburgh, Roslin, Arthur's Seat, Craig-Millar, &c., &c. Coming home one evening from some of those places, Mr D. said, ' We have made a party to go a-fishing to Inch-Keith to-morrow, if the morning is fine, and have bespoke our boat ; we shall be off at six ;' no objection being made, they separated for the night.

'Mrs Griffiths, had not been long asleep, till she screamed out in the most violent agitated manner, ' The boat is sinking ; save, oh, save them !' The Major awaked her, and said, ' Were you uneasy about the fishing party ?' ' Oh no,' said she, ' I had not once thought of it.' She then composed herself, and soon fell asleep again ; in about an hour, she cried out in a dreadful fright, ' I see the boat is going down.' The Major again awoke her, and she said, ' It has been owing to the other dream I had ; for I feel no uneasiness about it.' After some conversation, they both fell sound asleep, but no rest could be obtained for her ; in the most extreme agony, she again screamed, ' They are gone ; the boat is sunk !' When the Major awakened her, she said, ' Now I cannot rest ; Mr D. must not go, for I feel, should he go, I would be miserable till his return ; the thoughts of it would almost kill me.'

' She instantly arose, threw on her wrapping-gown, went to his bedside, for his room was next their own, and with great difficulty she got his promise to remain at home. ' But what am I to say to my young friends whom I was to meet at Leith at six o'clock ?' ' With great truth you may say your aunt is ill, for I am so at present ; consider, you are an only son, under our protection, and should any thing happen to you, it would be my death.' Mr D. immediately wrote a note to his friends, saying he was prevented from joining them, and sent his servant with it to Leith. The morning came in most beautifully, and continued so till three o'clock, when a violent storm arose, and in an instant the boat, and all that were in it, went to the bottom, and were never heard of, nor was any part of it ever seen.'*

Equally singular is the following case, from the 'Memoirs of Lady Fanshawe.'

' My mother being sick to death of a fever, three months after I was born, which was the occasion she gave me suck no longer, her friends and servants thought to all outward appearnce she was dead, and so lay almost two days and a night ; but Dr Winston coming to comfort my father, went into my mother's room, and looking earnestly on her face, said, ' She was so handsome, and now looks so lovely, I cannot think she is dead ;' and suddenly took a lancet out of his pocket, and with it cut the sole of her foot, which bled. Upon this, he immediately caused her to be laid upon the bed again, and to be rubbed, and such means, as she came to life, and opening her eyes, saw two of her kinswomen stand by her, my Lady Knollys and my Lady Russell, both with great wide sleeves, as the fashion then was, and said, ' Did not you promise me fifteen years, and are you come again' which they not understanding, persuaded her to keep her spirits quiet in that great weakness wherein she then was; but some hours after, she desired my father and Dr Howlsworth might be left alone with her, to whom she said, ' I will acquaint you, that during the time of my trance I was in great quiet, but in a place I could neither distinguish nor describe ; but the sense of leaving my girl, who is dearer to me than all my children, remained a trouble upon my spirits. Suddenly I saw two by me, clothed in long white garments, and methought I fell down upon my face upon the dust ; and they asked why I was so troubled in so great happiness. I re-plied, O let me have the same grant given to Hezekiah, that I may live fifteen years to see my daughter a woman : to which they answered, It is done : and then, at that instant, I awoke out of my trance !' and Dr Howlsworth did there affirm, that that day she died made just fifteen years from that time.'

A sufficiently striking instance of such coincidence occurs in the case of Dr Donne, the metaphysical poet ; but I believe that, in this case, it was a spectral illusion rather than a common dream. Two days after he had arrived in Paris, he was left alone in a room where he had been dining with Sir Robert Drury and a few companions. 'Sir Robert returned about an hour afterwards. He found his friend in a state of ecstacy, and so altered in his countenance, that he could not look upon him without amazement. The Doctor was not able for some time to answer the ques-tion, *what had befallen him ?*—but a long and perplexed pause, at last said, 'I have seen a dreadful vision since I saw you ; I have seen my dear wife pass twice by me through this room, with her hair hanging about her shoulders, and a dead child in her arms. This I have seen since I saw you.' To which Sir Robert answered, 'Sure, Sir, you have slept since I went out ; and this is the result of some melancholy dream, which I desire you to forget, for you are now awake.' Donne replied, 'I cannot be more sure that I now live, than that I have not slept since I saw you ; and am as sure that at her second appearing she stopped, looked me in in the face and vanished.''* It is certainly very curious that Mrs Donne, who was then in England, was at this time sick in bed, and had been delivered of a dead child, on the same day, and about the same hour, that the vision occurred. There were distressing circumstances in the marriage of Dr Donne which ac-count for his mind being strongly impressed with the image of his wife, to whom he was exceedingly at-tached ; but these do not render the coincidence above related less remarkable.

I do not doubt that the apparition of Julius Cæsar, which appeared to Brutus, and declared it would meet him at Philippi, was either a dream or a spectral illu-sion—probably the latter. Brutus, in all likelihood, had some idea that the battle which was to decide his fate would be fought at Philippi : probably it was a good military position, which he had fixed upon as a fit place to make a final stand ; and he had done enough to Cæsar to account for his own mind being painfully and constantly engrossed with the image of the assasin-ated Dictator. Hence the verification of this supposed warning—hence the easy explanation of a supposed supernatural event.

At Newark-upon-Trent, a curious custom, founded upon the preservation of Alderman Clay and his family by a dream, has prevailed since the days of Cromwell. On the 11th March, every year, penny loaves are given away to any one who chooses to appear at the town hall and apply for them, in commemoration of the al-derman's deliverance, during the siege of Newark by the parliamentary forces. This gentleman, by will, dated 11th December, 1694, gave to the mayor and al-dermen one hundred pounds, the interest of which was to be given to the vicar yearly, on condition of his preaching an annual sermon. Another hundred pounds were also appropriated for the behoof of the poor, in the way above mentioned. The origin of this bequest is singular. During the bombardment of Newark by Oli-ver Cromwell's forces, the alderman dreamed three nights successively that his house had taken fire, which produced such a vivid impression upon his mind, that he and his family left it ; and in a few days the cir-cumstances of his vision actually took place, by the house being burned down by the besiegers.

Dr Abercrombie relates the case of a gentleman in

* Hibbert's Philosophy of Apparitions, p. 354.

Edinburgh, who was affected with an aneurism of the popliteal artery, for which he was under the care of two eminent surgeons. About two days before the time appointed for the operation, his wife dreamed that a change had taken place in the disease, in consequence of which an operation would not be required. 'On examining the tumor in the morning, the gentleman was astonished to find that the pulsation had entirely ceased ; and, in short, this turned out to be a spontane-ous cure. To persons not professional, it may be right to mention that the cure of popliteal aneurism, without an operation, is a very uncommon occurrence, not hap-pening, perhaps, in one out of numerous instances, and never to be looked upon as probable in any individual case. It is likely, however, that the lady had heard of the possibility of such a termination, and that her anx-iety had very naturally embodied this into a dream : the fulfilment of it, at the very time when the event took place, is certainly a very remarkable coincidence.'*

Persons are said to have had the period of their own death pointed out to them in dreams. I have often heard the case of the late Mr M. of D—— related in support of this statement. It is certainly worth telling, not on account of any supernatural character belonging to it, but simply from the extraordinary coincidence between the dream and the subsequent event. This gentleman dreamed one night that he was out riding, when he stopped at an inn on the road side for refresh-ment, where he saw several people whom he had known some years before, but who were all dead. He was received kindly by them, and desired to sit down and drink, which he accordingly did. On quitting this strange company, they exacted a promise from him that he would visit them that day six weeks. This he promised faithfully to do ; and, bidding them farewell, he rode homewards. Such was the substance of his dream, which he related in a jocular way to his friends, but thought no more about it, for he was a person above all kind of superstition. The event, however, was cer-tainly curious enough, as well as melancholy ; for on that very day six weeks on which he had engaged to meet his friends at the inn, he was killed in attempting to spring his horse over a five-barred gate. The famous case of Lord Lyttleton† is also cited as an example of a similar kind, but with less show of reason, for this case is now very generally supposed to be an imposi-tion ; and so will almost every other of the same kind, if narrowly investigated. At the same time, I do not mean to doubt that such an event, foretold in a dream, may occasionally come to pass ; but I would refer the whole to fortuitous coincidence. Men dream, every now and then, that they will die on a certain day, yet how seldom do we see those predictions fulfiled by the result ! In very delicate people, indeed, such a vision-ary communication, by acting fatally upon the mind, might be the means of occasioning its own fulfilment. In such cases, it has been customary for the friends of the individual to put back the clock an hour or two, so as to let the fatal period pass by without his being aware of it ; and as soon as it was fairly passed, to inform him of the circumstance, and laugh him out of his ap-prehension.

There is another way in which the apparent fulfil-ment of a dream may be brought about. A good illus-tration in point is given by Mr Combe. The subject of it was one Scott, executed in 1823, at Jedburg, for murder. 'It is stated in his life, that some years be-

* Abercrombie's Inquiries concerning the Intellectual Pow-ers, p. 282, 1st edit.
† Of late it has been said and published, that the unfortu-nate nobleman had previously determined to take poison, and of course had it in his own power to ascertain the execution of the prediction. It was, no doubt, singular that a man, who medi-tated his exit from the world, should have chosen to play such a trick upon his friends. But it is still more credible that a whimsi-cal man should do so wild a thing, than that a messenger should be sent from the dead, to tell a libertine at what precise hour he should expire.'—*Scott's Letters on Demonology, p. 361.*

fore the fatal event, he had dreamed that he had committed a murder, and was greatly impressed, with the idea. He frequently spoke of it, and recurred to it as something ominous, till at last it was realized. · The organ of *Destructiveness* was large in the head, and so active that he was an enthusiast in poaching, and prone to outrage and violence in his habitual conduct. This activity of the organ might take place during sleep, and then it would inspire his mind with destructive feelings, and the dream of murder would be the consequence. From the great natural strength of the propensity, he probably may have felt, when awake, an inward tendency to this crime ; and, joining this and the dream together, we can easily account for the strong impression left by the latter on the mind.' *

One method in which death may appear to be foretold is, by the accession of frightful visions immediately before the fatal illnesses. This, however, goes for nothing in the way of argument, for it was the state of the system shortly before the attack of disease which induced such dreams. According to Silamachus, the epidemic fever which prevailed at Rome, was ushered in by attacks of nightmare ; and Sylvius Deleboe, who describes the epidemic which raged at Leyden in 1669, states, that previous to each paroxysm of the fever, the patient fell asleep, and suffered a severe attack of nightmare. The vulgar belief, therefore, that unpleasant dreams are ominous of death, is not destitute of foundation ; but the cause why they should be so is perfectly natural. It is the incipient disease which produces the dreams, and the fatal event which often follows, is a natural consequence of that disease.

It is undoubtedly owing to the faculty possessed by sleep, of renewing long-forgotten ideas, that persons have had important facts communicated to them in dreams. There have been instances, for example, where valuable documents, sums of money, &c, have been concealed, and where either the person who secreted them or he who had the place of their concealment communicated to him, may have forgotten every thing therewith connected. He may then torture his mind in vain, during the walking state, to recollect the event; and it may be brought to his remembrance, at once, in a dream. in such cases, an apparition is generally the medium through which the seemingly mysterions knowledge is communicated. The imagination conjures up some phantom that discloses the secret ; which circumstance, proceeding, in reality, from a simple operation of the mind, is straightway converted into something supernatural, and invested with all the attributes of wonder and awe. When such spectral forms appear, and communicate some fact which turns out to be founded on truth, the person is not always aware that the whole occurred in a dream, but often fancies that he was broad awake when the apparition appeared to him and communicated the particular intelligence. When we have, therefore, of hidden treasures, wills, &c, being disclosed in such a manner, we are not always to scout the report as false. The spectre divulging the intelligence was certainly the mere chimera of the dreamer's brain, but the facts revealed, apparently by this phantom, may, from the above circumstance, be substantially true. The following curious case is strikingly in point, and is given by Sir Walter Scott in his notes to the new edition of 'The Antiquary'

'Mr R——d of Bowland, a gentleman of landed property in the Vale of Gala, was prosecuted for a very considerable sum, the accumulated arrears of tiend, (or tithe,) for which he was said to be indebted to a noble family, the titulars (lay impropriators of the tithes.) Mr R——d was strongly impressed with the belief that his father had, by a form of process peculiar to the law of Scotland, purchased these lands from the titular, and, therefore, that the present prosecution was groundless.

* Combe's System of Phrenology, p. 511, 3d edit.

But after an industrious search among his father's papers, an investigation of the public records, and a careful inquiry among all persons who had transacted law business for his father, no evidence could be recovered to support his defence. The period was now near at hand when he conceived the loss of his lawsuit to be inevitable, and he had formed the determination to ride to Edinburgh next day, and make the best bargain he could in the way of compromise. He went to bed with this resolution, and, with all the circumstances of the case floating upon his mind, had a dream to the following purpose. His father, who had been many years dead, appeared to him, he thought, and asked him why he was disturbed in his mind. In dreams, men are not surprised at such apparitions. Mr R——d thought that he informed his father of the cause of his distress, adding, that the payment of a considerable sum of money was the more unpleasant to him, because he had a strong consciousness that it was not due, though he was unable to recover any evidence in support of his belief. 'You are right, my son,' replied the paternal shade ; 'I did acquire right to these tiends, for payment of which you are now prosecuted. The papers relating to the transaction are now in the hands of Mr ——, a writer, (or attorney,) who is now retired from professional business, and resides at Inveresk, near Edinburgh. He was a person whom I employed on that occasion for a particular reason, but who never on any other occasion transacted business on my account. It is very possible,' pursued the vision, 'that Mr —— may have forgotten a matter which is now of a very old date ; but you may call it to his recollection by this token, that when I came to pay his account, there was difficulty in getting change for a Portugal piece of gold, and we were forced to drink out the balance at a tavern.'

'Mr R——d awoke in the morning with all the words of the vision imprinted on his mind, and thought it worth while to walk across the country to Inveresk, instead of going straight to Edinburgh. When he came there, he waited on the gentleman mentioned in the dream, a very old man. Without saying anything of the vision, he inquired whether he remembered having conducted such a matter for his diseased father. The old gentleman could not at first bring the circumstance to his recollection, but on mention of the Portugal piece of gold, the whole returned upon his memory ; he made an immediate search for the papers, and recovered them—so that Mr R——d carried to Edinburgh the documents necessary to gain the cause which he was on the verge of losing.

'The author has often heard this story told by persons who had the best access to know the facts, who were not likely themselves to be deceived, and were certainly incapable of deception. He cannot, therefore, refuse to give it credit, however extraordinary the circumstances may appear. The circumstantial character of the information given in the dream, takes it out of the general class of impressions of the kind, which are occasioned by the fortuitous coincidence of actual events with our sleeping thoughts. On the other hand, few will suppose that the laws of nature were suspended, and a special communication from the dead to the living permitted, for the purpose of saving Mr. R——d a certain number of hundred pounds. The author's theory is, that the dream was only the recapitulation of information which Mr R——d had really received from his father while in life, but which at first he merely recalled as a general impression that the claim was settled. It is not uncommon for persons to recover, during sleep, the thread of ideas which they have lost during their waking hours. It may be added, that this remarkable circumstance was attended with bad consequences to Mr R——d ; whose health and spirits were afterwards impaired, by the attention which he thought himself obliged to pay to the visions of the night.' This result is a melancholy proof of the effect sometimes produced by ignorance of the natural laws. Had Mr R——d been acquainted with the nature of the brain, and of the manner in which it is affected in sleep, the circumstance above related would have given him no annoyance. He would have traced the whole chain of events to their true source ; but, being ignorant of this, he became the victim of superstition, and his life was rendered miserable.

CHAPTER V.

NIGHTMARE.

Nightmare may be defined a painful dream, accompanied with difficult respiratory action, and a torpor in the powers of volition. The reflecting organs are generally more or less awake ; and, in this respect, nightmare differs from simple dreaming, where they are mostly quiescent.

This affection, the EPHIALTES of the Greeks, and INCUBUS of the Romans, is one of the most distressing to which human nature is subject. Imagination cannot conceive the horrors it frequently gives rise to, or language describe them in adequate terms. They are a thousand times more frightful than the visions conjured up by necromancy or *diablere* ; and far transcend every thing in history or romance, from the fable of the writhing and asp-encircled Laocoon to Dante's appalling picture of Ugolino and his famished offspring, or the hidden tortures of the Spanish inquisition. The whole mind, during the paroxysm, is wrought up to a pitch of unutterable despair : a spell is laid upon the faculties, which freezes them into inaction ; and the wretched victim feels as if pent alive in his coffin, or overpowered by resistless and immitigable pressure.

The modifications which nightmare assumes are infinite ; but one passion is almost never absent—that of utter and incomprehensible dread. Sometimes the sufferer is buried beneath overwhelming rocks, which crush him on all sides, but still leave him with a miserable consciousness of his situation. Sometimes he is involved in the coils of a horrid, slimy monster, whose eyes have the phosphorescent glare of the sepulchre, and whose breath is poisonous as the marsh of Lerna. Every thing horrible, disgusting, or terrific in the physical or moral world, is brought before him in fearful array ; he is hissed at by serpents, tortured by demons, stunned by the hollow voices and cold touch of apparitions. A mighty stone is laid upon his breast, and crushes him to the ground in helpless agony; mad bulls and tigers pursue his palsied footsteps : the unearthly shrieks and gibberish of hags, witches, and fiends float around him. In whatever situation he may be placed, he feels superlatively wretched ; he is Ixion working for ages at his wheel : he is Sisyphus rolling his eternal stone : he is stretched upon the iron bed of Procrustes : he is prostrated by inevitable destiny beneath the approaching wheels of the car of Juggernaut. At one moment, he may have the consciousness of a malignant demon being at his side : then to shun the sight of so appalling an object, he will close his eyes, but still the fearful being makes its presence known ; for its icy breath is felt diffusing itself over his visage, and he knows that he is face to face with a fiend. Then, if he look up, he beholds horrid eyes glaring upon him, and an aspect of hell grinning at him with even more than hellish malice. Or, he may have the idea of a monstrous hag squatted upon his breast—mute, motionless, and malignant ; an incarnation of the evil spirit— whose intolerable weight crushes the breath out of his body, and whose fixed, deadly, incessant stare petrifies him with horror and makes his very existence insufferable.

In every instance, there is a sense of oppression and helplessness ; and the extent to which these are carried, varies according to the violence of the paroxysm. The individual never feels himself a free agent ; on the contrary he is spell-bound by some enchantment, and remains an unresisting victim for malice to work its will upon. He can neither breathe, nor walk, nor run, with his wonted facility. If pursued by an imminent danger, he can hardly drag one limb after another ; if engaged in combat, his blows are utterly ineffective ; if involved in the fangs of any animal, or in the grasp of an enemy, extrication is impossible. He struggles, he pants, he toils, but it is all in vain : his muscles are rebels to the will, and refuse to obey its calls. In no case is there a sense of complete freedom : the benumbing stupor never departs from him ; and his whole being is locked up in one mighty spasm. Sometimes he is forcing himself through an aperture too small for the reception of his body, and is there arrested and tortured by the pangs of suffocation produced by the pressure to which he is exposed ; or he loses his way in a narrow labyrinth, and gets involved in its contracted and inextricable mazes ; or he is entombed alive in a sepulchre, beside the mouldering dead. There is, in most cases, an intense reality in all that he sees, or hears, or feels. The aspects of the hideous phantoms which harass his imagination are bold and defined ; the sounds which greet his ear appalling distinct ; and when any dimness or confusion of imagery does prevail, it is of the most fearful kind, leaving nothing but dreary and miserable impressions behind it.

Much of the horror experienced in nightmare will depend upon the natural activity of the imagination, upon the condition of the body, and upon the state of mental exertion before going to sleep. If, for instance, we have been engaged in the perusal of such works as ' The Monk,' ' The Mysteries of Udolpho,' or ' Satan's Invisible World Discovered ;' and if an attack of nightmare should supervene, it will be aggravated into sevenfold horror by the spectral phantoms with which our minds have been thereby filled. We will enter into all the fearful mysteries of these writings, which, instead of being mitigated by slumber, acquire an intensity which they never could have possessed in the waking state. The apparitions of murdered victims, like the form of Banquo, which wrung the guilty conscience of Macbeth, will stalk before us ; we are surrounded by sheeted ghosts, which glare upon us with their cold sepulchral eyes ; our habitation is among the vaults of ancient cathedrals, or among the dungeons of ruined monasteries, and our companions are the dead.

At other times, an association of ludicrous images passes through the mind : every thing becomes incongruous, ridiculous, and absurd. But even in the midst of such preposterous fancies, the passion of mirth is never for one moment excited : the same blank despair, the same freezing *inertia*, the same stifling tortures, still harass us ; and so far from being amused by the laughable drama enacted before us, we behold it with sensations of undefined horror and disgust.

In general, during an attack, the person has the consciousness of an utter inability to express his horror by cries. He feels that his voice is half choked by impending suffocation, and that any exertion of it, farther than a deep sigh or groan, is impossible. Sometimes, however, he conceives that he is bellowing with prodigious energy, and wonders that the household are not alarmed by his noise. But this is an illusion : those outcries which he fancies himself uttering, are merely obscure moans, forced with difficulty and pain from the stifled penetralia of his bosom.

Nightmare takes place under various circumstances. Sometimes, from a state of perfect sleep, we glide into it, and feel ourselves unconsciously overtaken by its attendant horrors : at other times, we experience it stealing upon us like a thief, at a period when we are all but awake, and aware of its approach. We have then our senses about us, only, perhaps a little deadened and confused by incipient slumber ; and we feel the gradual advance of the fiend, without arousing ourselves, and scaring him away, although we appear to possess the full ability of doing so. Some persons, immediately previous to an attack, have sensations of vertigo and ringing in the ears.

At one time, nightmare melts into unbroken sleep or pleasing dreams ; and when we awake in the morning with merely the remembrance of having had one of its attacks ; at another, it arouses us by its violence, and we start out of it with a convulsive shudder. At the moment of throwing off the fit, we seem to turn round upon the side with a mighty effort, as if from beneath the pressure of a superincumbent weight ; and, the more thoroughly to awake ourselves, we generally kick violently, beat the breast, rise up in bed, and cry out once or twice. As soon as we are able to exercise the voice or voluntary muscles with freedom, the paroxysm is at an end ; but 'for some time after, we experience extreme terror, and often cold shivering, while the heart throbs violently, and the respiration is hurried. These two latter circumstances are doubted by Dr Darwin, but I am convinced of their existence, both from what I have experienced in my own person, and from what I have been told by others : indeed, analogy would irresistibly lead us to conclude that they must exist ; and whoever carefully investigates the subject, will find that they do almost universally.

An opinion prevails, that during incubus the person is always upon his back ; and the circumstances of his usually feeling as if in that posture, together with the relief which he experiences on turning round upon his side, are certainly strong presumptions in favour of its accuracy. The sensations, however, which occur, in this state, are fallacious in the highest degree. We have seldom any evidence either that he was on his back, or that he turned round at all. The fact, that he supposed himself in the above position during the fit, and the other fact, that, on recovering from it, he was lying on his side, may have produced the illusion ; and, where he never moved a single muscle, he may conceive that he turned round after a prodigious effort. I have had an attack of this disorder while sitting in an arm-chair, or with my head leaning against a table. In fact, these are the most likely positions to bring it on, the lungs being then more completely compressed than in almost any other posture. I have also had it most distinctly while lying on the side, and I know many cases of a similar description in others. Although, therefore, nightmare may take place more frequently upon the back than upon the side, the opinion that it occurs only in the former of these postures, is altogether incorrect ; and where we are much addicted to its attacks, no posture whatever will protect us.

Persons not particulary subject to incubus, feel no inconvenience, save temporary terror or fatigue, from any occasional attack which they may have ; but those with whom it is habitual, are apt to experience a certain degree of giddiness, ringing in the ears, tension of the forehead, flashing of light before the eyes, and other symptoms of cerebral congestion. A bad taste in the mouth, and more or less fulness about the pit of the stomach, are sometimes experienced after an attack.

The illusions which occur, are perhaps the most extraordinary phenomena of nightmare ; and so strongly are they often impressed upon the mind, that, even on awaking, we find it impossible not to believe them real. We may, for example, be sensible of knockings at the door of our apartment, hear familiar voices calling upon us, and see individuals passing through the chamber. In many cases, no arguments, no efforts of the under-

standing will convince us that these are merely the chimeras of sleep. We regard them as events of actual occurrence, and will not be persuaded to the contrary. With some, such a belief has gone down to the grave : and others have maintained it strenuously for years, till a recurrence of the illusions under circumstances which rendered their real existence impossible, has shown them that the whole was a dream. Many a good ghost story has had its source in the illusions of nightmare.

The following case related by Mr Waller gives a good idea of the strength of such illusive feelings.

'In the month of February, 1814, I was living in the same house with a young gentlemen, the son of a peer of the United Kingdom, who was at that time under my care, in a very alarming state of health ; and who had been, for several days, in a state of violent delirium. The close attention which his case required from me, together with a degree of personal attachment to him, had rendered me extremely anxious about him ; and as my usual hours of sleep suffered a great degree of interruption from the attendance given to him, I was from that cause alone, rendered more than usually liable to the attacks of nightmare, which consequently intruded itself every night upon my slumbers. The young gentleman in question, from the violence of his delirium, was with great difficulty kept in bed ; and had one or twice eluded the vigilance of his attendants, and jumped out of bed, an accident of which I was every moment dreading a repetition.' I awoke from one sleep one morning about four o'clock—at least it apppeared to me that I awoke—and heard distinctly the voice of this young gentleman, who seemed to be coming hastily up the stairs leading to my apartment, calling me by name in the manner he was accustomed to do in his delirium ; and, immediately after, I saw him standing by my bedside, holding the curtains open, expressing all that wildness in his looks which accompanies a violent delirium At the same moment, I heard the voices of his two attendants coming up the stairs in search of him, who likewise came into the room and took him away. During all this scene I was attempting to speak, but could not articulate ; I thought, however, that I succeeded in attempting to get out of bed, and assisting his attendants in removing him out of the room ; after which, I returned to bed, and instantly fell asleep. When I waited upon my patient in the morning, I was not a little surprised to find that he was asleep ; and was uttterly confounded on being told that he had been so all night ; and as this was the first sleep he had enjoyed for three or four days, the attendants were very minute in detailing the whole particulars of it. Athough this account appeared inconsistent with what I conceived I had seen, and with what I concluded they knew as well as myself, I did not, for some time, perceive the error into which I had been led, till I observed that some of my questions and remarks were not intelligible ; then I began to suspect the true source of the error, which I should never have discovered had not experience rendered these hallucinations familiar to me. But the whole of this transaction had so much consistency and probability in it, that I might, under different circumstances, have remained forever ignorant of having been imposed upon in this instance, by my senses.'*

During nightmare, the deepness of the slumber varies much at different times. Sometimes we are in a state closely approximating upon perfect sleep ; at other times we are almost completely awake ; and it will be remarked, that the more awake we are, the greater is the violence of the paroxysm. I have experienced the affection stealing upon me while in perfect possession of my faculties, and have undergone the greatest tortures, being haunted by spectres, hags, and every sort of phantom—having, at the same time, a full conscious-

* Waller's Treatise.

ness that I was labouring under incubus, and that all the terrifying objects around me were the creations of my own brain. This shows that the judgment is often only very partially affected, and proves also that nightmare is not merely a disagreeable dream, but a painful bodily affection. Were it nothing more than the former, we could rarely possess a knowledge of our condition ; for, in simple visions, the reflecting organs are almost uniformly quiescent, and we scarcely ever, for a moment, doubt the reality of our impressions. In nightmare, this is often, perhaps generally, the case ; but we frequently meet with instances, in which, during the worst periods of the fit, consciousness remains almost unimpaired.

There are great differences in the duration of the paroxysm, and also in the facility with which it is broken. I know not of any method by which the period to which it extends can be estimated, for the sufferer has no data to go by, and time, as in all modifications of dreaming, is subjected to the most capricious laws—an actual minute often appearing to embrace a whole hour. Of this point, therefore, we must be contented to remain in ignorance ; but it may be conceived that the attack will be as various in its duration, as in the characters which it assumes—in one case being ten times as long as in another. With regard to the breaking of the fit, the differences are equally great. At one time, the slightest agitation of the body, the opening of the chamber door, or calling softly to the sufferer, will arouse him ; at another, he requires to be shaken violently, and called upon long and loudly, before he is released.

Some people are much more prone to incubus than others. Those whose digestion is healthy, whose minds are at ease, and who go supperless to bed, will seldom be troubled with it. Those, again, who keep late hours, study hard, eat heavy suppers, and are subject to bile, acid, or hypochondria, are almost sure to be more or less its victims. There are particular kinds of food, which pretty constantly lead to the same result, such as cheese, cucumbers, almonds, and whatever is hard to be digested. Hildesheim, in his 'De Affectibus Capitis,' justly remarks, that ' he who wishes to know what nightmare is, let him eat chestnuts before going to sleep, and drink feculent wine after them.'

Certain diseases, also, are apt to induce it, such as asthma, hydrothorax, agina pectoris, and other varieties of dyspnœa. Men are more subject to it than women, probably from their stomachs being more frequently disordered by intemperance, and their minds more closely occupied. Sailors, owing to the hard and indigestible nature of their food, are very frequently its victims ; and it is a general remark that it oftener occurs at sea than on shore. It seems probable that much of the superstitious belief of these men, in apparitions, proceeds from the phantoms which nightmare calls into existence. Unmarried women are more annoyed by it than those who are married ; and the latter, when pregnant, have it oftener than at other times. Persons who were extremely subject to the complaint in their youth, sometimes get rid of it when they reach the age of puberty, owing, probably, to some change in the constitution which occurs at this period.

There have been different opinions with regard to the proximate cause of incubus, and authors have generally looked upon it as involved in considerable obscurity. An impeded circulation of blood in the pulmonary arteries, compression of the diaphragm by a full stomach, and torpor of the intercostal muscles, are all mentioned as contributing wholly, or partially, to the event. I am of opinion that either of these states may cause nightmare, but that, in most cases, they are all combined. Any thing, in fact, which impedes respiration, may give rise to the disorder, whether it be asthma, hydrothorax, distended stomach, muscular torpor, or external compression. The causes, then, are various,

but it will be found that, whatever they may be, their ultimate operation is upon the lungs.

We have already seen that, in ordinary sleep, particular states of the body are apt to induce visions : it is, therefore easily conceivable that a sense of suffocation, such as occurs in nightmare, may give birth to all the horrid phantoms seen in that distemper. The physical sufferings in such a case, exalts the imagination to its utmost pitch : fills it with spectres and chimeras ; and plants an immovable weight or malignant fiend upon the bosom to crush us into agony. Let us see how such physical sufferings is brought about.

Any disordered state of the stomach may produce it. This organ may be so distended with food or wind as to press upon the diaphragm, lessen the dimensions of the chest, obstruct the movements of the heart, and thereby impede respiration. Circumstances like these alone are sufficient to produce nightmare ; and the cause from the first is purely mechanical.

Secondly. The state of the stomach may call forth incubus by means circuitous or indirect. In this case, the viscus is unequal to the task imposed upon it of digesting the food, either from an unusual quantity being thrown upon it, from the food being of an indigestible nature, or from actual weakness. Here the sensorial power latent in this organ, is insufficient to carry it through with its operations, and it is obliged to draw upon the rest of the body—upon the brain, the respiratory muscles, &c, for the supply of which it is deficient. The muscles of respiration, in giving their portion, reduce themselves to a state of temporary debility, and do not retain a sufficient share to execute their own actions with due vigour. The pectorels, the intercostals, and the diaphragm became thus paralyzed ; and, the chest not being sufficiently dilated for perfect breathing, a feeling of suffocation inevitably insues. In like manner, the muscles of volition, rendered inert by the subtraction of their quota of sensorial power, are unable to exercise their functions, and remain, during the paroxysm, in a state of immovable torpor. This unequal distribution of nervous energy continues till, by producing some excessive uneasiness, it stimulates the will to a violent effort, and breaks the fit ; and so soon as this takes place, the balance becomes redressed, and the sensorial equilibrium restored.

Physical suffering of that kind which impedes breathing, may also be occasioned by many other causes—by pneuomonia, by empyema, by aneurism of the aorta, by laryngitis by croup, by external pressure ; and, accordingly, either of these may give rise to nightmare. If we chance to lie down with a pillow or heavy cloak upon the breast, or to sleep with the body bent forward, and the head supported upon a table, as already mentioned, we may be seized with it ; and, in truth, whatever, either directly or indirectly, acts upon the respiratory muscles, and impedes their operation, is pretty sure to bring it on. Even a weak or disordered stomach, in which there is no food, by attracting to itself a portion of their sensorial power to aid its own inadequacies, may induce it. The disorder, therefore, takes place under various circumstances—either by direct pressure upon the lungs, as in distended stomach, or hydrothorax ; or by partial torpor of the stomach or muscles of respiration, owing to a deficiency of nervous energy. These physical impediments coexisting with, or giving rise to a distempered state of the brain, sufficiently account for the horrors of nightmare.

Why are hard students, deep thinkers, and hypochondriacs unusually subject to incubus? The cause is obvious. Such individuals have often a bad digestion : their stomachs are subject to acidity, and other functional derangements, and therefore, peculiarly apt to generate the complaint. The sedentary life, and habits of intellectual or melancholy reflection in which they indulge, have a tendency not merely to disturb the digestive apparatus, but to act upon the whole cerebral system : hence, they are far more liable to dreams of every kind than other people, in so far as their minds are more intently employed ; and when, in sleep, they are pained by any physical endurance, the activity of their mental powers will naturally associate the most horrible ideas with such suffering, and produce incubus, and all its frightful accompaniments.

Nightmare is sometimes attended with danger, when it becomes habitual. It may then give rise to apoplexy, and destroy life ; or, in very nervous subjects, may occasion epileptic and hysterical affections, which prove extremely harassing. According to Cœlius Aurelianus, many people die of this complaint. Probably some of those who are found dead in bed have lost their lives in a fit of incubus, the circumstance being imputed to some other cause. Nightmare is thus, in some cases dangerous : and in all, when it becomes habitual, is such a source of misery, that sleep, instead of being courted as a period of blissful repose, is looked upon with horror, as the appointed season of inexpressible suffering and dread. It becomes, on this account, a matter of importance to contrive some method for preventing the attacks of so distressful a malady. The cause, whatever it may be, must, if practicable, be removed, and the symptoms thence arising will naturally disappear. If the disorder proceed from heavy suppers, or indigestible food, these things ought to be given up, and the person should either go supperless to bed, or with such a light meal as will not hurt his digestion. Salted provisions of all kinds must be abandoned, nor should he taste any thing which will lie heavily upon the stomach, or run into fermentation. For this reason, nuts, cucumbers, cheese, ham, and fruits are all prejudicial. If he be subject to heart-burn, flatulence, and other dyspeptic symptoms, he should make use of occasional doses of magnesia, or carbonate of potash or soda. I have known a tea-spoonful of either of the two latter, or three times that quantity of the former, taken before stepping into bed, prevent an attack, where, from the previous state of the stomach, I am convinced it would have taken place, had those medicines not been used. Great attention must be paid to the state of the bowels. For this purpose, the colocynth, the compound rhubarb, or the common aloetic pill, should be made use of, in doses of one, two, or three, according to circumstances, till the digestive organs are brought into proper play. The common blue pill, used with proper caution, is also an excellent medicine. In all cases, the patient should take abundant exercise, shun late hours, or too much study, and keep his mind in as cheerful a state as possible. The bed he lies on ought to be hard, and the pillow not very high. When the attacks are frequent, and extremely severe, Dr Darwin recommends that an alarm clock might be hung up in the room, so that the repose may be interrupted at short intervals. It is a good plan to have another person to sleep in the same bed, who might arouse him from the paroxysm ; and he should be directed to lie as little as possible upon the back.

These points comprehend the principal treatment, and when persevered in, will rarely fail to mitigate or remove the disease. Sometimes, however, owing to certain peculiarities of constitution, it may be necessary to adopt a different plan, or combine other means along with the above : thus, Whyatt, who was subject to nightmare, could only insure himself against an attack, by taking a small glassful of brandy, just before going to bed ; and some individuals find that a light supper prevents the fit, while it is sure to occur if no supper at all be taken. But these are rare exceptions to the general rule, and, when they do occur, must be treated in that manner which experience proves most effectual, without being bound too nicely by the ordinary modes of cure. Blood-letting, which some writers recommend, is useless or hurtful, except in cases where there is reason to suppose that the affection is

P

brought on by plethora. With regard to the other causes of nightmare, such as asthma, hydrothorax, &c., these must be treated on general principles, and it, as one of their symptoms, will depart so soon as they are removed.

Some persons recommend opium for the cure of nightmare, but this medicine I should think more likely to aggrave than relieve the complaint. The late Dr Polydori, author of 'The Vampyre,' and of an 'Essay on Positive Pleasure,' was much subject to incubus, and in the habit of using opium for its removal. One morning he was found dead, and on the table beside him stood a glass, which had evidently contained laudanum and water. From this, it was supposed he had killed himself by his own treatment ; but whether the quantity of laudanum taken by him would have destroyed life in ordinary circumstances, has never been ascertained.

CHAPTER VI.

DAYMARE.

I have strong doubts as to the propriety of considering this affection in any way different from the incubus, or nightmare. It seems merely a modification of the latter, only accompanied by no aberration of the judgment. The person endures precisely many of the same feelings, such as difficult respiration, torpor of the voluntary muscles, deep sighing, extreme terror, and inability to speak. The only difference which seem to exist between the two states is, that in daymare, the reason is *always* unclouded—whereas in incubus it is *generally* more or less disturbed.

Dr Mason Good, in his 'Study of Medicine,' takes notice of a case, recorded by Forestus, 'that returned periodically every third day, like an intermittent fever. The patient was a girl, nine years of age, and at these times was suddenly attacked with great terror, a constriction of both the lower and upper belly, with urgent difficulty of breathing. Her eyes continued open, and were permanently continued to one spot; with her hands she forcibly grasped hold of things, that she might breathe the more easily. When spoken to, she returned no answer. In the meantime, the mind seemed to be collected : she was without sleep ; sighed repeatedly ; the abdomen was elevated, and the thorax still violently contracted, and oppressed with laborious respiration and heavy panting : she was incapable of utterance.'

During the intensely hot summer of 1825, I experienced an attack of daymare. Immediately after dining, I threw myself on my back upon a sofa, and, before I was aware, was seized with difficult respiration, extreme dread, and utter incapability of motion or speech. I could neither move nor cry, while the breath came from my chest in broken and suffocating paroxysms. During all this time, I was perfectly awake : I saw the light glaring in at the windows in broad sultry streams ; I felt the intense heat of the day pervading my frame ; and heard distinctly the different noises in the street, and even the ticking of my own watch, which I had placed on the cushion beside me. I had, at the same time, the consciousness of flies buzzing around, and settling with annoying pertinacity upon my face. During the whole fit, judgment was never for a moment suspended. I felt assured that I laboured under a species of incubus. I even endeavoured to reason myself out of the feeling of dread which filled my mind, and longed with insufferable ardour for some one to open the door, and dissolve the spell which bound me in its fetters. The fit did not continue above five minutes : by degrees I recovered the use of speech and motion : and as soon as they were so far restored as to enable me to call out and move my limbs, it wore insensibly away.

Upon the whole, I consider daymare and nightmare identical. They proceed from the same causes, and must be treated in a similar manner.

CHAPTER VII.

SLEEP-WALKING.

In simple dreaming, as I have already stated, some of the cerebral organs are awake, while others continue in the quiescence of sleep. Such, also, is the case in somnambulism, but with this addition, that the dream is of so forcible a nature as to stimulate into action the muscular system as well as, in most cases, one or more of the organs of the senses. If we dream that we are walking, and the vision possesses such a degree of vividness and exciting energy as to arouse the muscles of locomotion, we naturally get up and walk. Should we dream that we hear or see, and the impression be so vivid as to stimulate the eyes and ears, or, more properly speaking, those parts of the brain which take cognizance of sights and sounds, then we both see any objects, or hear any sounds, which may occur, just as if we were awake. In some cases, the muscles only are excited, and then we simply walk, without either seeing or hearing. In others, both the muscles and organs of sight are stimulated, and we not only walk, but have the use of our eyes. In a third variety, the activity of hearing is added, and we both walk, and see, and hear. Should the senses of smell, taste, and touch be stimulated into activity, and relieved from the torpor into which they were thrown by sleep, we have them also brought into operation. If, to all this, we add an active state of the organs of speech, inducing us to talk, we are then brought as nearly as the slumbering state admits, into the condition of perfect wakefulness. The following passage from Dr Mason Good will illustrate some of the foregoing points more fully.

'If,' observes he, 'the external organ of sense thus stimulated be that of sight, the dreamer may perceive objects around him, and be able to distinguish them; and if the tenor of the dreaming ideas should as powerfully operate upon the muscles of locomotion, these also may be thrown into their accustomed state of action, and he may rise from his bed, and make his way to whatever place the drift of his dream may direct him, with perfect ease, and free from danger. He will see more or less distinctly, in proportion as the organ of sight is more or less awake: yet, from the increased exhaustion, and, of course, increased torpor of the other organs, in consequence of an increased demand of sensorial power from the common stock, to supply the action of the sense and muscles immediately engaged, every other sense will probably be thrown into a deeper sleep or torpor than if the whole had been quiescent. Hence, the ears may not be roused even by a sound that might otherwise awake the sleeper. He may be insensible not only to a slight touch, but a severe shaking of the limbs; and may even cough violently, without being recalled from his dream. Having accomplished the object of his visionary pursuit, he may safely return, even over the most dangerous precipices —for he sees them distinctly—to his bed: and the organ of sight being now quite exhausted, or there being no longer any occasion for its use, it may once more associate in the general inactivity, and the dream take a new turn, and consist of a new combination of images.'*

I suspect that sleep-walking is sometimes hereditary, at least I have known instances which gave countenance to such a supposition. Its victims are generally pale, nervous, irritable persons; and it is remarked that they

are subject, without any apparent cause, to frequent attacks of cold perspiration. Somnambulism, I have had occasion to remark, is very common among children; and I believe that it more frequently affects childhood than any other age. In females, it sometimes arises from amenorrhœa; and any source of bodily or mental irritation may produce it. It is a curious, and not easily explained fact, that the aged, though they dream more than the middle-aged, are less addicted to somnambulism and sleep-talking. Indeed, these phenomena are seldom noticed in old people.

It has been matter of surprise to many, that somnambulists often get into the most dangerous situations without experiencing terror. But the explanation of this ought not to be attended with any real difficulty; for we must reflect, that alarm cannot be felt unless we apprehend danger, and that the latter however great it may be, cannot excite emotion of any kind, so long as we are ignorant of its existence. This is the situation in which sleep-walkers, in a great majority of cases, stand. The reasoning faculties, which point out the existence of danger, are generally in a state of complete slumber, and unable to produce corresponding emotions in the mind. And even if danger should be perceived by a sleep-walker and avoided, as is sometimes the case, his want of terror is to be imputed to a quiescent state of the organ of *cautiousness*; the sense of fear originating in high excitement of this particular part of the brain. That the reasoning faculties, however, are sometimes only very partially suspended we have abundant evidence, in the fact of the individual not only now and then studiously avoiding danger, but performing offices which require no small degree of judgment. In the higher ranks of somnambulism, so many of the organs of the brain are in activity, and there is such perfect wakefulness of the external senses and locomotive powers, that the person may almost be said to be awake.

Somnambulism bears a closer analogy than a common dream to madness. 'Like madness, it is accompanied with muscular action, with coherent and incoherent conduct, and with that complete oblivion (in most cases) of both, which takes place in the worst grade of madness.'*

Somnambulists generally walk with their eyes open, but these organs are, nevertheless frequently asleep, and do not exercise their functions. This fact was well known to Shakspeare, as is apparent in the fearful instance of Lady Macbeth:

'*Doctor.* You see her eyes are open.'
'*Gentleman.* Ay, but their sense is shut.'

The following is a remarkable instance in point, and shows that though the power of vision was suspended, that of hearing continued in full operation.

A female servant in the town of Chelmsford, surprised the family, at four o'clock one morning, by walking down a flight of stairs in her sleep, and rapping at the bed-room door of her master, who inquired what she wanted? when, in her usual tone of voice, she requested some cotton, saying that she had torn her gown, but hoped that her mistress would forgive her: at the same time bursting into tears. Her fellow-servant, with whom she had been conversing for some time, observed her get out of bed, and quickly followed her, but not before she had related the pitiful story. She then returned to her room, and a light having been procured, she was found groping to find her cotton-box. Another person went to her, when, perceiving a difference in the voice, she called out, 'That is a different voice, that is my mistress,' which was not the case—thus clearly showing; that she *did not see* the object before her, although her eyes were *wide open*. Upon inquiry as to what was the matter, she only said that she wanted some cotton, but that her fellow-servant had been to her master and mistress, making a fuss about it   It

* Good's Study of Medicine, vol. iv. p. 175, 3d edit.

* Rush's Medical Inquiries.

was now thought prudent that she should be allowed to remain quiet for some short time, and she was persuaded to lie down with her fellow-servant, until the usual hour of rising, thinking that she might then awake in her accustomed manner. This failing in effect, her mistress went up to her room, and rather angrily desired her to get up, and go to her work, as it was now six o'clock; this she refused, telling her mistress that if she did not please her, she might look out for another servant, at the same time saying, that she would not rise up at two o'clock, (pointing to the window,) to injure her health for any one. For the sake of a joke, she was told to pack up her things, and start off immediately, but to this she made no reply. She rebuked her fellow-servant for not remaining longer in bed, and shortly after this became quiet. She was afterwards shaken violently, and awoke. She then rose, and seeing the cotton-box disturbed, demanded to know why it had been meddled with, not knowing that she alone was the cause of it. In the course of the day, several questions were put to her in order to try her recollection, but the real fact of her walking, was not made known to her; and she is still quite unconscious of what has transpired.

The next case is of a different description, and exhibits a dormant state of the sense of hearing, while sight appears, throughout, to have been in active operation.

A young man named Johns, who works at Cardrew, near Redruth, being asleep in the sump-house of that mine, was observed by two boys to rise and walk to the door, against which he leaned; shortly after, quitting that position, he walked to the engine-shaft, and safely descended to the depth of twenty fathoms, where he was found by his comrades soon after, with his back resting on the ladder. They called to him, to apprize him of the perilous situation in which he was, but he did not hear them, and they were obliged to shake him roughly till he awoke, when he appeared totally at a loss to account for his being so situated.

In Lodge's 'Historical Portraits,' there is a likeness, by Sir Peter Lely, of Lord Culpepper's brother, so famous as a dreamer. In 1686, he was indicted at the Old Bailey, for shooting one of the Guards, and his horse to boot. He pleaded somnambulism, and was acquitted on producing nearly fifty witnesses, to prove the extraordinary things he did in his sleep.

A very curious circumstance is related of Dr Franklin, in the memoirs of that eminent philosopher, published by his grandson. 'I went out,' said the Doctor, 'to bathe in Martin's salt water hot bath, in Southampton, and, floating on my back, fell asleep, and slept nearly an hour, by my watch, without sinking or turning —a thing I never did before, and should hardly have thought possible.'

A case still more extraordinary occurred some time ago in one of the towns on the coast of Ireland. About two o'clock in the morning, the watchmen on the Revenue quay, were much surprised at descrying a man disporting himself in the water, about a hundred yards from the shore. Intimation having been given to the Revenue boat's crew, they pushed off and succeeded in picking him up, but strange to say, he had no idea whatever of his perilous situation: and it was with the utmost difficulty they could persuade him he was not still in bed. But the most singular part of this novel adventure, and which was afterwards ascertained, was that the man had left his house at twelve o'clock that night, and walked through a difficult, and, to him, dangerous road, a distance of nearly two miles, and had actually swum one mile and a half when he was fortunately discovered and picked up.

Not very long ago a boy was seen fishing off Brest, up to the middle in water. On coming up to him, he was found to be fast asleep.

I know a gentleman who, in consequence of dreaming that the house was broken into by thieves, got out of bed, dropped from the window (fortunately a low one) into the street; and was a considerable distance on his way to warn the police, when he was discovered by one of them, who awoke him, and conducted him home.

A case is related of an English clergyman who used to get up in the night, light his candle, write sermons, correct them with interlineations, and retire to bed again; being all the time asleep. The Archbishop of Bourdeaux mentions a similar case of a student, who got up to compose a sermon while asleep, wrote it correctly, read it over from one end to the other; or at least appeared to read it, made corrections on it, scratched out lines, and substituted others, put in its place a word which had been omitted, composed music, wrote it accurately down, and performed other things equally surprising. Dr Gall takes notice of a miller who was in the habit of getting up every night and attending to his usual avocations at the mill, then returning to bed; on awaking in the morning, he recollected nothing of what passed during night. Martinet speaks of a saddler who was accustomed to rise in his sleep and work at his trade; and Dr Pritchard of a farmer who got out of bed, dressed himself, saddled his horse, and rode to the market, being all the while asleep. Dr Blacklock, on one occasion, rose from bed, to which he had retired at an early hour, came into the room where his family were assembled, conversed with them, and afterwards entertained them with a pleasant song, without any of them suspecting he was asleep, and without his retaining after he awoke, the least recollection of what he had done. It is a singular, yet well authenticated fact, that in the disastrous retreat of Sir John Moore, many of the soldiers fell asleep, yet continued to march along with their comrades.

The stories related of sleep-walkers are, indeed, of so extraordinary a kind, that they would almost seem fictitious, were they not supported by the most incontrovertible evidence. To walk on the house-top, to scale precipices, and descend to the bottom of frightful ravines, are common exploits with the somnambulist; and he performs them with a facility far beyond the power of any man who is completely awake. A story is told of a boy, who dreamed that he got out of bed, and ascended to the summit of an enormous rock, where he found an eagle's nest, which he brought away with him, and placed beneath his bed. Now, the whole of these events actually took place; and what he conceived on awaking to be a mere vision, was proved to have had an actual existence, by the nest being found in the precise spot where he imagined he had put it, and by the evidence of the spectators who beheld his perilous adventure. The precipice which he ascended, was of a nature that must have baffled the most expert mountaineer, and such as, at other times, he never could have scaled. In this instance, the individual was as nearly as possible, without actually being so, awake. All his bodily, and almost the whole of his mental powers, appear to have been in full activity. So far as the latter are concerned, we can only conceive a partial defect of the judgment to have existed, for that it was altogether abolished is pretty evident from the fact of his proceeding to work precisely as he would have done, had he, in his waking hours, seriously resolved to make such an attempt; the defect lay in making the attempt at all; and still more in getting out of bed to do so in the middle of the night.

Somnambulism, as well as lunacy, sometimes bestows supernatural strength upon the individual. Mr Dubrie, a musician in Bath, affords an instance of this kind. One Sunday, while awake, he attempted in vain to force open the window of his bed-room, which chanced to be nailed down; but having got up in his sleep, he repeated the attempt successfully, and threw himself out, by which he unfortunately broke his leg.

Sleep-walking is sometimes periodical. Martinet describes the case of a watchmaker's apprentice who had an attack of it every fortnight. In this state, though insensible to all external impressions, he would perform his work with his usual accuracy, and was always astonished. on awaking, at the progress he had made. The paroxysm began with a sense of heat in the epigastrium extending to the head, followed by confusion of ideas and complete insensibility, the eyes remaining open with a fixed and vacant stare. This case, which undoubtedly originated in some diseased state of the brain, terminated in epilepsy. Dr Gall relates that he saw at Berlin a young man, sixteen years of age, who had, from time to time, very extraordinary fits. He moved about unconsciously in bed, and had no perception of any thing that was done to him; at last he would jump out of bed. and walk with rapid steps about the room, his eyes being fixed and open. Several obstacles which were placed by Dr Gall in his way, he either removed or cautiously avoided. He then threw himself suddenly again upon bed, moved about for some time, and finished by jumping up awake, not a little surprised at the number of curious people about him.

The facility with which somnambulists are awakened from the paroxysm, differs extremely in different cases. One man is aroused by being gently touched or called upon, by a flash of light, by stumbling in his peregrinations, or by setting his foot in water. Another remains so heavily asleep, that it is necessary to shout loudly, to shake him with violence, and make use of other excitations equally powerful. In this condition, when the sense of vision chances to be dormant, it is curious to look at his eyes. Sometimes they are shut; at other times wide open; and when the latter is the case, they are observed to be fixed and inexpressive, 'without speculation,' or energy, while the pupil, is contracted, as in the case of perfect sleep.

It is not always safe to arouse a sleep walker; and many cases of the fatal effects thence arising have been detailed by authors. Nor is it at all unlikely that a person, even of strong nerves, might be violently agitated by awaking in a situation so different from that in which he lay down. Among other examples, that of a young lady, who was addicted to this affection, may be mentioned. Knowing her failing, her friends, made a point of locking the door, and securing the window of her chamber in such a manner that she could not possibly get out. One night, these precautions were, unfortunately overlooked; and in a paroxysm of somnambulism, she walked into the garden behind the house. While there, she was recognised by some of the family, who were warned by the noise she made on opening the door, and they followed and awoke her; but such was the effect produced upon her nervous system, that she almost instantly expired.

The remote causes of sleep walking are so obscure, that it is seldom we are able to ascertain them. General irritability of frame, a nervous temperament, and bad digestion, will dispose to the affection. Being a modification of dreaming, those who are much troubled with the latter will, consequently be most prone to its attacks. The causes, however, are, in a great majority of cases, so completely unknown, that any attempt to investigate them would be fruitless; and we are compelled to refer the complaint to some idiosyncracy of constitution beyond the reach of human knowledge.

According to the report made by a Committee of the Royal Academy of Sciences in Paris, animal magnetism appears to have the power of inducing a peculiar species of somnambulism. The circumstances seem so curious, that, even authenticated as they are by men of undoubted integrity and talent, it is extremely difficult to place reliance upon them. The person who is thrown into the magnetic sleep is said to a acquire a new consciousness, and entirely to forget all the events of his ordinary life. When this sleep is dissolved, he gets into his usual state of feeling and recollection, but forgets every thing that happened during the sleep; being again magnetized, however, the remembrance of all that occurred in the previous sleep is brought back to his mind. In one of the cases above related, the patient, a lady of sixty-four years, had an ulcerated cancer in the right breast. She had been magnetized for the purpose of dissolving the tumor, but no other effect was produced than that of throwing her into a species of somnambulic sleep, in which sensibility was annihilated, while her ideas retained all their clearness. In this state her surgeon, M. Chapelain, disposed her to submit to an operation, the idea of which she rejected with horror *when awake*. Having formally given her consent she undressed herself, sat down upon a chair, and the diseased glands were carefully and deliberately dissected out, the patient conversing all the time and being perfectly insensible of pain. On awaking, she had no consciousnes whatever of having been operated upon; but being informed of the circumstance, and seeing her children around her, she experienced the most lively emotion, which the magnetizer instantly checked by again setting her asleep. These facts appear startling and incredible. I can give no opinion upon the subjcet from any thing I have seen myself; but the testimony of such men as Cloquet, Georget, and Itard, is not to be received lightly on any physiological point; and they all concur in bearing witness to such facts as the above. In the present state of knowledge and opinion, with regard to animal magnetism, and the sleep occasioned by it, I shall not say more at present, but refer the reader to the ample details contained in the Parisian Report; an able translation of which into English has been made by by Mr Colquhoun.

When a person is addicted to somnambulism, great care should be taken to have the door and windows of his sleeping apartment, secured, so as to prevent the possibility of egress, as he sometimes forces his way through the panes of glass: this should be put out of his power, by having the shutters closed, and bolted, in such a way that they cannot be opened without the aid of a key or screw, or some such instrument, which should never be left in the room where he sleeps, but carried away, while the door is secured on the outside. Some have recommended that a tub of water should be put by the bedside, that, on getting out, he might step into it, and be awaked by the cold; but this, from the suddenness of its operation, might be attended with bad consequences in very nervous and delicate subjects. It is a good plan to fix a cord to the bedpost, and tie the other end of it securely round the person's wrist. This will effectually prevent mischief if he attempt to get up. Whenever it can bo managed, it will be prudent for another person to sleep along with him. In all cases, care should be taken to arouse him suddenly. This must be done as gently as possible, and when he can be conducted to bed without being awakened at all, it is still better. Should he be perceived in any dangerous situation as on the house-top, or the brink of a precipice, the utmost caution is requisite; for, if we call loudly upon him, his dread, on recovering, at finding himself in such a predicament, may actually occasion him to fall, where, if he had been left to himself, he would have escaped without injury.

To prevent a recurrence of somnambulism, we should remove, if possible, the cause which gave rise to it. Thus, if it proceed from a disordered state or the stomach, or biliary system, we must employ the various medicines used in such cases. Plenty of exercise should be taken, and late hours and much study avoided. If it arises from plethora, he must be blooded, and live low; should hysteria produce it, antispasmodics, such as valerian, ammonia, assafœtida, and opium may be necessary.

But, unfortunately, we can often refer sleep-walking to no complaint whatever. In this case, all that can be done is to carry the individual as safely as possible through the paroxysm, and prevent him from injury by the means we have mentioned. In many instances, the affection will wear spontaneously away : in others, it will continue in spite of every remedy.

CHAPTER VIII.

SLEEP-TALKING.

This closely resembles somnambulism, and proceeds from similar causes. In somnambulism, those parts of the brain which are awake call the muscles of the limbs into activity ; while, in sleep-talking, it is the muscles necessary for the production of speech which are animated by the waking cerebral organs. During sleep, the organ of *language* may be active, either singly or in combination with other parts of the brain ; and of this activity sleep-talking is the result.* If, while we dream that we are conversing with some one, the organ of *language* is in such a high state of activity as to rouse the muscles of speech, we are sure to talk. It often happens, however, that the cerebral parts, though sufficiently active to make us dream that we are speaking, are not excited so much as to make us actually speak. We only suppose we are carrying on a conversation, while, in reality, we are completely silent. To produce sleep-talking, therefore, the brain, in some of its functions, must be so much awake as to put into action the voluntary muscles by which speech is produced.

The conversation in this state, is of such subjects as our thoughts are most immediately occupied with ; and its consistency or incongruity depends upon that of the prevailing ideas—being sometimes perfectly rational and coherent ; at other times, full of absurdity. The voice is seldom the same as in the waking state. This I would impute to the organs of hearing being mostly dormant, and consequently unable to guide the modulations of sound. The same fact is observable in very deaf persons, whose speech is usually harsh, unvaried, and monotonous. Sometimes the faculties are so far awake, that we can manage to converse with the individual, and extract from him the most hidden secrets of his soul : circumstances have thus been ascertained which would otherwise have remained in perpetual obscurity. By a little address in this way, a gentleman lately detected the infidelity of his wife from some expressions which escaped her while asleep, and succeeded in finding out that she had a meeting arranged with her paramour for the following day. Lord Byron describes a similar case in his ' Parisina :'

' And Hugo is gone to his lonely bed,
    To covet there another's bride ;
But she must lay her conscious head
    A husband's trusting heart beside.

* Among the insane, the organ just mentioned is occasionally excited to such a degree that even, in the waking state, the patient, however *desirous*, is literally *unable* to refrain from speaking. Mr. W. A. F. Browne has reported two cases of this nature in the 37th No. of the Phrenological Journal. The first is that of a woman in the hospital of ' La Salpetrière' in Paris. Whenever she encounters the physician or other of the attendants, she bursts forth into an address which is delivered with incredible rapidity and vehemence, and is generally an abusive or ironical declamation against the tyranny, cruelty, and injustice to which she is exposed. In the midst of her harangues, however, she introduces frequent and earnest parenthetical declarations ' that she does not mean what she says ; that though she vows vengeance and showers imprecations on her medical attendant, she loves him, and feels grateful for his kindness and forbearance ; and that, though anxious to evince her gratitude and obedience by silence, she is constrained by an invisible agency to speak.' In the other case, the individual speaks constantly ; sleep itself does not yield an intermission ; and there is strong reason to believe that a part, at least of his waking orations is delivered either without the cognizance of the other powers, or without consciousness on the part of the speaker.'

But fever'd in her sleep she seems,
And red her cheek with troubled dreams,
And *mutters she in her unrest*
    A name she dare not breathe by day,
    And clasps her lord unto her breast
    Which pants for one away.'

From what has been said of somnambulism, the reader will be prepared for phenomena equally curious as regards sleep-talking. Persons have been known, for instance, who delivered sermons and prayers during sleep ; among others, Dr Haycock, Professor of Medicine in Oxford. He would give out a text in his sleep, and deliver a good sermon upon it : nor could all the pinching and pulling of his friends prevent him. ' One of the most remarkable cases of speaking during sleep,' observes a writer in Frazer's Magazine, ' is that of an American lady, now (we believe) alive, who preached during her sleep, performing regularly every part of the Presbyterian service, from the psalm to the blessing. This lady was the daughter of respectable and even wealthy parents ; she fell into bad health, and, under its influence, she disturbed and annoyed her family by her nocturnal eloquence. Her unhappy parents, though at first surprised, and perhaps flattered by the exhibition in their family of so extraordinary a gift, were at last convinced that it was the result of disease ; and, in the expectation that their daughter might derive benefit from change of scene, as well as from medical skill, they made a tour with her of some length, and visited New York and some of the other great cities of the Union. We know individuals who have heard her preach during the night in steamboats ; and it was customary, at tea parties in New York, (at the houses of medical practitioners,) to put the lady to bed in a room adjacent to the drawing-room, in order that the dilletanti might witness so extraordinary a phenomenon. We have been told by ear-witnesses, that her sermons, though they had the appearance of connected discourses, consisted chiefly of texts of scripture strung together. It is strongly impressed upon our memory, that some of her sermons were published in America.'

In the Edinburgh Journal of science, a lady who was subject to spectral illusions, is described as being subject to talk in her sleep with great fluency, to repeat great portions of poetry, especially when unwell, and even to *cap* verses for half an hour at a time, never failing to quote lines beginning with the final letter of the preceding till her memory was exhausted.

Dr Dyce, in the Edinburgh Philosophical Transactions, relates the case of Maria C——, who, during one paroxysm of somnambulism, recollected what took place in a preceding one, without having any such recollection during the interval of wakefulness. One of the occasions in which this young woman manifested the power in question, was of a very melancholy nature. Her fellow-servant, a female of abandoned character, having found out that, on awaking, she entirely forgot every thing which occurred during the fit, introduced by stealth into the house, a young man of her acquaintance, and obtained for him an opportunity of treating Maria in the most brutal and treacherous manner. The wretches succeeded in their object by stopping her mouth with the bed-clothes, by which and other means, they overcame the vigorous resistance she was enabled to make to their villany, even in her somnolent state. On awaking she had no consciousness whatever of the outrage ; but some days afterwards, having fallen into the same state, it recurred to her memory, and she related to her mother all the revolting particulars. The state of mind in this case was perfectly analogous to that which is said to occur in the magnetic sleep ; but the particular state of the brain which induces such conditions will, I believe, ever remain a mystery.*

* A case, in some respects similar, was published in the Medical Repository, by Dr Mitchell, who received the particulars of it from Major Ellicot, Professor of Mathematics in the United States Military Academy at West Point. The subject was a

The following singular case of sleep-talking, combined with somnambulism, will prove interesting to the reader:—

'A very ingenious and elegant young lady, with light eyes and hair, about the age of seventeen, in other respects well, was suddenly seized with this very wonderful malady. The disease began with violent convulsions of almost every muscle of her body, with great, but vain efforts to vomit, and the most violent hiccoughs that can be conceived : these were succeeded in about an hour with a fixed spasm ; in which, one hand was applied to her head, and the other to support it : in about half an hour these ceased, and the reverie began suddenly, and was at first manifest by the look of her eyes and countenance, which seemed to express attention. Then she conversed aloud with imaginary persons, with her eyes open, and could not, for about an hour, he brought to attend to the stimulus of external objects by any kind of violence which it was possible to use : these symptoms returned in this order every day for five or six weeks.

'These conversations were quite consistent, and we could understand what, she supposed her imaginary companions to answer, by the continuation of her part of the discourse. Sometimes she was angry, at other times showed much wit and vivacity, but was most frequently inclined to melancholy. In these reveries, she sometimes sung over some music with accuracy, and repeated whole passages from the English poets. In repeating some lines from Mr Pope's works, she had forgot one word, and began again, endeavouring to recollect it ; when she came to the forgotten word, it was shouted aloud in her ears, and this repeatedly, to no purpose ; but by many trials she at length regained it herself.

'Those paroxysms were terminated with the appearance of inexpressible surprise and great fear, from which she was some minutes in recovering herself, calling on her sister with great agitation, and very frequently underwent a repetition of convulsions, apparently from the pain of fear.

'After having thus returned for about an hour a-day, for two or three weeks, the reveries seemed to become less complete, and some of the circumstances varied, so that she could walk about the room in them, without running against any of the furniture ; though these motions were at first very unsteady and tottering. And afterwards, she once, drank a dish of tea, and the whole apparatus of the tea-table was set before her, and expressed some suspicion that a medicine was put into it ; and once seemed to smell at a tuberose, which was in flower in her chamber, and deliberated aloud about breaking it for the stem, saying, 'It would make her sister so charmingly angry.' At another time, in her melancholy moments, she heard the bell, and then taking off one of her shoes as she sat upon the bed, 'I love the color black,' says she ; 'a little wider and a little longer, and even this might make me a coffin !' Yet it is evident she was not sensible at this time, any more than formerly, of seeing or hearing any person about her ; indeed, when great light was thrown upon her by opening the shutters of the window ; she seemed less melancholy : and when I have forcibly held her hands, or covered her eyes, she appeared to grow impatient, and would say, she could not tell what to do, for she could neither see nor move. In all these circumstances, her pulse continued unaffected, as in health. And when the paroxysm was over, she could never recollect a single idea of what had passed.'*

Equally extraordinary is the following instance of combined sleep-talking and somnambulism :

'A remarkable instance of this affection occurred to a lad named George David, sixteen years and a half old, in the service of Mr Hewson, butcher, of Bridge-Road, Lambeth. At about twenty minutes after nine o'clock, the lad bent forward in his chair, and rested his forehead on his hands, and in ten minutes started up, went for his whip, put on his one spur, and went thence to the stable ; not finding his own saddle in the proper place, he returned to the house and asked for it. Being asked what he wanted with it, he replied, to go his rounds. He returned to the stable, got on the horse without the saddle, and was proceeding to leave the stable : it was with much difficulty and force that Mr Hewson, junior, assisted by the other lad, could remove him from the horse ; his strength was great, and it was with difficulty he was brought in doors. Mr Hewson, senior, coming home at this time, sent for Mr Benjamin Ridge, an eminent practitioner, in Bridge-Road, who stood by him for a quarter of an hour, during which time the lad considered himself as stopped at the turnpike-gate, and took sixpence out of his pocket to be changed ; and holding out his hand for the change, the sixpence was returned to him. He immediately observed, 'None of your nonsense—that is the sixpence again ; give me my change ;' when two pence halfpenny was given to him, he counted it over, and said, 'None of your gammon ; that is not right ; I want a penny more ;' making the three pence halfpenny, which was his proper change. He then said, 'Give me my castor, (meaning his hat,) which slang term he had been in the habit of using, and then began to whip and spur to get his horse on. His pulse at this time was 136, full and hard ; no change of countenance could be observed, nor any spasmodic affection of the muscles, the eyes remaining close the whole of the time. His coat was taken off his arm, shirt sleeves tucked up, and Mr Ridge bled him to 32 ounces ; no alteration had taken place in him during the first part of the time the blood was flowing ; at about 24 ounces, the pulse began to decrease ; and when the full quantity named above had been taken, it was at 80—a slight perspiration on the forehead. During the time of bleeding, Mr Hewson related a circumstance of a Mr Harris, optician, in Holborn, whose son, some years since, walked out on the parapet of the house in his sleep. The boy joined the conversation, and observed, 'He lived at the corner of Brownlow-Street.' After the arm was tied up, he unlaced one boot, and said he would go to bed ; in three minutes from this time, he awoke, got up, and asked what was the matter, (having then been one hour in the trance,) not having the slightest recollection of any thing that had passed, and wondered at his arm being tied up, and at the blood, &c. A strong aperient

young lady, of a good constitution, excellent capacity, and well educated. ' Her memory was capacious and well stored with a copious stock of ideas. Unexpectedly, and without any forewarning, she fell into a profound sleep, which continued several hours beyond the ordinary term. On waking, she was discovered to have lost every trait of acquired knowledge. Her memory was *tabula rasa*—all vestiges, both of words and things were obliterated and gone. It was found necessary for her to learn every thing again. She even acquired, by new efforts, the art of spelling, reading, writing, and calculating, and gradually became acquainted with the persons and objects around, like a being for the first time brought into the world. In these exercises she made considerable proficiency. But after a few months another fit of somnolency invaded her. On rousing from it, she found herself restored to the state she was in before the first paroxysm ; but was wholly ignorant of every event and occurrence that had befallen her afterwards. The former condition of her existence she now calls the Old State, and the latter the New State ; and she is as unconscious of her double character as two distinct persons are of their respective natures. For example, in her old state, she possesses all the original knowledge ; in her new state, only what she acquired since. If a lady or gentleman be introduced to her in the old state, and *vice versa*, (and so of all other matters) to know them satisfactorily, she must learn them in both states. In the old state, she possesses fine powers of penmanship, while in the new, she writes a poor, awkward hand, having not had time or means to become expert. During four years and upwards, she has had periodical transitions from one of these states to the other. The alterations are always consequent upon a long and sound sleep. Both the lady and her family are now capable of conducting the affair without embarrassment. By simply knowing whether she is in the old or new state, they regulate the intercourse and govern themselves accordingly.' .

medicine was then administered : he went to bed, slept well, and the next day appeared perfectly well, excepting debility from the bleeding, and operation of the medicine, and has no recollection whatever of what had taken place. None of his family or himself were ever affected in this way before.'*

Sleep-talking is generally such a trivial affection as not to require any treatment whatever. In every case the digestive organs must be attended to, and, if disordered, put to rights by suitable medicines. And should the affection proceed, or be supposed to proceed from hypochondria, hysteria, or the prevalence of any strong mental emotion, these states must be treated according to general principles. When it arises from idiosyncrasy, and becomes habitual, I believe that no means which can be adopted will be of much avail. As, in the case of somnambulism, it very frequently happens that the affection, after continuing for a long time, and baffling every species of treatment, disappears spontaneously.

CHAPTER IX.

SLEEPLESSNESS.

Sleep takes place as soon as the sensorial power that keeps the brain awake is expended, which, under common circumstances, occurs at our ordinary hour of going to rest, or even sooner, if any sophorific cause sufficiently strong should chance to operate. But the above power may be increased by various means, as in cases of physical suffering, or excited imagination, and, consequently, is not expended at the usual time. In this case, the person remains awake, and continues so till the period of its expenditure, which may not happen for several hours after he lies down, or even not at all, during the whole of that night. Now, whatever increases the sensorial power, whether it be balls, concerts, grief, joy, or bodily pain, is prejudicial to repose. By them the mind is exalted to a pitch of unnatural action, from which it is necessary it should descend before it can roll into the calm channel of sleep. Whatever stimulates the external senses, however slightly, may prevent sleep. Thus, the ticking of a clock has this effect with very sensitive people ; and a candle burning in the chamber is attended with the same result. Even when the eyes are shut this may take place, for the eye-lids are sufficiently transparent to transmit a sense of light to the retina. For the same reason, the light of day peering in at the window may awake us from or prevent slumber. It is said that Napoleon could never sleep if exposed to the influence of light, although, in other circumstances, slumber appeared at his bidding with surprising readiness.

A constitutional restlessness is sometimes brought on by habitually neglecting to solicit sleep when we lie down, by which means the brain is brought into such a state of irritability, that we can hardly sleep at all. Chronic wakefulness, originating from any mental or bodily affection, sometimes degenerates into a habit, in which the sufferer will remain for weeks, months, or even years, if authors are to be believed, awake. In the disease called delirium tremens, wakefulness is a constant symptom, and frequently continues for many successive days and nights. It is also an attendant upon all disorders accompanied by acute suffering, especially when the brain is affected, as in phrenitis, or fever. Maniacs, from the excited state of their sensorium, are remarkably subject to want of sleep ; and this symptom is often so obstinate as to resist the most powerful remedies we can venture to prescribe.

Certain stimulating agents, such as tea or coffee, taken shortly before going to bed, have often the effect

of preventing sleep. I would impute this to their irritative properties, which, by supplying the brain with fresh sensorial power, enable it to carry on uninterruptedly all its functions longer than it would otherwise do, and consequently prevent it from relapsing into slumber at the usual period.

Any uneasy bodily feeling has the same effect—both preventing the accession of sleep, and arousing us from it when it has fairly taken place. Thus, while moderate fatigue provoke slumber, excessive fatigue, owing to the pain and irritation it necessarily occasions, drives it away. Sickness, cold, heat, pregnancy, the ordinary calls of nature, a disagreeable bed, the want of an accustomed supper, too heavy a supper, or uneasiness of any kind, have the same result. Cold is most apt to induce sleeplessness, when partial, especially if it be confined to the feet ; for when general and sufficiently intense, it has the opposite effect, and give rise to drowsiness. Certain diseases, such as hemicrania, tic douloureux, &c., have actually kept the person awake for three successive months ; and all painful affections prevent sleep more or less. But the most violent tortures cannot altogether banish, however much they may retard it. Sooner or later the fatigue, which a want of it occasions, prevails, and slumber ultimately ensues.

Sleeplessness is sometimes produced by a sense of burning heat in the soles of the feet and palms of the hands, to which certain individuals are subject some time after lying down. This seems to proceed from a want of perspiration in these parts ; owing generally to impaired digestion.

Mental emotions, of every description, are unfavorable to repose. If a man, as soon as he lays his head upon a pillow, can banish thinking, he is morally certain to fall asleep. There are many individuals so constituted, that they can do this without effort, and the consequence is, they are excellent sleepers. It is very different with those whose minds are oppressed by care, or over stimulated by excessive study. The sorrowful man, above all others, has the most need of sleep ; but, far from shedding its benignant influence over him, it flies away, and leaves him to the communionship of his own sad thoughts :

> ' His slumbers—if he slumber—are not sleep,
> But a continuance of enduring thought.'

It is the same with the man of vivid imagination. His fancy, instead of being subdued by the spell of sleep, becomes more active than ever. Thoughts in a thousand fantastic forms—myriads of waking dreams—pass through his mind, whose excessive activity spurns at repose, and mocks all his endeavors to reduce it to quiescence. Great joy will often scare away sleep for many nights ; but, in this respect, it is far inferior to grief, a fixed attack of which has been known to keep the sufferer awake for several months. Those who meditate much, seldom sleep well in the early part of the night : they lie awake, for perhaps two or three hours, after going to bed, and do not fall into slumber till towards morning. Persons of this description often lie long, and are reputed lazy by early risers, although, it is probable, they actually sleep less than these early risers themselves. Long continued study is highly prejudicial to repose. Boerhaave mentions that, on one occasion, owing to this circumstance, he did not close his eyes for six weeks.

Nothing is so hurtful both to the mind and body as want of sleep. Deprived of the necessary portion, the person gets wan, emaciated and listless, and very soon falls into bad health ; the spirit becomes entirely broken, and the fire of even the most ardent dispositions is quenched. Nor is this law peculiar to the human race, for it operates with similar power upon the lower animals, and deprives them of much of their natural ferocity. An illustration of this fact is afforded in the taming of wild elephants. These animals, when first caught, are studiously prevented from sleeping; in consequence of which, they become, in a few days, comparatively mild and harmless. Restlessness, when long protracted, may terminate in delirium, or confirmed insanity ; and in many diseases, it is the most obstinate symptom we have to struggle against. By it alone, all the existing bad symptoms are aggravated ; and as soon as we can succeed in overcoming it, every thing disagreeable and dangerous frequently wears away, and the person is restored to health.

In restlessness, both the perspiration and urinary secretions are usually much increased ; there is also an accession of heat in the system, and a general feverish tendency, unless the want of sleep should proceed from cold.

With regard to the treatment of sleeplessness, a very few words will suffice : in f_{act}, upon this head little more can be said, than a recommendation to obviate the causes from whence it proceeds, and it will naturally disappear. I may mention, however, that when there is no specific disease, either of body or mind, to which the want of sleep can be imputed, the person should keep himself in as cheerful a mood as possible—should rise early, if his strength permits it, and take such exercise as to fatigue himself moderately ; and if all these means fail, that he ought to make use of opium. In all cases of restlessness, indeed, this medicine must be had recourse to, if the affection resists every other remedy, and continues so long as to endanger health. Those preparations of opium, the acetate and muriate of morphia, have lately been a good deal used, and with excellent effect, for the same purpose. When neither opium nor its preparations agrees with the constitution, it becomes necessary to employ other narcotics. especially hyosciamus or hop. A pillow of hops sometimes succeeds in inducing sleep when other means fail. Such was the case with his late majesty, George III., who, by this contrivance, was relieved from the protracted wakefulness under which he laboured for so long a time. In giving medicines to produce sleep, great attention must be paid to the disease which occasions the restlessness ; for, in phrenitis, high fever, and some other disorders, it would be most injurious to administer anodynes of any kind. In such cases, as the restlessness is merely a symptom of the general disease, its removal will depend upon that of the latter. When, however, the acute symptoms have been overcome, and nothing but chronic wakefulness, the result of debility, remains behind, it then becomes necessary to have recourse to opium, or such other remedies as may be considered applicable to the particular case. Studious men ought to avoid late reading ; and, on going to bed. endeavour to abstract their minds from all intrusive ideas. They should try to circumscribe their thoughts within the narrowest possible circle, and prevent them from becoming rambling or excursive. I have often coaxed myself asleep by internally repeating half a dozen of times, any well known rhyme. While doing so, the ideas must be strictly directed to this particular theme, and prevented from wandering ; for sometimes, during the process of repetition, the mind takes a strange turn, and performs two offices at the same time, being directed to the rhyme on the one hand, and to something else on the other ; and it will be found that the hold it has of the former, is oftentimes much weaker than of the latter. The great secret is, by a strong effort of the will to compel the mind to depart from the favourite train of thought into which it has run, and address itself solely to the internal repetition of what is substituted in its place. If this is persevered in, it will generally be found to succeed ; and I would recommend all those who are prevented from sleeping, in consequence of too active a flow of ideas, to try the experiment. As has been already remarked, the more the mind is made to turn upon a single impression, the more closely it is made to approach

to the state of sleep, which is the total absence of all impressions. People should never go to bed immediately after studying hard, as the brain is precisely in that state of excitement which must prevent sleep. The mind ought previously to be relaxed by light conversation, music, or any thing which requires little thought.

In some cases of restlessness, sleep may be procured by the person getting up, and walking for a few minutes about the room. It is not easy to explain on what principle this acts, but it is certain, that by such means sleep sometimes follows, where previously it had been solicited in vain. It is customary with some people to read themselves into slumber, but dangerous accidents have arisen from this habit, in consequence of the lighted candle setting fire to the bed curtains. A safer and more effectual way is to get another person to read ; in which case, sleep will very generally take place, especially if the subject in question is not one of much interest, or read in a dry monotonous manner. When sleeplessness proceeds from the heat of the weather, the person should lie very lightly covered, and let the air circulate freely through his room. A cold bath taken shortly before going to bed, or sponging the body with cold water, will often ensure a comfortable night's rest in the hot season of the year. When it arises from heat in the soles or palms, these parts should be bathed with cold vinegar and water, before lying down, and, if necessary, occasionally afterwards till the heat abates, which usually occurs in two or three hours. Attention must also be paid to the stomach and bowels.

An easy mind, a good digestion, and plenty of exercise in the open air, are the grand conducives to sound sleep ;—and, accordingly, every man whose repose is indifferent, should endeavour to make them his own as soon as possible. When sleeplessness becomes habitual, the utmost care ought to be taken to overcome the habit, by the removal of every thing that has a tendency to cherish it.

CHAPTER X.

DROWSINESS.

Drowsiness is symptomatic of apoplexy and some other diseases, but sometimes it exists as an idiopathic affection. There are persons who have a disposition to sleep on every occasion. They do so at all times, and in all places. They sleep after dinner ; they sleep in the theatre ; they sleep in church. It is the same to them in what situation they may be placed : sleep is the great end of their existence—their occupation—their sole employment. Morpheus is the deity at whose shrine they worship—the only god whose influence over them is omnipotent. Let them be placed in almost any circumstances, and their constitutional failing prevails. It falls upon them in the midst of mirth ; it assails them when travelling. Let them sail, or ride, or sit, or lie, or walk, sleep overtakes them—binds their faculties in torpor ; and makes them dead to all that is passing around. Such are our dull, heavy-headed. drowsy mortals, those sons and daughters of phlegm—with passions as inert as a Dutch fog, and intellects as sluggish as the movements of the hippopotamus or the leviathan. No class of society is so insufferable as this. There is a torpor and obtuseness about their faculties, which render them dead to every impression. They have eyes and ears, yet they neither see nor hear ; and the most exhilarating scenes may be passing before them without once attracting their notice. It is not uncommon for persons of this stamp to fall asleep in the midst of a party to which they have been invited ; Mr Mackenzie, in one of his papers, speaks of an honest farmer having done so alongside of a young lady, who was playing on the harp for his amusement. The cause of this constitutional disposition to doze upon every occasion, seems to be a certain want of activity in the brain, the result of which is, that the individual is singularly void of fire, energy, and passion. He is of a phlegmatic temperament, generally a great eater, and very destitute of imagination. Such are the general characteristics of those who are predisposed to drowsiness: the cases where such a state coexists with intellectual energy are few in number.

Boerhaave speaks of an eccentric physician who took it into his head that sleep was the natural state of man, and accordingly slept eighteen hours out of the twenty-four—till he died of apoplexy, a disease which is always apt to be produced by excessive sleep.

Cases of constitutional drowsiness are in a great measure without remedy, for the soporific tendency springs from some natural defect, which no medicinal means can overcome.

Equally impossible of cure is the affection when it arises, as it very often does, from old age. Even long before this period of life, as at the age of fifty or sixty, people very often get into somnolent habits, and are pretty sure to fall asleep if they attempt to read, or even if they place themselves in an easy chair before the fire. I know of no cure for this indolent propensity, unless indeed the habits arise, as it sometimes does, from corpulency, in which case it is more manageable, in so far as its cause is occasionally capable of being removed.

Drowsiness sometimes proceeds from a fulness of blood in the head, or a disordered state of the digestive organs. When it originates from the former cause, it becomes necessary to have recourse to general or local blood-letting. The person, likewise, should use, from time to time, mild laxatives, live temperately, and take abundance of exercise. Medicines of a similar kind are necessary when the affection arises from the state of the stomach and bowels: so soon as these organs are restored to health, the symptomatic drowsiness will naturally disappear.

Persons who feel the disposition to drowsiness gaining upon them, should struggle vigorously against it ; for when once the habit is fairly established, its eradication is very difficult. Exercise of body and mind, early rising and the cold bath, are among the best means for this purpose.

CHAPTER XI.

PROTRACTED SLEEP.

I have already mentioned a few instances of individuals remaining for days or weeks in a state of profound sleep. The nature of this extraordinary affection is in a great measure, unknown; it arises, in most cases, without any obvious cause, generally resists every method that can be adopted for removing it, and disappears of its own accord.

The case of Mary Lyall, related in the 8th volume of the 'Transactions of the Royal Society of Edinburgh,' is one of the most remarkable instances of excessive somnolency on record. This woman fell asleep on the morning of the 27th of June, and continued in that state till the evening of the 30th of the same month, when she awoke, and remained in her usual way till the 1st of July, when she again fell asleep, and continued so till the the 8th of August. She was bled, blistered, immersed in the hot and cold bath, and stimulated in almost every possible way, without having any consciousness of what was going on. For the first seven days she continued motionless, and exhibited no inclination to eat. At the end of this time she began to move her left hand ; and, by pointing to her mouth, signified a wish for food. She took readily what was given to her ; still she discovered no symptoms of hearing, and made no other kind of bodily movement than of her left hand. Her right hand and arm, particularly, appeared completely dead, and bereft of feeling ; and even when pricked with a pin, so as to draw blood, never shrunk in the least degree. At the same time, she instantly drew back her left arm whenever it was touched by the point of the pin. She continued to take food whenever it was offered to her. For the first two weeks, her pulse generally stood at 50, during the third and fourth week, about 60 ; and on the day before her recovery, at 70 or 72. Her breathing was soft and almost imperceptible, but during the night-time she occasionally drew it more strongly, like a person who has first fallen asleep. She evinced no symptom of hearing, till about four days before her recovery. On being interrogated, after this event, upon her extraordinary state, she mentioned that she had no knowledge of any thing that had happened—that she had never been conscious of either having needed or received food, or of having been blistered ; and expressed much surprise on finding her head shaved. She had merely the idea of having passed a long night in sleep.

The case of Elizabeth Perkins is also remarkable. In the year 1788, she fell into a profound slumber, from which nothing could arouse her, and remained in this state for between eleven and twelve days, when she awoke of her own accord, to the great joy of her relatives, and wonder of the neighbourhood. On recovering, she went about her usual business ; but this was only for a short period, for in a week after she relapsed again into a sleep which lasted some days. She continued, with occasional intervals of wakefulness, in a dozing state for several months, when she expired.

There was lately at Kirkheaton a remarkable instance of excessive sleep. A poor paralytic, twenty years of age, was seldom, for the period of twelve months, awake more than three hours in the twenty-four. On one occasion, he slept for three weeks ; he took not a particle of either food or drink ; nothing could rouse him, even for a moment ; yet his sleep appeared to be calm and natural.

The case of Elizabeth Armitage of Woodhouse, near Leeds, may also be mentioned. The age of this person was sixty-nine years. She had been for several months in a decline, during which she had taken very little sustenance, when she fell into a state of lethargic stupor, on the morning of the 1st of July, 1827, in which condition she remained, without uttering one word, receiving any food, or showing any signs of life, except breathing, which was at times almost imperceptible. In this state she continued for eight days, when she expired without a groan.

Excessively protracted sleep may ensue from the injudicious use of narcotics. A very striking instance of this kind occurred on 17th February, 1816, near Lymington. In consequence of a complaint with which a child had been painfully afflicted for some time previous, its mother gave it an anodyne, (probably laudanum,) for the purpose of procuring it rest. The consequence was, that it fell into a profound sleep, which continued for three weeks. In this case, in addition to an excessive dose, the child must have possessed some constitutional idiosyncrasy, which favoured the operation of the medicine in a very powerful manner.

One of the most extraordinary instances of excessive sleep, is that of the lady of Nismes, published in 1777, in the 'Memoirs of the Royal Academy of Sciences at Berlin.' Her attacks of sleep took place periodically, at sunrise and about noon. The first continued till within a short time of the accession of the second, and the second till between seven and eight in the evening —when she awoke, and continued so till the next sunrise. The most extraordinary fact connected with this.

case is, that the first attack commenced always at daybreak, whatever might be the season of the year, and the other always immediately after twelve o'clock. During the brief interval of wakefulness which ensued shortly before noon, she took a little broth, which she had only time to do, when the second attack returned upon her, and kept her asleep till the evening. Her sleep was remarkably profound, and had all the characters of complete insensibility, with the exception of a feeble respiration, and a weak but regular movement of the pulse. The most singular fact connected with her remains to be mentioned. When the disorder had lasted six months, and then ceased, she had an interval of perfect health for the same length of time. When it lasted one year, the subsequent interval was of equal duration. The affection at last wore gradually away; and she lived, entirely free of it, for many years after. She died in the eighty-first year of her age, of dropsy, a complaint which had no connexion with her preceding disorder.

There are a good many varieties in the phenomena of protracted sleep. In some cases, the individual remains for many days without eating or drinking ; in others, the necessity for these natural wants arouses him for a short time from his slumber, which time he employs in satisfying hunger and thirst, and then instantly gets into his usual state of lethargy. The latter kind of somnolency is sometimes feigned by impostors for the purpose of extorting charity ; on this account, when an instance of the kind occurs, it should be narrowly looked into, to see that there is no deception.

The power possessed by the body of subsisting for such a length of time in protracted sleep, is most remarkable, and bears some analogy to the abstinence of the polar bear in the winter season. It is to be observed, however, that during slumber, life can be supported by a much smaller portion of food than when we are awake, in consequence of the diminished expenditure of the vital energy which takes place in the former state.

All that can be done for the cure of protracted somnolency, is to attempt to rouse the person by the use of stimuli, such as blistering, pinching, the warm or cold bath, the application of sternutatories to the nose, &c. Blooding should be had recourse to, if we suspect any apopletic tendency to exist. Every means must be employed to get nourishment introduced into the stomach ; for this purpose, if the sleeper cannot swallow, nutritious fluids should be forced, from time to time, into this organ by means of Jukes' pump, which answers the purpose of filling as well as evacuating it.

CHAPTER XII.

SLEEP FROM COLD.

This kind of sleep is so peculiar, that it requires to be considered separately. The power of cold in occasioning slumber, is not confined to man, but pervades a very extensive class of animals. The hybernation, or winter torpidute of the brown and Polar bear, results from this cause. Those animals continue asleep for months ; and do not awake from their apathy till revived by the genial temperature of spring. The same is the case with the hedgehog, the badger, the squirrel, and several species of the mouse and rat tribes, such as the dormouse and marmot : as also with the land tortoise, the frog, and almost all the individuals of the lizard, insect, and serpent tribes. Fishes are often found imbedded in the ice, and though in a state of apparent death, become at once lively and animated on being exposed to heat. " The fish froze," says Cap-

tain Franklin, ' as fast as they were taken out of the nets, and in a short time became a solid mass of ice, and by a blow or two of the hatchet were easily split open, when the intestines might be removed in one lump. If, in this completely frozen state, they were thawed before the fire, they recovered their animation.' Sheep sometimes remain for several weeks in a state of torpidude, buried beneath wreaths of snow. Swallows are occasionally in the same state, being found torpid and insensible in the hollows of trees, and among the ruins of old houses during the winter season ; but with birds this more rarely happens, owing, probably, to the temperature of their blood being higher than that of other animals, and thereby better enabling them to resist the cold. Almost all insects sleep in winter. This is particularly the case with the crysalis, and such grubs as cannot, at that season, procure their food. In hybernating animals, it is impossible to trace any peculiarity of structure which disposes them to hybernate, and enables life to be sustained during that period. So far the subject is involved in deep obscurity. According to Dr Edwards, the temperature of such animal sinks considerably during sleep, even in summer.

Want of moisture produces torpor in some animals. This is the case with the garden snail, which revives if a little water is thrown on it. Snails, indeed, have revived after being dried for fifteen years. Mr Bancer has restored the *vibris tritici* (a species of worm) after perfect torpidute and apparent death for five years and eight months by merely soaking it in water. The *furcularia anostobea*, a small microscopic animal, may be killed and revived a dozen times by drying it and then applying moisture. According to Spallanzani, animalculi have been recovered by moisture after a torpor of twenty-seven years. Larger animals are thrown into the same state from want of moisture. Such according to Humboldt, is the case with the alligator and boa constrictor during the dry season in the plains of Venezuela, and with the *centenes solosous*, a species of hedge hog found in Madagascar ; so that dryness as well as cold, produces hybernation, if, in such a case, we may use that term.

The power of intense cold in producing sleep, is very great in the human subject, and nothing in the winter season is more common than to find people lying dead in fields and on the high highways from such a cause. An overpowering drowsiness steals upon them, and if they yield to its influence death is almost unevitable. This is the particularly the case in snowstorms, in which it is often impossible to get a place of shelter.

This state of torpor, with the exception perhaps of catalepsy, is the most perfect sleep that can be imagined : it approaches almost to death in its apparent annihilation of the animal functions. Digestion is at an end, and the secretions and excretions suspended : nothing seems to go on but circulation, respiration and absorption. The two former are extremely languid,* but the latter tolerably vigorous, if we may judge from the quantity of fat which the animal loses during its torpid state. The bear, for example, on going to its wintry rest, is remarkably corpulent ; on awaking from it, quite emaciated ; in which state, inspired by the pangs of hunger, it sallies forth with redoubled fury upon its prey. Life is sustained by the absorption of this fat, which for months serves the animal as provision. Such emaciation, however, is not common to all hybernating animals, some of whom lose little or nothing by their winter torpidute.

Hybernation may be prevented. Thus the polar bear in the menagerie at Paris never hybernated ; and

---

* The extremely languid, or almost suspended state of these two functions, is demonstrated by the fact, that an animal in a state of hybernation may be placed for an hour in a jar of hydrogen without suffering death.

in the marmot and hedgehog hybernation is prevented if the animals be kept in a higher temperature. It is also a curious fact, that an animal, if exposed to a more intense cold, while hybernating, is awaked from its lethargy. Exposing a hybernating animal to light has also, in many cases the same effect.

Some writers, and Buffon among the rest, deny that such a state of torpor as we have here described, can be looked upon as sleep. This is a question into which it is not necessary at present to enter. All I contend for is, that the state of the mind is precisely the same here as in the ordinary sleep—that, in both cases, the organs of the senses and of volition are equally inert ; and that though the condition of the secretive and circulating systems are different, so many circumstances are nevertheless identical, that we become justified in considering the one in a work which professes to treat of the other.

In Captain Cook's first voyage, a memorable instance is given of the power of intense cold in producing sleep. It occurred in the island of Terra del Fuego. Dr Solander, Mr Banks, and several other gentlemen had ascended the mountains of that cold region, for the purpose of botanizing and exploring the country. ' Dr Solander, who had more than once crossed the mountains which divide Sweden from Norway, well knew that extreme cold, especially when joined with fatigue, produces a torpor and sleepinesss that are almost irresistible. He, therefore, conjured the company to keep moving whatever pain it might cost them, and whatever relief they might be promised by an inclination to rest. ' Whoever sits down,' said he, ' will sleep ; and whoever sleeps, will wake no more,' Thus at once admonished and alarmed, they set forward ; but while they were still upon the naked rock, and before they had got among the bushes, the cold became suddenly so intense as to produce the effects that had been most dreaded. Dr Solander himself was the first who felt the inclination, against which he had warned others, irresistible ; and insisted upon being suffered to lie down. Mr Banks entreated and remonstrated in vain ; down he lay upon the ground, although it was covered with snow, and it was with great difficulty that his friend kept him from sleeping. Richmond, also, one of the black servants, began to linger, having suffered from the cold in the same manner as the Doctor. Mr Banks, therefore, sent five of the company, among whom was Buchan, forward, to get a fire ready at the first convenient place they could find ; and himself, with four others remained with the Doctor and Richmond, whom, partly by persuasion and entreaty, and partly by force, they brought on ; but when they had got through the greatest part of the birch and swamp, they both declared they could go no farther. Mr Banks again had recourse to entreaty and expostulation, but they produced no effect. When Richmond was told that, if he did not go on, he would in a short time be frozen to death, he answered, that he desired nothing but to lie down and die. The Doctor did not so explicitly renounce his life ; he said he was willing to go on, but that he must first take some sleep, though he had before told the company, to sleep was to perish. Mr Banks and the rest found it impossible to carry them ; and there being no remedy, they were both suffered to sit down, being partly supported by the bushes ; and in a few minutes they fell into a profound sleep. Soon after, some of the people who had been sent forward, returned, with the welcome news that a fire was kindled about a quarter of a mile farther on the way. Mr Banks then endeavored to awake Dr Solander, and happily succeeded. But though he had not slept five minutes, he had almost lost the use of his limbs, and the muscles were so shrunk, that the shoes fell from his feet : he consented to go forward with such assistance as could be given him, but no attempts to relieve poor Richmond were successful.

It is hardly necessary to say any thing about the treatment of such cases. If a person is found in a state of torpor from cold, common sense points out the necessity of bringing him within the influence of warmth. When, however, the limbs, &c., are frost-bitten, heat must be very cautiously applied, lest reaction, ensuing in such debilitated parts, might induce gangrene. Brisk friction with a cold towel, or even with snow, as is the custom in Russia, should, in the first instance, be had recourse to. When by this means the circulation is restored, and motion and feeling communicated to the parts, the heat may be gradually increased, and the person wrapped in blankets, and allowed some stimulus internally, such as a little negus, or spirits and water. This practice should be adopted from the very first, when the parts are not frost-bitten ; but when such is the case, the stimulating system requires to be used with great caution, and we must proceed carefully, proportioning the stimulus to the particular circumstance of the case.

If a person is unfortunate enough to be overtaken in a snow storm, and has no immediate prospect of extrication. he should, if the cold is very great, and the snow deep, sink his body as much as possible in the latter, leaving only room for respiration. By this plan, the heat of the body is much better preserved than when exposed to the influence of the atmosphere, and life has a greater chance of being saved ; for the temperature of the snow is not lower than that of the surrounding air, while its power of absorbing caloric is much less. It is on this principle that sheep live for such a length of time enveloped in snow wreaths, while, had they been openly exposed, for a much less period, to a similar degree of cold, death would inevitably have ensued.

One of the best methods to prevent the limbs from being frost-bitten in intensely cold weather, is to keep them continually in motion. Such was the method recommended by Xenophon to the Greek troops, in the memorable ' retreat of the ten thousand,' conducted by that distinguished soldier and historian

CHAPTER XIII

TRANCE.

There is some analogy between suspended animation and sleep. It is not so striking, however, as to require any thing like a lengthened discussion of the former, which I shall only consider in so far as the resemblance holds good between it and sleep. I have already spoken of that suspension of the mind, and of some of the vital functions, which occurs in consequence of intense cold ; but there are other varieties, not less singular in their nature. The principal of these are, fainting, apoplexy, hanging, suffocation, drowning and especially, trance. When complete fainting takes place, it has many of the characters of death—the countenance being pail, moist, and clammy ; the body cold ; the respiration extremely feeble ; the pulsation of the heart apparently at an end ; while the mind is in a state of utter abeyance. It is in the latter respect only that the resemblance exists between syncope and sleep ; in every other they are widely different. The same rule holds with regard to apoplexy, in which a total insensibility, even to the strongest stimuli, takes place, accompanied also with mental torpor. In recoverable cases of drowning, hanging, and suffocation, a similar analogy prevails, only in a much feebler degree ; the faculties of the mind being for the time suspended, and the actual existence of the vital spark only proved by the subsequent restoration of the individual to consciousness and feeling.

The most singular species, however, of suspended

animation is that denominated catalepsy, or trance. No affection, to which the animal frame is subject, is more remarkable than this. During its continuance, the whole body is cold, rigid, and inflexible ; the countenance, without color ; the eyes fixed and motionless ; while breathing and the pulsation of the heart are, to all appearance, at an end. The mental powers, also, are generally suspended, and participate in the universal torpor which pervades the frame. In this extraordinary condition, the person may remain for several days, having all, or nearly all, the characteristics of death impressed upon him. Such was the case with the celebrated Lady Russel, who only escaped premature interment by the affectionate prudence of her husband ; and other well authenticated instances of similar preservation from burying alive, have been recorded

The nature of this peculiar species of suspended animation, seems to be totally unknown ; for there is such an apparent extinction of every faculty essential to life, that it is inconceivable how existence should go on during the continuance of the fit. There can be no doubt, however, that the suspension of the heart and lungs is more apparent than real. It is quite certain that the functions of these organs must continue, so as to sustain life although in so feeble a manner as not to come under the cognizance of our senses. The respiration, in particular, is exceedingly slight ; for a mirror, held to the mouth of the individual, receives no tarnish whatever from his breath. One fact seems certain, that the functions of the nervous system are wholly suspended, with the exception of such a faint portion of energy, as to keep up the circulatory and respiratory phenomena : consciousness, in a great majority of cases, is abolished ; and there is nothing wanting to indicate the unquestionable presence of death, but that decomposition of the body which invariably follows this state, and which never attends the presence of vitality.

The remote causes of trance are hidden in much obscurity ; and, generally, we are unable to trace the affection to any external circumstance. It has been known to follow a fit of terror. Sometimes it ensues after hysteria, epilepsy, or other spasmodic diseases, and is occasionally an accompaniment of menorrhagia and, intestinal worms. Nervous and hypochondriac patients are the most subject to its attacks ; but sometimes it occurs when there is no disposition of the kind, and when the person is in a state of the most seeming good health.

' A girl named Shorigny, about twenty-five years old, residing at Paris, had been for two years past subject to hysteria. On the twenty-eighth day after she was first attacked, the physician who came to visit her was informed that she had died during the night, which much surprised him, as when he had left her the night before, she was better than usual. He went to see her, in order to convince himself of the fact ; and, on raising the cloth with which she was covered, he perceived that though her face was very pale, and her lips discoloured, her features were not otherwise in the least altered. Her mouth was open, her eyes shut, and the pupils very much dilated ; the light of the candle made no impression on them. There was no sensible heat in her body ; but it was not cold and flabby like corpses in general. The physician returned the next day, determined on seeing her again before she was buried ; and, finding that she had not become cold, he gave orders that the coffin should not be soldered down until putrefaction had commenced. He continued to observe her during five days, and at the end of that period, a slight movement was observed in the cloth which covered her. In two hours, it was found that the arm had contracted itself ; she began to move ; and it was clear that it had only been an apparent death. The eyes soon after were seen opened, the senses returned, and the girl began gradually to recover. This is an extraordinary, but incontestible fact : the girl is still alive, and a great many persons who saw her while she was in the state of apathy described, are ready to satisfy the doubts of any one who will take the trouble to inquire.'*

The case which follows is from the *Canton Gazette*, and is not less curious :—

' On the western suburbs of Canton, a person named Le, bought as a slave-woman a girl named Leaning. At the age of twenty-one, he sold her to be a concubine to a man named Wong. She had lived with him three years. About six months ago she became ill, in consequence of a large imposthume on her side, and on the 25th of the present moon died. She was placed in a coffin, the lid of which remained unfastened, to wait for her parents to come and see the corpse, that they might be satisfied she died a natural death. On the 28th, while carrying the remains to be interred in the north side of Canton, a noise or voice was heard proceeding from the coffin ; and, on removing the covering, it was found the woman had come to life again. She had been supposed dead for three days.'

The case of Colonel Townsend, however, is much more extraordinary than either of the above mentioned. This gentleman possessed the remarkable faculty of throwing himself into a trance at pleasure. The heart ceased, apparently, to throb at his bidding, respiration seemed at an end, his whole frame assumed the icy chill and rigidity of death ; while his face became colourless, and shrunk, and his eye fixed, glazed, and ghastly : even his mind ceased to manifest itself ; for during the trance it was utterly devoid of consciousness as his body of animation. In this state he would remain for hours, when these singular phenomena wore away, and he returned to his usual condition. Medical annals furnish no parallel to this extraordinary case. Considered whether in a physiological or metaphysical point of view, it is equally astonishing and inexplicable.

A variety of stories are related of people having had circumstances revealed to them in a trance, of which they were ignorant when awake : most of these tales have their origin in fiction, although there is no reason why they may not be occasionally true ; as the mind, instead of being in torpor, as is very generally the case, may exist in a state analogous to that of dreaming, and may thus, as in a common dream, have long forgotten events impressed upon it.

The following case exhibits a very singular instance, in which the usual characteristic—a suspension of the mental faculties—was wanting. It seems to have been a most complete instance of suspended volition, wherein the mind was active, while the body refused to obey its impulses, and continued in a state of apparent death.

' A young lady, an attendant on the Princess ——, after having been confined to her bed, for a great length of time, with a violent nervous disorder, was at last, to all appearance, deprived of life. Her lips were quite pale, her face resembled the countenance of a dead person, and the body grew cold.

' She was removed from the room in which she died, was laid in a coffin, and the day of her funeral fixed on. The day arrived, and, according to the custom of the country, funeral songs and hymns were sung before the door. Just as the people were about to nail on the lid of the coffin, a kind of perspiration was observed to appear on the surface of her body. It grew greater every moment ; and at last a kind of convulsive motion was observed in the hands and feet of the corpse. A few minutes after, during which time fresh signs of returning life appeared, she at once opened her eyes and uttered a most pitiable shriek. Physicians were quickly procured, and in the course of a few days she was considerably restored, and is probably alive at this day.

' The description which she gave of her situation is extremely remarkable, and forms a curious and authentic addition to psychology.

' She said it seemed to her, as if in a dream, that she was really dead ; yet she was perfectly conscious of all that happened around her in this dreadful state. She distinctly heard her friends speaking and lamenting her death, at the side of her coffin. She felt them pull on the dead-clothes, and lay her in it. This feeling produced a mental anxiety, which is indescribable. She tried to cry, but her soul was without power, and could not act on her body. She had the contradictory feeling as if she were in her body, and yet not in it, at one and the same time. It was equally impossible for her to stretch out her arm, or to open her eyes, or to cry, although she continually endeavored to do so. The internal anguish of her mind was, however, at its utmost height when the funeral hymns began to be sung, and when the lid of the coffin was about to be nailed on. The thought that she was to be buried alive, was the one that gave activity to her soul, and caused it to operate on her corporeal frame.'*

The following is different from either of the foregoing ; I have given it on account of its singularity, although it does not altogether come under the denomination of trance.

' George Grokatzhi, a Polish soldier, deserted from his regiment in the harvest of the year 1677. He was discovered, a few days after, drinking and making merry in a common ale-house. The moment he was apprehended, he was so much terrified, that he gave a loud shriek, and was immediately deprived of the power of speech. When brought to a court martial, it was impossible to make him articulate a word ; nay, he then became as immovable as a statue, and appeared not to be conscious of any thing that was going forward. In the prison, to which he was conducted, he neither ate nor drank. The officers and priests at first threatened him, and afterwards endeavored to soothe and calm him, but all their efforts were in vain. He remained senseless and immovable. His irons were struck off, and he was taken out of the prison, but he did not move. Twenty days and nights were passed in this way, during which he took no kind of nourishment : he then gradually sunk and died.'†

It would be out of place to enter here into a detail of the medical management of the first mentioned varieties of suspended animation, such as drowning, strangulation, &c., &c. ; and with regard to the treatment of trance, properly so called, a very few words will suffice.

If we have reason to suppose that we know the cause of the affection, that, of course, must be removed whenever practicable. We must then employ stimuli to arouse the person from his torpor, such as friction, the application of sternutatories and volatile agents to the nostrils, and electricity. The latter remedy is likely to prove a very powerful one, and should always be had recourse to when other means fail. I should think the warm bath might be advantageously employed. When even these remedies do not succeed, we must trust to time. So long as the body does not run into decay, after a case of suspended animation arising without any very obvious cause, interment should not take place ; for it is possible that life may exist, although, for the time being, there is every appearance of its utter extinction. By neglecting this rule, a person may be interred alive ; nor can there be a doubt that such dreadful mistakes have occasionally been committed, especially in France, where it is customary to inter the body twenty-four hours after death. Decomposition is the only infallible mark that existence is at an end, and that the grave has triumphed.

CHAPTER XIV.

VOLUNTARY WAKING DREAMS.

The young and the imaginative are those who indulge most frequently in waking dreams. The scenes which life presents do not come up to the desires of the heart ; and the pencil of fancy is accordingly employed in depicting others more in harmony with its own designs. Away into the gloomy back-ground goes reality with its stern and forbidding hues, and forward, in colours more dazzling than those of the rainbow, start the bright and airy phantoms of imagination. ' How often,' observes Dr Good,* ' waking to the roar of the midnight tempest, while dull and gluttonous indolence snores in happy forgetfulness, does the imagination of those who are thus divinely gifted mount the dizzy chariot of the whirlwind, and picture evils that have no real existence ; now figuring to herself some neat and thrifty cottage where virtue delights to reside, she sees it swept away in a moment by the torrent, and despoiled of the little harvest just gathered in ; now following the lone traveller in some narrow and venturous pathway, over the edge of the Alpine precipices, where a single slip is instant destruction, she tracks him alone by fitful flashes of lightning ; and at length, struck by the flash, she beholds him tumbling headlong from rock to rock, to the bottom of the dread abyss, the victim of a double death. Or possibly she takes her stand on the jutting foreland of some bold terrific coast, and eyes the foundering vessel straight below ; she mixes with the spent and despairing crew ; she dives into the cabin, and singles out, perhaps from the rest, some lovely maid, who, in all the bloom of recovered beauty, is voyaging back to her native land from the healing airs of a foreign climate, in thought just bounding over the scenes of her youth, or panting in the warm embraces of a father's arms.' Such are waking dreams ; and there are few who, at some happy moment or other, have not yielded to their influence. Often under the burning clime of India, or upon the lonely banks of the Mississippi, has the stranger let loose the reins of his imagination, calling up before him the mountains of his own beloved country, his native streams, and rocks, and valleys, so vividly, that he was transported back into the midst of them, and lived over again the days of his youth. Or the waking dream may assume a more selfish character. If the individual pines after wealth, his mind may be filled with visions of future opulence. If he is young and unmarried, he may conjure up the form of a lovely female, may place her in a beautiful cottage by the banks of some romantic stream, may love her with unfathomable affection, and become the fondest and most happy of husbands. The more completely a person is left to solitude, the more likely is his imagination to indulge in such fancies. We seldom build castles in the air in the midst of bustle, or when we have any thing else to think of. Waking dreams are the luxuries of an otherwise unemployed mind—the aristocratic indulgences of the intellect. As people get older and more coversant with life in all its diversified features, they are little inclined to indulge in such visions. They survey events with the eye of severe truth, amuse themselves with no impracticable notions of fancied happiness, and are inclined to take a gloomy, rather than a flattering, view of the future. With youthful and poetical minds, however, the case is widely different. Much of that portion of their existence, not devoted to occupation, is a constant dream. They lull themselves into temporary happiness with scenes which they know only to exist in their own imagination ; but which are nevertheless so beautiful, and so much in harmony with every thing their souls desire, that they fondly clasp at the illusion, and submit themselves unhesitatingly to its spell. These curious states of mind may occur at any time ; but the most common periods of their accession are shortly after lying down, and shortly before getting up. Men, especially young men, of vivid, sanguine, imaginative temperaments, have dreams of this kind almost

---

* ' Psychological Magazine,' vol. v. part iii. page 15.
† Bonetus, ' Medic Septentrion.' lib. i. sec. xvi. cap. 6.
* Book of Nature, vol. iii. p. 422.

every morning and night. Instead of submitting to the sceptre of sleep, they amuse themselves with creating a thousand visionary scenes. Though broad awake, their judgment does not exercise the slightest sway, and fancy is allowed to become lord of the ascendant. Poets are notorious castle-builders, and poems are, in fact, merely waking dreams—at least their authors were under the hallucination of such dreams while composing. Milton's mind, during the composition of Paradise Lost, must have existed chiefly in the state of a sublime waking dream; so must Raphael's, while painting the Sistine Chapel; and, Thorwaldson's, while designing the triumphs of Alexander. In waking dreams, whatever emotion prevails has a character of exaggeration, at least in reference to the existing condition of the individual. He sees every thing through the serene atmosphere of imagination, and imbues the most trite circumstances with poetical colouring. The aspect, in short, which things assume, bears a strong resemblance to that impressed upon them by ordinary dreams, and differs chiefly in this, that, though verging continually on the limits of extravagance, they seldom transcend possibility.

CHAPTER XV.

SPECTRAL ILLUSIONS.

Of the various faculties with which man is endowed, those which bring him into communication with the material world, constitute an important class. The organs of these faculties—termed perceptive—are situated in the middle and lower parts of the forehead. Their function is to perceive and remember the existence, phenomena, qualities, and relations of external objects. *Individuality* takes cognizance of the existence of material bodies; *Eventuality*, of their motions or actions; *Form*, of their shape; *Size*, of their magnitude and proportions; *Weight*, of the resistance which they offer to a moving or restraining power; *Colouring*, of their colours; and *Locality*, of their relative position. *Time* and *Number* perceive and remember duration and numbers; *Language* takes cognizance of artificial signs of feeling and thought; and *Order* delights in regularity and arrangement. In ordinary circumstances, the mode of action of these organs is this. If any object—a horse for example—be placed before us, the rays of light reflected from its surface to our eye, form a picture of the animal upon the retina or back part of that organ. This picture gives rise to what, for want of more precise language, is called an impression, which is conveyed by the optic nerve to the cerebral organs already mentioned; and by them, in reality, the horse is perceived. The eye and optic nerve, it will be observed, do no more than transmit the impression from without, so as to produce that state of the internal organs which is accompanied by what is termed perception or *sensation*. When the horse is withdrawn, the impression still remains, to a certain extent, in the brain; and though the animal is not actually perceived, we still remember its appearance, and can almost imagine that it is before us. This faint semi-perception is called an *idea*, and differs from sensation only in being less vivid. The brain is more highly excited when it perceives a sensation, than when an idea only is present; because, in the former case, there is applied, through the medium of the senses, a stimulus from without, which, in the latter case, is not present. If, however, the brain be brought to internal causes to a degree of excitement, which, in general, is the result only of external impressions, ideas not less vivid than sensations ensue; and the individual has the same consciousness as if an impression were transmitted from an actual object through the senses. In

other words, the brain, in a certain state, perceives external bodies; and any cause which induces that state, gives rise to a like perception, independently of the usual cause—the presence of external bodies themselves. The chief of these internal causes is inflammation of the brain: and when the organs of the perceptive faculties are so excited—put into a state similar to that which follows actual impressions from without—the result is a series of false images or sounds, which are often so vivid as to be mistaken for realities. During sleep, the perceptive organs seem to be peculiarly susceptible of such excitement. In dreaming, for instance, the external world, is inwardly represented to our minds with all the force of reality: we speak and hear as if we were in communication with actual existences. Spectral illusions are phenomena strictly analogous; indeed, they are literally nothing else than involuntary waking dreams.

In addition to the occasional cause of excitement of the perceptive organs above alluded to, there is another, the existence of which is proved by numerous facts, though its mode of action is somewhat obscure. I allude to a large development of the organ of *Wonder*. Individuals with such a development are both strongly inclined to believe in the supernaturality of ghosts, and peculiarly liable to be visited by them. This organ is large in the head of Earl Grey, and he is said to be haunted by the apparition of a bloody head. Dr Gall mentions, that in the head of Dr Jung Stilling, who saw visions, the organ was very largely developed. A gentleman who moves in the best society in Paris, once asked Gall to examine his head. The doctor's first remark was, 'You sometimes see visions, and believe in apparitions.' The gentleman started from this in astonishment, and said that he *had* frequent visions: but never till that moment had he spoken on the subject to any human being, through fear of being set down as absurdly credulous. How a large development of *Wonder* produces the necessary excitement of the perceptive organs is unknown, but the fact seems indisputable.

In former times, individuals who beheld visions, instead of ascribing them to a disordered state of the brain, referred them to outward impressions, and had a false conviction of the presence of supernatural beings. Hence the universal belief in ghosts which in these periods prevailed, even among the learned, and from which the illiterate are not yet entirely exempt.

We read in history of people being attended by familiar spirits; such was the case with Socrates in ancient, and with the poet Tasso, in modern times: their familiar spirits were mere spectral illusions. 'At Bisaccio, near Naples,' says Mr Hoole, in his account of the illustrious author of the Jerusalem Delivered, 'Manso had an opportunity of examining the singular effects of Tasso's melancholy, and often disputed him concerning a *familiar spirit* which he pretended conversed with him: Manso endeavoured in vain to persuade his friend that the whole was the illusion of a disturbed imagination; but the latter was strenuous in maintaining the reality of what he asserted, and to convince Manso, desired him to be present at one of the mysterious conversations. Manso had the complaisance to meet him the next day, and while they were engaged in discourse, on a sudden he observed that Tasso kept his eyes fixed on a window, and remained in a manner immovable; he called him by his name, but received no answer; at last Tasso cried out, 'There is the friendly spirit that is come to converse with me; look! and you will be convinced of all I have said.'

Manso heard him with surprise; he looked, but saw nothing except the sunbeams darting through the window; he cast his eyes all over the room, but could perceive nothing; and was just going to ask where the pretended spirit was, when he heard Tasso speak with great earnestness, sometimes putting questions to the spirit, sometimes giving answers · delivering the whole in such a pleasing manner, and in such elevated expressions, that he listened with admiration, and had not the least inclination to interrupt him. At last the uncommon conversation ended with the departure of the spirit, as appeared by Tasso's own words, who, turning to Manso, asked him if his doubts were removed. Manso was more amazed than ever; he scarce knew what to think of his friend's situation, and waived any farther conversation on the subject.'

The visions of angels, and the communications from above, with which religious enthusiasts are often impressed, arise from the operation of spectral illusions. They see forms and hear sounds which have no existence; and, believing in the reality of such impressions, consider themselves highly favored by the almighty. These feelings prevailed very much during the persecutions in Scotland. Nothing was more common than for the Covenanter by the lonely hill side to have what he supposed a special message from God, and even to see the angel who brought it, standing before him, and encouraging him to steadfastness in his religious principles. Much of the crazy fanaticism exhibited by the disciples of Campbell and Irving, undoubtedly arises from a similar cause; and it is probable that both of these individuals see visions and hear supernatural voices, as well as many of their infatuated followers.

Various causes may so excite the brain as to produce these phantasmata, such as great mental distress, sleeplessness, nervous irritation, religious excitement, fever, epilepsy, opium, delirium tremens, excessive study, and dyspepsia. I have known them to arise without the apparent concurrence of any mental or bodily distemper. I say apparent, for it is very evident there must be some functional derangement, however much it may be hidden from observation. An ingenious friend has related to me a case of this kind which occurred in his own person. One morning, while lying in bed broad awake, and, as he supposed, in perfect health, the wall opposite to him appeared to open at its junction with the ceiling, and out of the aperture came a little uncouth, outlandish figure, which descended from the roof, squatted upon his breast, grinned at him maliciously, and seemed as if pinching and pummelling his sides. This illusion continued for some time, and with a timorous subject might have been attended with bad consequences; but he referred it at once to some disordered state of the stomach under which he imagined he must have labored at the time, although he had no direct consciousness of any such derangement of this organ. The same gentleman has related to me the case of one of his friends which attracted much notice at the time it happened, from the melancholy circumstance that attended it. It is an equally marked instance of hallucination arising without the individual being conscious of any physical cause by which it might be occasioned. It is as follows:—

Mr H. was one day walking along the street, apparently in perfect health, when he saw, or supposed he saw his acquaintance, Mr C., walking before him. He called aloud to the latter, who, however, did not seem to hear him, but continued moving on. Mr H. then quickened his pace for the purpose of overtaking him; the other increased his also, as if to keep ahead of his pursuer, and proceeded at such a rate that Mr H. found it impossible to make up to him. This continued for some time, till, on Mr C. coming to a gate he opened it, passed in, and slammed it violently in Mr H.'s face. Confounded at such treatment, the latter instantly opened the gate, looked down the long lane into which it led, and, to his astonishment, no one was visible. Determined to unravel the mystery, he went to Mr C.'s house; and what was his surprise when he learned that he was confined to his bed, and had been so for several days. A week or two afterwards, these gentlemen chanced to meet in the house of a common friend, when Mr H. mentioned the circumstance, and told Mr

C. jocularly that he had seen his wraith, and that, as a natural consequence, he would soon be a dead man. The person addressed laughed heartily, as did the rest of the company, but the result turned out to be no laughing matter; for, in a very few days, Mr C. was attacked with putrid sore throat, and died; and within a very short period of his death Mr H. was also in the grave.

Some of the most vivid instances of spectral illusion are those induced by opium. Several of the 'English Opium-Eater's' visions were doubtless of this nature. Dr Abercrombie relates a striking instance of the kind which occurred to the late Dr Gregory. 'He had gone to the north country by sea to visit a lady, a near relation, in whom he felt deeply interested, and who was in an advanced state of consumption. In returning from the visit, he had taken a moderate dose of laudanum. with the view of preventing sea-sickness, and was lying on a couch in the cabin, when the figure of the lady appeared before him in so distinct a manner that her actual presence could not have been more vivid. He was quite awake, and fully sensible that it was a phantasm produced by the opiate, along with his intense mental feeling; but he was unable by any effort to banish the vision.'* Indeed, any thing on which the mind dwells excessively, may by exciting the perceptive organs, give rise to spectral illusions. It is to this circumstance that the bereaved husband sees the image of a departed wife, to whom he was fondly attached—that the murderer is haunted by the apparition of his victim—and that the living with whom we are familiar, seem to be presented before our eyes, although at a distance from us. Dr Conolly relates the case of a gentleman, who, when in danger of being wrecked near the Eddystone lighthouse, saw the images of his whole family.

These illusive appearance sometimes occur during convalescence from diseases. In the summer of 1832, a gentleman in Glasgow, of dissipated habits, was seized with cholera, from which he recovered. His recovery was unattended with any thing particular, except the presence of a phantasmata—consisting of human figures about three feet high, neatly dressed in pea-green jackets, and knee-breeches of the same color. Being a person of a superior mind, and knowing the cause of the illusions, they gave him no alarm, although he was very often haunted by them. As he advanced in strength the phantoms appeared less frequently, and diminished in size, till at last they were not taller than his finger. One night, while seated alone, a multitude of these Lilliputian gentlemen made their appearance on his table, and favored him with a dance; but being at the time otherwise engaged, and in no mood to enjoy such an amusement, he lost temper at the unwelcome intrusion of his pigmy visiters, and striking his fist violently upon the table, he exclaimed in a violent passion, 'Get about your business you little impertinent rascals! What the devil are you doing here?' when the whole assembly instantly vanished, and he was never troubled with them more.

It generally happens that the figures are no less visible when the eyes are closed than when they are open. An individual in the west of Scotland, whose case is related in the Phrenological Journal,† whenever he shut his eyes or was in darkness, saw a procession move before his mind as distinctly as it had previously done before his eyes. Some years ago, a farmer from the neighbourhood of Hamilton, informed me, with feelings of great horror, that he had frequently the vision of a hearse drawn by four black horses, which were driven by a black driver. Not knowing the source of this illusion he was rendered extremely miserable by it; and, to aggravate his unhappiness, was regarded by the ignorant country people, to whom he told his story, as

* Inquiries concerning the Intellectual Powers, p. 357.
† Vol. ii. p. 111.

having been guilty of some grievous crime. This vision was apparent to him chiefly by night, and the effect was the same whether his eyes were open or shut. Indeed, so little are these illusions dependant on sight, that the blind are frequently subject to them. A respected elderly gentleman, a patient of my own, who was afflicted with loss of sight, accompanied by violent headaches, and severe dispeptic symptoms, used to have the image of a black cat presented before him, as distinctly as he could have seen it before he became blind. He was troubled with various other spectral appearances, besides being subject to illusions of sound equally remarkable ; for he had often the consciousness of hearing music so strongly impressed upon him, that it was with difficulty his friends could convince him it was purely ideal.

Considering the age in which Bayle lived, his notions of the true nature of spectral illusions were wonderfully acute and philosophical. Indeed, he has so well described the theory of apparitions, that the modern phrenological doctrine on this point seems little more than an expanded version of his own. ' A man,' says he, ' would not only be very rash, but also very extravagant, who should pretend to prove that there never was any person that imagined he saw a spectre ; and I do not think that the most obstinate and extravagant unbelievers have maintained this. All they say, comes to this : that the persons who have thought themselves eye-witnesses of the apparition of spirits had a disturbed imagination. They confess that there are *certain places in our brain* that, being affected in a certain manner, *excite the image of an object which has no real existence out of ourselves*, and make the man, whose brain is thus modified, believe he sees, at two paces distant, a frightful spectre, a hobgoblin, a threatening phantom. The like happens in the heads of the most incredulous, either in their sleep, or in the paroxysms of a violent fever. Will they maintain after this, that it is impossible for a man awake, and not in a delirium, to receive, *in certain places of his brain, an impression* almost like that which, by the law of nature, is connected with the appearance of a phantom.' In one of Shenstone's Essays, entitled ' An Opinion of Ghosts,' the same theory is clearly enunciated.

It is worthy of remark, that the phenomena of apparitions are inconsistent with the prevalent theory that the brain is a single organ, with every part of which each faculty is connected. Were this theory sound, the same cause that vivifies the perceptive faculties must also vivify, or excite to increased action, the propensities, sentiments, and reflecting powers. This, however, is by no means the case.

The case of Nicolai, the Prussian bookseller, which occurred in the beginning of 1791, is one of the most remarkable instances of spectral illusion on record. ' I saw,' says he, ' in a state of mind completely sound, and—after the first terror was over—with perfect calmness, for nearly two months, almost constantly and involuntarily, a vast number of human and other forms, and even heard their voices, though all this was merely the consequence of a diseased state of the nerves, and an irregular circulation of the blood.' ' When I shut my eyes, these phantoms would sometimes vanish entirely, though there were instances when I beheld them with my eyes closed ; yet when they disappeared on such occasions, they generally returned when I opened my eyes. I conversed sometimes with my physician and my wife of the phantasms which, at the moment surrounded me ; they appeared more frequently walking than at rest ; nor were they constantly present. They frequently did not come for some time, but always reappeared for a longer or shorter period either singly or in company, the latter, however, being most frequently the case. I generally saw human forms of both sexes ; but they usually seemed not to take the smallest notice of each other, moving as in a market-place, where all are eager to press through the crowd ; at times, however, they seemed to be transacting business with each other. I also saw, several times, people on horseback. dogs, and birds. All these phantasms appeared to me in their natural size, and as distinct as if alive, exhibiting different shades of carnation in the uncovered parts. as well as in different colours and fashions in their dresses, though the colours seemed somewhat paler than in real nature ; none of the figures appeared particularly comical, terrible, or disgusting, most of them being of an indifferent shape, and some presenting a pleasing aspect.'

Perhaps the most remarkable visionary, of whom we have any detailed account, was Blake the painter. This extraordinary man not only believed in his visions, but could often call up at pleasure whatever phantasms he wished to see ; and so far from their being objects of annoyance, he rather solicited than wished to avoid their presence. He was in the habit of conversing with angels, demons, and heroes, and taking their likenesses ; for they proved most obedient sitters, and never showed any aversion to allow him to transfer them to paper. ' His mind ;' says Mr Cunningham, ' could convert the most ordinary occurrences into something mystical and supernatural.' '' Did you ever see a fairy's funeral, madam ?' he once said to a lady who happened to sit by him in company, ' never, sir,' was the answer. ' I have,' said Blake, ' but not before last night. I was walking alone in my garden, there was great stillness among the branches and flowers, and more than common sweetness in the air ; I heard a low and pleasant sound, and knew not whence it came. At last I saw the broad leaf of a flower move, and underneath I saw a procession of creatures of the size and color of the green and grey grasshoppers, bearing a body laid out on a rose leaf, which they buried with songs, and then disappeared. It was a fairy funeral.'' On being asked to draw the likeness of Sir William Wallace, that hero immediately stood before him, and he commenced taking his portrait. ' Having drawn for some time with the same care of hand and steadiness of eye, as if a living sitter had been before him, Blake stoped suddenly and said, ' I cannot finish him—Edward the first has stepped in between him and me.' 'That's lucky,' said his friend, ' for I want the portrait of Edward too.' Blake took another sheet of paper and sketched the features of Plantagenet ; upon which his majesty politely vanished, and the artist finished the head of Wallace.'* The greater part of his life was passed in beholding visions and in drawing them. On one occasion he saw the ghost of a flea and took a sketch of it. No conception was too strange or incongruous for his wild imagination, which totally overmastered his judgment, and made him mistake the chimeras of an excited brain for realities.

What is called the *Second sight* originated, in most cases, from spectral illusions ; and the seers of whom we so often read, were merely individuals visited by these phantoms. The Highland mountains, and the wild lawless habits of those who inhabited them, were peculiarly adapted to foster the growth of such impressions in imaginative minds ; and, accordingly, nothing was more common than to meet with persons who not only fancied they saw visions, but, on the strength of this belief, laid claim to the gift of prophesy. The more completely the mind is abstracted from the bustle of life, the more solitary the district in which the individual resides ; and the more romantic and awe-inspring the scenes that pass before his eyes, the greater is his tendency to see visions, and to place faith in what he sees. A man, for instance, with the peculiar temperament which predisposes to see, and believe in, spectral illusions, is informed that his chieftain and clan have set out on a dangerous expedition. Full of the subject, he forces their images before him—sees them engaged

* Cunningham's Lives of the British Painters, Sculptors, and Architects, vol. ii., Life of Blake.

in fight—beholds his chieftian cut down by the claymore of an enemy—the clansmen routed and dispersed, their houses destroyed, their cattle carried off. This vision he relates to certain individuals. If, as is not unlikely, it is borne out by the event, his prophecy is spread far and wide, and looked upon as an instance of the second sight; while, should nothing happen, the story is no more thought of by those to whom it was communicated. In some instances, it is probable that the accidental fulfilment of an ordinary dream was regarded as second sight.

The belief in fairies, no doubt, had also its origin in spectral illusions. In the days of ignorance and superstition nothing was more easy than for an excited brain to conjure up those tiny forms, and see them perform their gambols upon the greensward beneath the light of the moon.

The dimensions of the figures which are exhibited in spectral illusions vary exceedingly. Sometimes they appear as miniatures, sometimes of the size of life, at other times of colossal proportions. The same differences apply to their colour. In one case they are pale, misty, transparent; in another black, red, blue, or green. Sometimes we have them fantastically clothed in the costume of a former age, sometimes in that of our own. Now they are represented grinning, now weeping, now in smiles. 'White or grey Ghosts,' says Mr Simpson ' result from excited *Form*, with quiescent *Colouring*, the transparent cobweb effect being colourless. Pale spectres, and shadowy yet coloured forms, are the effect of partially excited *Colouring*. Tall ghosts and dwarf goblins, are the illusions of over-excited *Size*.' The jabbering of apparitions arises from an excited state of that part of the brain which gives us cognizance of sounds. This explanation seems highly probable, or rather quite satisfactory. There are points, however, which it is likely no one will ever be able to explain. Why, for instance should the disordered brain conjure up *persons* and *faces* rather than *trees* and *houses?* why should a ghost be dressed in *red* rather than *blue*, and why should it *smile* rather than *grin?* These are minutiæ beyond the reach of investigation at least in the present state of our knowledge.

Mr Simpson, in the second volume of the Phrenological Journal, has published a case of spectral illusion, which, for singularity and interest, equals any thing of the same kind which has hitherto been recorded. The subject of it was a young lady under twenty years of age, of good family, well educated, free from any superstitious fears, in perfect bodily health and of sound mind. She was early subject to occasional attacks of such illusions, and the first she remembered was that of a carpet which descended in the air before her, then vanished away. After an interval of some years, she began to see human figures in her room as she lay wide awake in bed. These figures were *whitish* or rather *grey*, and *transparent* like *cobweb*, and generally above the size of life. At this time she had acute headaches, very singularly confined to one small spot of the head. On being asked to indicate the spot, she touched, with her fore-finger and thumb, each side of the root of the nose, the commencement of the eyebrows, and the spot immediately over the top of the nose, the ascertained seats of *Form, Size*, and *Lower Individuality*. On being asked if the pain was confined to these spots, she answered that some time afterwards it extended to the right and left, along the eyebrows, and a little above them, and completely round the eyes, which felt as if they would burst from their sockets. On this taking place the visions varied. The organs of *Weight, Colouring, Order, Number*, and *Locality*, were affected, and the phantasmata assumed a change corresponding to the irritated condition of these parts. The whitish or cobweb spectres assumed the natural *colour* of the objects, but they continued often to present themselves, though not always, above the *size of* life.' ' *Colouring* being over-excited, began to occasion its specifie and fantastical illusions. Bright spots, like stars on a back ground, filled the room in the dark, and even in day-light; and sudden, and sometimes gradual, illumination of the room during the night took place, so that the furniture in it became visible. Innumerable balls of fire seemed one day to pour like a torrent out of one of the rooms of the house down the staircase. On one occasion, the pain between the eyes, and along the lower ridge of the brow, struck her suddenly with great violence—when, *instantly*, the room filled with stars and bright spots. On attempting, on that occasion, to go to bed, she said she was conscious of an *inability to balance herself, as if she had been tipsy*, and she fell, having made repeated efforts to seize the bed-post; which, in the most unaccountable manner eluded her grasp *by shifting its place*, and also by presenting her with *a number of bed-posts instead of one*. If the organ of *Weight* situated between *Size* and *Colouring*, be the organ of the instinct to preserve, and power of preserving equilibrium, it must be the necessary consequence of the derangement of that organ to overset the balance of the person. Over-excited *Number* we should expect to produce multiplication of objects, and the first experience she had of this illusion, was the multiplication of the bed-posts, and subsequently of any inanimate object she looked at.'

' For nearly two years, Miss S. L. was free from her frontal headaches, and—mark the coincidence—untroubled by visions or any other illusive perceptions. Some months ago, however, all her distressing symptoms returned in great aggravation, when she was conscious of a want of health. The pain was more acute than before along the frontal bone, and round and in the eyeballs; and all the organs there situated recommenced their game of illusion. Single figures of absent and deceased friends were terribly real to her, both in the day and in the night, sometimes *cobweb*, but generally coloured. She sometimes saw friends on the street, who proved phantoms when she approached to speak to them; and instances occurred, where, from not having thus satisfied herself of the illusion, she affirmed to such friends that she had seen them in certain places, at certain times, when they proved to her the clearest *alibi*. The *confusion* of her spectral forms now distressed her.—(*Order* affected.) The oppression and perplexity were intolerable, when figures presented themselves before her in inextricable disorder, and still more when they changed—as with Nicolai—from whole figures to parts of figures—faces and half faces, and limbs—sometimes of inordinate size and dreadful deformity. One instance of illusive *Disorder*, which she mentioned, is curious; and has the farther effect of exhibiting (what cannot be put in terms except those of) the derangement of the just perception of gravitation or equilibrium. (*Weight*.) One night as she sat in her bed-room, and was about to go to bed, a *stream* of spectres, persons' faces, limbs, in the most shocking confusion, seemed to her to pour into her room from the window, in the manner of a cascade! Although the cascade continued, apparently, in rapid descending motion; there was no accumulation of figures in the room, the supply unaccountably vanishing, after having formed the cascade. *Colossal* figures are her frequent visiters. (*Size*.)'

In the fifth volume of the Phrenological Journal, page 319, a case is mentioned where the patient was tortured with horrid faces glaring at her, and approaching close to her in every possible aggravation of horror. ' She was making a tedious recovery in child-bed when these symptoms troubled her. Besides the forms, which were of natural colour, though often bloody, she was perplexed by their variation in size, from colossal to minute. She saw also entire human figures, but

Q

they were always as minute as pins, or even pin-heads, and were in great confusion and numbers.' 'She described the pain which *accompanied* her illusions, viz. acute pain in the upper part or root of the nose, the seat of the organ of *Form*, and all along the eyebrows, which takes in *Individuality, Form, Size, Weight, Order* and *Number*.' In the same volume, page 430, Mr Levison relates, that on asking an individual who saw apparitions, whether or not he felt pain at any part of his head, he answered, 'that every time before he experienced this peculiar power of seeing figures, he invariably felt pain in and between his eyes, and, in short, all over the eyebrows.' It does not appear, however, that pain is universally felt in such cases in the lower part of the forehead. Dr Andrew Combe informs me that, so far as he has observed, the pain, when it does exist, is more frequently in the exciting organ, generally *Wonder.*

Spectral illusions constitute the great pathognomonic sign of delirium tremens. In this disease they are usually of a horrible, a disgusting, or a frightful nature ; the person being irresistibly impressed with the notion that reptiles, insects, and all manner of vermin are crawling upon him, which he is constantly endeavoring to pick off—that he is haunted by hideous apparitions —that people are in the room preparing to murder and rob him, and so forth. In the following case, with which I have been favored by Dr Combe, the illusive appearances were of a more pleasing kind than generally happen. 'In a case,' says he, 'of delirium tremens in an inn-keeper, about whom I was consulted, the spectral illusions continued several days, and had a distinct reference to a large and active cerebullum, (the organ of *Amativeness*) conjoined with *Wonder*. The man refused to allow me to look at a blister which had been placed between his shoulders, ' because he could not take off his coat *before the ladies who were in the room !*' When I assured him that there was nobody in the room, he smiled at the joke, as he conceived it to, be, and, in answer to my questions, described them as several in number, well dressed, and good-looking. At my request he rose up to shake hands with them, and was astonished at finding them elude his grasp, and his hand strike the wall. This, however, convinced him that it was an illusion, and he forthwith took off his coat, but was unwilling to converse longer on the subject. In a few days the ladies vanished from his sight.'

Spectral illusions are more frequently induced by fever than by any other cause. Indeed, the premonitory stages of most fevers are accompanied by illusive appearances of one kind or another, such as luminous bodies, especially when the eyes are shut, hideous faces, streaks of fire, &c.; and in the advanced stages, they are not uncommon. A medical friend informed me, that when ill of fever in Portugal, he was terribly harrassed by the vision of a soldier, whose picture was hanging in the room. Removing the picture failed to dissipate the illusion, which did not disappear till he was conveyed to another apartment. Dr Bostock, while under a febrile attack, was visited by spectral illusions of an unusual kind. The following are the particulars of his case, as described by himself :—

'I was laboring,' says he, 'under a fever, attended with symptoms of general debility, especially of the nervous system, and with a severe pain of the head, which was confined to a small spot situated above the right temple. After having passed a sleepless night, and being reduced to a state of considerable exhaustion, I first perceived figures presenting themselves before me, which I immediately recognised as similar to those described by Nicolai, and upon which, as I was free from delirium, and as they were visible about three days and nights with little intermission, I was able to make my observations. There were two circumstance which appeared to me very remarkable ; first, that the spectral appearances always followed the motion of the eyes; and, secondly, that the objects which were the best defined and remained the longest visible, were such as I had no recollection of ever having previously seen. For about twenty-four hours I had constantly before me a human figure, the features and dress of which were as distinctly visible as that of any real existence, and of which, after an interval of many years, I still retain the most lively impression ; yet, neither at the time nor since have I been able to discover any person whom I had previously seen who resembled it.

'During one part of this disease, after the disappearance of this stationary phantom, I had a very singular and amusing imagery presented to me. It appeared as if a number of objects, principally human faces or figures on a small scale, were placed before me, and gradually removed like a succession of medallions. They were all of the same size, and appeared to be all situated at the same distance from the face. After one had been seen for a few minutes, it became fainter, and then another, which was more vivid, seemed to be laid upon it or substituted in its place, which, in its turn, was superseded by a new appearance. During all this succession of scenery, I do not recollect that, in a single instance, I saw any object with which I had been previously acquainted, nor, as far as I am aware, were the representations of any of those objects, with which my mind was the most occupied at other times, presented to me ; they appeared to be invariably new creations, or, at least, new combinations of. which I could not trace the original materials.'[*]

The following very curious instance, is not less interesting : the subject of it was a member of the English bar.

'In December, 1823, A. was confined to his bed by inflammation of the chest, and was supposed by his medical attendant to be in considerable danger. One night, while unable to sleep from pain and fever, he saw sitting on a chair, on the left side of his bed, a female figure which he immediately recognised to be that of a young lady who died about two years before. His first feeling was surprise, and perhaps a little alarm ; his second, that he was suffering from delirium. With this impression, he put his head under the bed-clothes, and, after trying in vain to sleep, as a test of the soundness of his mind, he went through a long and complicated process of metaphysical reasoning. He then peeped out and saw the figure in the same situation and position. He had a fire, but would not allow a candle or nurse in the room. A stick was kept by his side to knock for the nurse when he required her attendance. Being too weak to move his body, he endeavored to touch the figure with the stick, but, on a real object being put on the chair, the imaginary one disappeared, and was not visible again that night.

The next day he thought of little but the vision, and expected its return without alarm, and with some pleasure. He was not disappointed. It took the same place as before, and he employed himself in observations. When he shut his eyes or turned his head, he ceased to see the figure ; by interposing his hand he could hide part of it ; and it was shown, like any mere material substance, by the rays of the fire which fell upon and were reflected from it. As the fire declined it became less perceptible, and as it went out, invisible. A similar appearance took place on several other nights ; but it became less perceptible, and its visits less frequent, as the patient recovered from his fever.

'He says the impressions on his mind were always pleasing, as the spectre looked at him with calmness and regard. He never supposed it real ; but was unable to account for it on any philosophical principles within his knowledge.

'In the autumn of 1825. A.'s health was perfectly

restored, and he had been free from any waking vision for nearly eighteen months. Some circumstances occurred which produced in him great mental excitement. One morning he dreamed of the figure, which stood by his side in an angry posture, and asked for a locket which he usually wore. He awoke and saw it at the toilet, with the locket in its hand. He rushed out of bed and it instantly disappeared. During the next six weeks its visits were incessant, and the sensations which they produced were invariably horrible. Some years before, he had attended the dissection of a woman in a state of rapid decomposition. Though much disgusted at the time, *the subject* had been long forgotten ; but was recalled by the union of its putrescent body with the spectre's features. The visits were not confined to the night, but frequently occurred while several persons were in the same room. They were repeated at intervals during the winter ; but he was able to get rid of them by moving or sitting *in an erect position*. Though well, his pulse was hard, and generally from 90 to 100.'*

In March, 1829, during an attack of fever, accompanied with violent action in the brain, I experienced illusions of a very peculiar kind. They did not appear except when the eyes were shut or the room perfectly dark ; and this was one of the most distressing things connected with my illness ; for it obliged me either to keep my eyes open or to admit more light into the chamber than they could well tolerate. I had the consciousness of shining and hideous faces grinning at me in the midst of profound darkness, from which they glared forth in horrid and diabolical relief. They were never stationary, but kept moving in the gloomy background : sometimes they approached within an inch or two of my face : at other times, they receded several feet or yards from it. They would frequently break into fragments, which after floating about would unite —portions of one face coalescing with those of another, and thus forming still more uncouth and abominable images. The only way I could get rid of those phantoms was by admitting more light into the chamber and opening my eyes, when they instantly vanished ; but only to reappear when the room was darkened or the eyes closed. One night, when the fever was at its height, I had a splendid vision of a theatre, in the arena of which Ducrow, the celebrated equestrian, was performing. On this occasion, I had no consciousness of a dark back ground like to that on which the monstrous images floated ; but every thing was gay, bright, and beautiful. I was broad awake, my eyes were closed, and yet I saw with perfect distinctness the whole scene going on in the theatre, Duerow performing his wonders of horsemanship—and the assembled multitude, among whom I recognized several intimate friends ; in short, the whole process of the entertainment as clearly as if I were present at it. When I opened my eyes the whole scene vanished like the enchanted palace of the necromancer ; when I closed them, it as instantly returned. But though I could thus dissipate the spectacle, I found it impossible to get rid of the accompanying music. This was the grand march in the Opera of Aladdin, and was performed by the orchestra with more superb and imposing effect, and with greater loudness, than I ever heard it before ; it was executed, indeed, with tremendous energy. This air I tried every effort to dissipate, by forcibly endeavouring to call other tunes to mind, but it was in vain. However completely the vision might be dispelled, the music remained in spite of every effort to banish it. During the whole of this singular state, I was perfectly aware of the illusiveness of my feelings ; and, though labouring under violent headache, could not help speculating upon them and endeavoring to trace them to their proper cause. This theatrical vision continued for about five hours ; the previous delusions for a couple of days. The whole evidently

* Phrenological Journal, vol. v. p. 210.

proceeded from such an excited state of some parts of the brain, as I have already alluded to. *Ideality, Wonder, Form, Colour,* and *Size,* were all in intensely active operation, while the state of the reflecting organs was unchanged. Had the latter participated in the general excitement, to such an extent as to be unable to rectify the false impressions of the other organs, the case would have been one of pure delirium.

Spectral illusions can only be cured by removing the causes which give rise to them. If they proceed from the state of the stomach, this must be rectified by means of purgatives and alterative medicines. Should plethora induce them, local or general blood-letting and other antiphlogistic means are requisite. If they accompany fever or delirium tremens, their removal will, of course, depend upon that of these diseases. Arising from sleeplessness, they will sometimes be cured by anodynes ; and from nervous irritation, by the shower-bath and tonics. Where they seem to arise without any apparent cause, our attention should be directed to the state of the bowels, and blood-letting had recourse to

---

CHAPTER XVI.

REVERIE.

A state of mind somewhat analogous to that which prevails in dreaming, also takes place during reverie. There is the same want of balance in the faculties, which are almost equally ill regulated, and disposed to indulge in similar extravagancies. Reverie proceeds from an unusual quiescence of the brain, and inability of the mind to direct itself strongly to any one point : it is often the prelude of sleep. There is a defect in the *attention*, which, instead of being fixed on one subject, wanders over a thousand, and even on these is feebly and ineffectively directed. We sometimes see this while reading, or, rather, while attempting to read. We get over page after page, but the ideas take no hold whatever upon us ; we are in truth ignorant of what we peruse, and the mind is either an absolute blank, or vaguely addressed to something else. This feeling every person must have occasionally noticed in taking out his watch, looking at it, and replacing it without knowing what the hour was. In like manner he may hear what is said to him without attaching any meaning to the words, which strike his ear, yet communicate no definite idea to the sensorium. Persons in this mood may, from some ludicrous ideas flashing across them, burst into a loud fit of laughter during sermon or at a funeral, and thus get the reputation of being either grossly irreverent or deranged. That kind of reverie in which the mind is nearly divested of all ideas, and approximates closely to the state of sleep, I have sometimes experienced while gazing long and intently upon a river. The thoughts seem to glide away, one by one, upon the surface of the stream, till the mind is emptied of them altogether. In this state we see the glassy volume of the water moving past us, and hear its murmur, but lose all power of fixing our attention definitively upon any subject : and either fall asleep, or are aroused by some spontaneous reaction of the mind, or by some appeal to the senses sufficiently strong to startle us from our reverie. Grave, monotonous, slowly repeated sounds—as of a mill, a waterfall, an Eolian harp, or the voice of a dull orator, have the effect of lulling the brain into repose, and giving rise to a pleasing melancholy, and to calmness and inanity of mind. Uniform gentle motions have a tendency to produce a similar state of reverie, which is also very apt to ensue in the midst of perfect silence ; hence, in walking alone in the country, where there is no sound to distract our meditations, we frequently get into this state. It is also apt to take place when we are seated without books, companions, or amusement of any kind, by the hearth on a winter evening, especially when the fire is beginning to burn out, when the candles are becoming faint for want of topping, and a dim religious light, like that filling a hermit's cell from his solitary lamp, is diffused over the apartment. This is the situation most favourable for reveries, waking dreams, and all kinds of brown study, abstraction, ennui, and hypochondria.

Reverie has been known to arise from the mind sustaining temporary weakness, in consequence of long and excessive application to one subject. It is also, I believe, frequently induced by forcing young people to learn what they dislike. In this case, the mind, finding it impossible to direct itself to the hated task, goes wandering off in another direction, and thus acquires a habit of inattention, which, in extreme cases, may terminate in imbecility. Sometimes reveries arise from peculiarity of temperament, either natural or induced by mental or bodily weakness. The best regulated minds and strongest bodies, may, however, and, in fact, often have, occasional attacks : but when the feeling grows into a habit, and is too much indulged in, it is apt to injure the usefulness of the individual, and impair the whole fabric of his understanding. ' It is,' says Dr Good, ' upon the faculty of attention that every other faculty is dependent for its vigour and expansion : without it, the perception exercises itself in vain ; the memory can lay up no store of ideas ; the judgment draw forth no comparisons ; the imagination must become blighted and barren ; and where there is no attention whatever, the case must necessarily verge upon fatuity.' I conceive that persons in whom the organ of *Concentrativeness* is very small, are peculiarly apt to fall into reverie.

The following is a remarkable instance of reverie arising from excessive application :—The subject of it was Mr Spalding, a gentleman well known as an eminent literary character in Germany, and much respected by those who knew him. The case was drawn up by himself, and published in the *Psychological Magazine.*

' I was this morning engaged with a great number of people who followed each other quickly, and to each of whom I was obliged to give my attention. I was also under the necessity of writing much ; but the subjects, which were various and of a trivial and uninteresting nature, had no connexion the one with the other ; my attention, therefore, was constantly kept on the stretch, and was continually shifting from one subject to another. At last it became necessary that I should write a receipt for some money I had received, on account of the poor. I seated myself and wrote the two first words, but in a moment found that I was incapable of proceeding, for I could not recollect the words which belonged to the ideas that were present in my mind. I strained my attention as much as possible, and tried to write one letter slowly after the other, always having an eye to the preceding one, in order to observe whether they had the usual relationship to each other ; but I remarked, and said to myself at the time, that the characters I was writing were not those which I wished to write, and yet I could not discover where the fault lay. I therefore desisted, and partly by broken words and syllables, and partly by gesture, I made the person who waited for the receipt understand he should leave me. For about half an hour there reigned a kind of tumultuary disorder in my senses, in which I was incapable of remarking any thing very particular, except that one series of ideas forced themselves involuntarily on my mind. The trifling nature of these thoughts I was perfectly aware of, and was also conscious that I made several efforts to get rid of them, and supply their place with better ones, which lay at the bottom of my soul. I endeavoured as much as lay in my power, considering the great crowd of confused images which presented themselves to my mind, to recall my principles

of religion, of conscience, and of future expectation ; these I found equally correct, and fixed as before. There was no deception in my external senses, for I saw and knew every thing around me ; but I could not free myself from the strange ideas which existed in my head. I endeavoured to speak in order to discover whether I was capable of saying any thing that was connected ; but although I made the greatest efforts of attention, and proceeded, with the utmost caution, I perceived that I uniformly spoke other words than those I intended. My soul was at present as little master of the organs of speech, as it had been before of my hand in writing. Thank God, this state did not continue very long, for, in about half an hour, my head began to grow clearer, the strange and tiresome ideas became less vivid and turbulent, and I could command my own thoughts with less interruption.

' I now wished to ring for my servant, and desire him to inform my wife to come to me ; but I found it still necessary to wait a little longer to exercise myself in the right pronunciation of the few words I had to say : and the first half hour's conversation I had with her was, on my part, preserved with a slow and anxious circumspection, until at last I gradually found myself as clear and serene as in the beginning of the day, all that now remained was a slight headache. I recollected the receipt I had begun to write, and in which I knew I had blundered ; and upon examining it, I observed to my great astonishment, that instead of the words *fifty dollars*, *being one half year's rate*, which I ought to have written, the words were *fifty dollars through the salvation of Bra—*, with a break after it, for the word *Bra* was at the end of a line. I cannot recollect any perception, or business which I had to transact, that could, by means of an obscure influence, have produced this phenomenon.'

Reverie, when proceeding, as in this case, from excessive application, will seldom be difficult of cure ; the removal of the exciting cause will of itself naturally constitute the remedy. When it arises from such a defect in education as that already mentioned, the cure will be more difficult, although even then it is not always impracticable. In such a case, the person should be strongly directed to those subjects in which he feels most interest, and never be made to study what he has not a positive liking for. Active employment and gay and pleasant society, may effect much in restoring the intellectual balance. In all cases, whatever, he should never be left long alone ; as nothing has such a tendency to foster this state of mind as solitude.

CHAPTER XVII.

ABSTRACTION.

Abstraction, or absence of mind, has been confounded with reverie, but it is, in reality, a different intellectual operation ; for as in the latter a difficulty is experienced in making the mind bear strongly on any one point, in the former its whole energies are concentrated towards a single focus, and every other circumstance is, for the time, utterly forgotten. Such was the case with Sir Isaac Newton when, in a fit of absence, he made a tobacco stopper of the lady's finger, and with Archimedes, who remained unconscious and unmoved during the noise and slaughter of captured Syracuse. Though, in general, abstraction is easily broken by outward impressions, there have been instances where it has been so powerful as to render the individuals labouring under it insensible to pain. Pinel in his *Nosographie Philosophique* speaks of a priest who in a fit of mental absence was unconscious of the pain of burning ; and Cardan brought himself into such a state as to be insensible to all external impression.

Some men are naturally very absent ; others acquire this habit from particular pursuits, such as mathematics, and other studies demanding much calculation. Indeed, all studies which require deep thinking, are apt to induce mental absence, in consequence of the sensorial power being drained from the general circumference of the mind, and directed strongly to a certain point. This draining, while it invigorates the organ of the particular faculty towards which the sensorial energy is concentrated, leaves the others in an inanimate state, and incapacitates them from performing their proper functions ; hence persons subject to abstraction are apt to commit a thousand ludicrous errors ; they are perpetually blundering—committing a multitude of petty, yet harmless offences against established rules, and for ever getting into scrapes and absurd situations. Nothing is more common than for an absent man to take the hat of another person instead of his own, to give away a guinea for a shilling, to mistake his lodgings, forget invitations, and so forth. When the fit of abstraction is very strong, he neither hears what is said to him, nor sees what is passing around. ‘While you fancy,’ says Budgell, in the 77th No. of the Spectator, ‘he is admiring a beautiful woman, it is an even wager that he is solving a proposition in Euclid ; and while you imagine he is reading the Paris Gazette, it is far from being impossible that he is pulling down and rebuilding his coultry house.’ In some cases the individual requires to be shaken before he can be brought to take notice of any occurrence ; and it is often difficult to make him comprehend even the simplest proposition. Abstraction, therefore, bears an analogy to dreaming ; inasmuch as, in each of these states, some faculties are active, while others are at rest. In dreaming, however, the organs of the quiescent faculties are in a much deeper slumber, and less easily roused into activity than in abstraction ; hence in the great majority of cases, abstraction is broken with greater facility than sleep.

It appears from the observations of the Edinburgh phrenologists, that individuals who have a large development of the organ of *Concentrativeness* are peculiarly liable to fall into a state of abstraction. The effect of such a development is fixity of ideas—the power and tendency to think consecutively and steadily upon one subject. ‘In conversing with some individuals,’ says Mr Combe,* ‘ we find them fall naturally into a connected train of thinking ; either dwelling on a subject which interests them, till they have placed it clearly before the mind, or passing naturally and gracefully to a connected topic. Such persons uniformly have this organ large. We meet with others, who in similar circumstances, never pursue one idea for two consecutive seconds, who shift from topic to topic, without regard to natural connexion, and leave no distinct impression on the mind of the listener ; and this happens even with individuals in whom reflection is not deficient ; but this organ (*Concentrativeness*) is, in such persons, uniformly small.’ A good endowment of the power in question adds very much to the efficiency of the intellect, by enabling its possessor to apply his mind continuously to a particular investigation, unannoyed by the intrusion of foreign and irrelevant ideas. It seems to have been very strong in Sir Isaac Newton, whose liability to abstraction has already been alluded to. ‘ During the two years,’ says Biot, ‘which he spent in preparing and developing his immortal work, *Philosophæ Naturalis Principia Mathematica*, he lived only to calculate and to think. Oftentimes lost in the contemplation of these grand objects, he acted unconsciously ; his thoughts appearing to preserve no connexion with the ordinary affairs of life. It is said, that frequently, on rising in the morning, he would sit down on his bedside, arrested by some new conception, and would remain for hours together engaged in tracing it out, without dressing

* System of Phrenology, p. 135.

himself.’ ‘ To one who asked him, on some occasion, by what means he had arrived at his discoveries, he replied, ‘ By always thinking unto them.’ And at another time, he thus expressed his method of proceeding, —‘ I keep the subject constantly before me, and wait till the first dawning opens slowly, by little and little, into a full and clear light.’ Again, in a letter to Dr . Bentley, he says, ‘ If I have done the public any service this way, it is due to nothing but industry and patient thought.’ Biot mentions farther, that, ‘ in general, the intensity of thinking was with him so great that it entirely abstracted his attention from other matters, and confined him exclusively to one object. Thus, we see that he never was occupied at the same time with two different scientific investigations.’

The instances of abstraction upon record are so numerous that a volume might easily be filled with them. Hogarth, the illustrious painter, affords a good specimen. Having got a new carriage, he went in it to the Mansion-House, for the purpose of paying a visit to the Lord Mayor. On leaving the house he went out by a different door from that by which he entered, and found that it rained hard. Notwithstanding this, he walked homewards, and reached his own dwelling drenched to the skin. His wife seeing him in this state, asked him how it happened, and what had become of his carriage since he had not returned home in it. The truth was, that he had actually forgotten he had a carriage, or had gone in one at all.

The following case, from the pleasant style in which it is told, will amuse the reader.

‘ It is a case of one of the most profound and clearheaded philosophical thinkers, and one of the most amiable of men, becoming so completely absorbed in his own reflections, as to loose the perception of external things, and almost that of his own identity and existence. There are few that have paid any attention to the finance of this country, but must have heard of Dr Robert Hamilton’s ‘ essay on the National debt,’ which fell on the houses of parliament like a bombshell, or, rather, which rose and illuminated their darkness like an orient sun. There are other writings of his in which one knows not which most to admire—the profound and accurate, science, the beautiful arrangement, or the clear expression. Yet, in public, the man was a shad dow ; pulled off his hat to his own wife in the streets, and apologized for not having the pleasure of her acquaintance ; went to his classes in the college on the dark mornings, with one of her white stockings on the one leg, and one of his own black ones on the other, often spent the whole time of the meeting in moving from the table the hats of the students, which they as constantly returned ; sometimes invited them to call on him, and then fined them for coming to insult them. He would run against a cow in the road, turn round, beg her pardon, ‘ madam,’ and hope she was not hurt. at other times he would run against posts, and chide them for not getting out of his way ; and yet his con versation at the same time, if any body happened to be with him, was perfect logic and perfect music. Were it not that there may be a little poetic license in Aberdeen story-telling, a volume might be filled with anecdotes of this amiable and excellent man, all tending, to prove how wide the distinction is between first rate thought and that merely animal use of the organs of sense which prevents ungifted mortals from walking into wells. The fish-market at Aberdeen, if still where-it used to be, is near the Dee, and has a stream passing through it that falls into that river. The fish women expose their wares in large baskets. The doctor one day marched into that place, where his attention was attracted by a curiously figured stone in a stack of chimneys. He advanced towards it, till he was interrupted by one of the benches, from which, however, he tumbled one of the baskets into the stream, which was bearing the fish to their native element. The visage of the lady was instantly in lightning, and her voice in thunder; but the object of her wrath was deaf to the loudest sounds, and blind to the most alarming colors. She stamped, gesticulated, scolded, brought a crowd that filled the place; but the philosopher turned not from his eager gaze and his inward meditations on the stone. While the woman's breath held good, she did not seem to heed, but when that began to fail, and the violence of the act moved not one muscle of the object, her rage felt no bounds: she seized him by the breast, and yelling, in an effort of despair, 'spagh ta ma, or I'll burst,' sank down among the remnant of her fish in a state of complete exhaustion; and before she had recovered, the doctor's reverie was over, and he had taken his departure.'*

Many curious anecdotes of a similar kind are related of the Rev Dr George Harvest, one of the ministers of Thames Ditton. So confused on some occasion, were the ideas of this singular man, that he has been known to write a letter to one person, address it to a second, and send it to a third. He was once on the eve of being married to the bishop's daughter, when having gone a gudgeon-fishing, he forgot the circumstance, and overstaid the canonical hour, which so offended the lady, that she indignantly broke off the match. If a beggar happened to take off his hat to him on the streets, in hopes of receiving alms, he would make him a bow, tell him he was his most humble servant, and walk on. He has been known on Sunday to forget the days on which he was to officiate, and would walk into church with his gun under his arm, to ascertain what the people wanted there. Once, when he was playing at backgammon, he poured out a glass of wine, and it being his turn to throw, having the box in one hand and the glass in the other, and being extremely dry, and unwilling to lose any time, he swallowed down both the dice, and discharged the wine upon the dice-board. 'Another time,' says the amusing narrative which has been published of his peculiarities, in one of his absent fits, he mistook his friend's house, and went into another, the door of which happened to stand open; and no servant being in the way, he rambled all over the house, till, coming into a middle room, where there was an old lady ill in bed of the quincy, he stumbled over the night stool, threw a close-horse down, and might not have ended there, had not the affrighted patient made a noise at his intrusion, which brought up the servants, who, on finding Dr Harvest in the room, instead of the apothecary that was momentarily expected, quieted the lady's fears, who by this time was taken with such an immoderate fit of laughter at his confusion, that it broke the quincy in her throat, and she lived many years afterwards to thank Dr Harvest for his unlucky mistake. 'His notorious heedlessness was so apparent, that no one would lend him a horse, as he frequently lost his beast from under him, or, at least from out of his hands, it being his frequent practice to dismount and lead the horse, putting the bridle under his arm, which the horse sometimes shook off, or the intervention of a post occasioned it to fall; sometimes it was taken off by the boys, when the parson was seen drawing his bridle after him; and if any one asked him after the animal, he could not give the least account of it, or how he had lost it.' In short the blunders which he committed were endless, and would be considered incredible, were they not authenticated by incontestible evidence. Yet, notwithstanding all this, Harvest was a man of uncommon abilities, and an excellent scholar.

Bacon, the celebrated sculptor, exhibited on one occasion, a laughable instance of absence of mind. 'Bacon was remarkably neat in his dress, and, according to the costume of the old school, wore, in fine weather, a powdered wig, ruffles, silver buckles. with silk stockings, &c., and walked with his gold-headed cane.

* 'New Monthly Magazine,' vol. xxxviii. p. 510.

Thus attired, he one day called at St. Paul's, shortly after having erected the statue of the benevolent Howard, and before the boarding which enclosed the statue had been removed. One of his sons was employed, at this time, in finishing the statue. After remaining a short time, he complained of feeling somewhat cold, on which the son proposed, as no one could overlook them, that he should put on, as a kind of temporary spencer, an old torn, green shag waistcoat, with a red stuff back, which had been left there by one of the workmen. He said it was a 'good thought,' and accordingly buttoned the waistcoat over his handsome new coat. Shortly afterwards, he was missing, but returned in about an hour, stating that he had been to call on a gentleman in Doctor's Commons, and had sat chatting with his wife and daughters, whom he had never seen before; that he found them to be exceedingly pleasant women, though perhaps a little disposed to laugh and titter about he knew not what. 'Sir,' said the son, 'I am afraid I can explain their mysterious behavior; surely you have not kept on that waistcoat all the time?' 'But, as-sure as I am a living man, I have,' said he, laughing heartily, 'and I can now account not only for the strange behavior of the ladies, but for all the jokes that have been cracked about me as I walked along the street—some crying let him alone, he does it for a wager, &c. &c.; all which, from being quite unconscious of my appearance, I thought was levelled at some other quiz that might be following near me; and I now recollect that, whenever I looked round for the object of their pleasantry, the people laughed, and the more so, as, by the merry force of sympathy, I laughed also, although I could not comprehend what it all meant.'

I shall conclude by mentioning an anecdote of Mr Warton, the accomplished Professor of Poetry in the University of Oxford. 'This good divine having dined with some jolly company at a gentleman's house in that city, passing through the streets to the church, it being summer-time, his ears were loudly saluted with the cry of 'Live mackerel!' This so much dwelt upon the Doctor's mind, that after a nap while the psalm was performing, as soon as the organ ceased playing, he got up in the pulpit, and with eyes half open, cried out 'All alive, alive oh!' thus inadvertently keeping up the reputation of a Latin proverb, which is translated in the following lines:—

'Great wits to madness nearly are allied,
    And thin partitions do their bounds divide.'

'The Professor of Poetry perhaps supposed himself yet with his companions at the convivial table.'

Mental absence is generally incurable. In stout subjects, depletion, purging, and low diet, will sometimes be of use. Where the affection seems to arise from torpor of the nervous system, blistering the head and internal stimuli afford the most probable means of relief. The person should associate as much as possible with noisy, bustling people, and shun solitude and all such studies as have a tendency to produce abstraction.

CHAPTER XVIII.

SLEEP OF PLANTS.

During night, plants seem to exist in a state analogous to sleep. At this period they get relaxed, while their leaves droop and become folded together. Such is peculiarly the case with the tamarind tree, and the leguminous plants with pinnated leaves; but with almost all plants it takes place in a greater or lesser degree, although in some the change is much more striking than in others. The trefoil, the Oxalis, and other herbs with ternate leaves, sleep with their leaflets folded together in the erect posture. The cause of the different states in which plants exist during the day and night has never been correctly ascertained—some attributing it to the influence of light, some to the vicissitudes of temperature, and others to atmospherical humidity. Probably the whole of these influences are concerned. It is very evident that the presence of certain stimuli during the day puts the leaves in a state of activity, and excites their development ; while the want of such stimuli in the night time throws them into repose, relaxes them, and occasions them to be weighed down, as if the sustaining principle which kept them in energy was suspended in the torpor of sleep. The principal of these stimuli is unquestionably light ; indeed, Linnæus, from the observation of stove plants, seems to have demonstrated that it is the withdrawing of light, and not of heat, which produces the relaxation, or *Sleep of Plants*, as it is commonly denominated. The effect of light upon the leaves of the *Acacia* is peculiarly striking. At sunrise they spread themselves out horizontally ; as the heat increases they become elevated, and at noon shoot vertically upwards : but as soon as the sun declines they get languid and droop, and during night are quite pendant and relaxed. During day, the leaves of some plants are spread out, and displayed, and at the same time inclined towards the sun. Those of the *Helianthus annuus*, the *Helianthemum annuum*, and *Croton tinctorium* follow the course of the sun in their position ; and most buds and flowers have a tendency to turn their heads in the direction of the great luminary of day. As an instance of this let us look at the sun flower, which confronts the source of light with its broad yellow expansion of aspect, and hangs its gorgeous head droopingly so soon as the object of its worship declines. The leaves of a great number of vegetables present changes in their position corresponding to the different hours of the day. 'Who does not know,' says Wildenow, ' that the species of *Lupinus*, especially *Lupinus luteus* turn, in the open air, their leaves and stalks towards the sun, and follow its course in so steady a manner, as to enable us to specify the hour of the day from their direction.' Such phenomena were not unknown to Pliny and Theophrastus.

The analogy between animal and vegetable life is still farther demonstrated by the well known fact, that while some creatures, such as the cat and owl, sleep during the day, and continue awake at night, certain plants do the same thing. Such is the case with the *Tragopogon luteum*, which becomes closed, or in other words, goes to sleep at nine in the morning, and opens at night. Every hour of the day, indeed, has some particular plant which then shuts itself up : hence the idea of the Flower Dial by means of which the hour of the day can be told with tolerable accuracy. Some plants, which shut themselves up in the day time, flower at night. The night-flowering *Cereus*, a species of Cactus, is a beautiful instance of the kind ; and there are other plants which exhibit the same interesting phenomenon. Nothing, indeed, can be more beautiful than the nocturnal flowering of certain members of the vegetable world. Linnæus used to go out at night with a lantern into his garden to have an opportunity of witnessing this remarkable peculiarity in the plants by which it is exhibited.

The analogy between the two kingdoms is rendered yet more striking, when it is recollected that (with such exceptions as the above,) plants increase much more rapidly during night, which is their time of sleep, than in the day-time, which may be considered the period of their active or waking existence.

The state in which plants exists in the winter season resembles the hybernation of animals : there is the same torpor and apparent extinction of vitality. Heat and light have the power of both reviving plants and putting an end to hybernation. Between plants and

animals, however, there is this difference : that while *most* plants become torpid in winter, only a *small number* of animals get into that state ; but even in such dissimilitude we can trace an analogy ; for as there are animals upon which winter has no torpifying influence, so are there likewise plants. The *Helleborus hymalis* or christmas rose, flowers at the end of December, and the *Galanthus nivilis*, or snow-drop, in the month of February.

CHAPTER XIX.

GENERAL MANAGEMENT OF SLEEP.

In the foregoing pages, I have detailed at length all the principal phenomena of sleep ; and it now only remains to state such circumstances as affect the comfort and healthfulness of the individual while in that condition. The first I shall mention is the nature of the chamber in which we sleep ; this should be always large and airy. In modern houses, these requisites are too much overlooked ; and, while the public rooms are of great dimensions, those appropriated for sleeping are little better than closets. This error is exceedingly detrimental to health. The apartments wherein so great a portion of life is passed, should always be roomy, and, if possible, not placed upon the ground-floor, because such a situation is more apt to be damp and ill ventilated than higher up.

The next consideration applies to the bed itself, which ought to be large, and not placed close to the wall, but at some distance from it, both to avoid any dampness which, may exist in the wall. and admit a freer circulation of air. The curtains should never be drawn closely together, even in the coldest weather ; and when the season is not severe, it is a good plan to remove them altogether. The bed or mattress ought to be rather hard. Nothing is more injurious to health than soft beds ; they effeminate the individual. render his flesh soft and flabby, and incapacitate him from undergoing any privation. The texture of which the couch is made, is not of much consequence, provided it is not too soft : hence, feather-beds, or mattresses of hair or straw are almost equally good, if suitable in this particular. I may mention, however, that the hair mattress, from being cooler, and less apt to imbibe moisture, is preferable during the summer season. to a bed of feathers. Those soft yielding feather-beds, in which the body sinks deeply, are highly improper, from the unnatural heat and perspiration which they are sure to induce. Air-beds have been lately recommended, but I can assert, from personal experience that they are the worst that can possibly be employed. They become very soon heated to such an unpleasant degree as to render it impossible to repose upon them with any comfort. For bed-ridden persons, whose skin has become irritated by long lying, the hydrostatic bed, lately brought into use in some of the public hospitals, is the best.

The pillow as well as the bed, should be pretty hard. When very soft, the head soon sinks in it. and becomes unpleasantly heated. The objection made to air-beds applies with equal force to air-pillows. which I several times attempted to use. but was compelled to abandon, owing to the disagreeable heat that was generated in a few minutes.

With regard to the covering, there can be no doubt that it is more wholesome to lie between sheets than blankets. For the same reason, people should avoid sleeping in flannel nightshirts. Such a degree of warmth as is communicated by those means is only justifiable in infancy and childhood, or when there is actual disease or weakness of constitution. Parents often commit a great error in bringing up their young people under so effeminate a system.

22*

A common custom prevails of warming the bed before going to sleep. This enervating practice should be abandoned except with delicate people, or when the cold is very intense. It is far better to let the bed be chafed by the natural heat of the body, which, even in severe weather, will be sufficient for the purpose, provided the clothing is abundant.

We ought never to sleep overloaded with clothes, but have merely what is sufficient to maintain a comfortable warmth.

When a person is in health, the atmosphere of his apartment should be cool; on this account, fires are exceedingly hurtful, and should never be had recourse to, except when the individual is delicate, or the weather intolerably severe. When they become requisite, smoke must be carefully guarded against, as fatal accidents have arisen from this cause.

The window-shutters ought never to be entirely closed, neither ought they to be kept altogether open. In the first case, we are apt to oversleep ourselves, owing to the prevailing darkness with which we are surrounded; and in the second, the light which fills the apartment, especially if it be in the summer season, may disturb our repose, and waken us at an earlier hour than there is any occasion for. Under both circumstances, the eyes are liable to suffer; the darkness in the one instance, disposes them to be painfully affected, on exposure to the brilliant light of day, besides directly debilitating them—for, in remaining too much in the gloom, whether we be asleep or awake, these organs are sure to be more or less weakened. In the other case, the fierce glare of the morning sun acting upon them, perhaps for several hours before we get up, does equal injury, making them tender and easily affected by the light. The extremes of too much and too little light must, therefore, be avoided, and such a moderate portion admitted into the chamber as not to hurt the eyes, or act as too strong a stimulus in breaking our slumbers.

During the summer heats, the covering requires to be diminished, so as to suit the atmospheric temperature; and a small portion of the window drawn down from the top, to promote a circulation of air; but this must be done cautiously, and the current prevented from coming directly upon the sleeper, as it might give rise to colds, and other bad consequences. The late Dr Gregory was in the habit of sleeping with the window drawn slightly down during the whole year: and there can be no doubt that a gentle current pervading our sleeping apartments, is in the highest degree essential to health.

Nothing is so injurious as damp beds. It becomes every person, whether at home or abroad, to look to this matter, and see that the bedding on which he lies is thoroughly dry, and free from even the slightest moisture. By neglecting such a precaution, rheumatism, colds, inflammations, and death itself may ensue. Indeed these calamities are very frequently traced to sleeping incautiously upon damp beds. For the same reason, the walls and floor should be dry, and wet clothes never hung up in the room.

We should avoid sleeping in a bed that has been occupied by the sick, till the bedding has been cleansed and thoroughly aired. When a person has died of any infectious disease, not only the clothes in which he lay, but the couch itself ought to be burned. Even the bed-stead should be carefully washed and fumigated.

Delicate persons who have been accustomed to sleep upon feather-beds, must be cautious not to exchange them rashly for any other.

On going to sleep, all sorts of restraints must be removed from the body; the collar of the night-shirt should be unbuttoned and the neckcloth taken off. With regard to the head, the more lightly it is covered the better: on this account, we should wear a thin cotton or silk night-cap; and this is still better if made of net-work. Some persons wear worsted, or flannel caps, but these are never proper, except in old or rheumatic subjects. The grand rule of health is to keep the head cool, and the feet warm; hence, the night-cap cannot be too thin. In fact, the chief use of this piece of clothing is to preserve the hair, and preserve it from being disordered and matted together.

Sleeping in stockings is a bad and uncleanly habit. By accustoming ourselves to do without any covering upon the feet, we shall seldom experience cold in these parts, if we have clothing enough to keep the rest of the system comfortable; and should they still remain cold, this can easily be obviated by wrapping a warm flannel cloth around them, or by applying to them, for a few minutes, a heated iron, or a bottle of warm water.

The posture of the body must be attended to. The head should be tolerably elevated, especially in plethoric subjects; and the position, from the neck downwards, as nearly as possible horizontal. The half-sitting posture, with the shoulders considerably raised, is injurious, as the thoracic and abdominal viscera are thereby compressed, and respiration, digestion, and circulation, materially impeded. Lying upon the back is also improper, in consequence of its tendency to produce nightmare. Most people pass the greater part of the night upon the side, which is certainly the most comfortable position that can be assumed in sleep. According to Dr A. Hunter, women who love their husbands generally lie upon the right side. This interesting point I have no means of ascertaining, although, doubtless, the ladies are qualified to speak decidedly upon the subject. I have known individuals who could not sleep except upon the back; but these are rare cases.

I have mentioned the necessity of a free circulation of air. On this account, it is more wholesome to sleep single, than double, for there is then less destruction of oxygen; and the atmosphere is much purer and cooler. For the same reason, the practice, so common in public schools, of having several beds in one room, and two or three individuals in each bed, must be deleterious. When more than one sleep in a single bed, they should take care to place themselves in such a position as not to breath in each other's faces. Some persons have a dangerous custom of covering their heads with the bedclothes. The absurdity of this practice needs no comment.

Before going to bed, the body should be brought into that state which gives us the surest chance of dropping speedily asleep. If too hot, its temperature ought to be reduced by cooling drinks, exposure to the open air, sponging, or even the cold bath; if too cold, it must be brought into a comfortable state by warmth; for both cold and heat act as stimuli, and their removal is necessary before slumber can ensue. A full stomach, also, though it sometimes promotes, generally prevents sleep; consequently, supper ought to be dispensed with, except by those who, having been long used to this meal, cannot sleep without it. As a general rule, the person who eats nothing for two or three hours before going to rest, will sleep better than he who does. His sleep will also be more refreshing, and his sensations upon waking much more gratifying. The Chinese recommended brushing the teeth previous to lying down: this is a good custom.

Sleeping after dinner is pernicious. On awaking from such indulgence, there is generally some degree of febrile excitement, in consequence of the latter stages of digestion being hurried on: it is only useful in old people, and in some cases of disease.

The weak, and those recovering from protracted illnesses, must be indulged with more sleep than such as are vigorous. Sleep, in them, supplies, in some measure, the place of nourishment, and thus becomes a most powerful auxiliary for restoring them to health. Much repose is likewise necessary to enable the system to recover from the effects of dissipation.

Too little and too much sleep are equally injurious. Excessive wakefulness, according to Hippocrates, prevents the aliment from being digested, and generates crude humours. Too much sleep produces lassitude and corpulency, and utterly debases and stupifies the mind. Corpulent people being apt to indulge in excessive sleep, they should break this habit at once, as, in their case, it is peculiarly unwholesome. They ought to sleep little, and that little upon hard beds.

The practice of sleeping in the open air, cannot be too strongly reprobated. It is at all times dangerous, especially when carried into effect under a burning sun, or amid the damps of night. In tropical climates, where this custom is indulged in during the day, it is not unusual for the person to be struck with a *coup-de-soleil*, or some violent fever; and in our own country, nothing is more common than inflammations, rheumatisms, and dangerous colds, originating from sleeping upon the ground, either during the heat of the day, or when the evening has set in with its attendant dews and vapours.

As respects the repose of children it may be remarked that the custom of rocking them asleep in the cradle, is not to be recommended, sanctioned though it be by the voice of ages. This method of procuring slumber, not only heats the infant unnecessarily, but, in some cases, disorders the digestive organs, and, in most, produces a sort of artificial sleep, far less conducive to health, than that brought on by more natural means. According to some writers, it has also a tendency to induce water in the head, a circumstance which I think possible, although I never knew a case of that disease which could be traced to such a source. the cradle, then, should be abandoned, so far as the rocking is concerned, and the child simply lulled to repose in the nurse's arms, and then deposited quietly in bed. Sleep will often be induced by gently scratching or rubbing the top of the child's head. This fact is well known to some nurses, by whom the practice is had recourse to for the purpose of provoking slumber in restless children. For the first month of their existence, children sleep almost continually, and they should be permitted to do so, for at this early age they cannot slumber too much: calm and long-continued sleep is a favourable symptom, and ought to be cherished rather than prevented, during the whole period of infancy. When, however, a child attains the age of three or four months, we should endeavour to manage so that its periods of wakefulness may occur in the daytime, instead of at night. By proper care, a child may be made to sleep at almost any hour; and, as this is always an object of importance, it should be sedulously attended to in the rearing of children. Until about the third year, they require a little sleep in the middle of the day, and pass half their time in sleep. Every succeeding year, till they attain the age of seven, the period allotted to repose should be shortened one hour, so that a child of that age may pass nine hours or thereabouts, out of the twenty-four, in a state of sleep. Children should never be awakened suddenly, or with a noise, in consequence of the terror and starting which such a method of arousing them produces: neither should they be brought all at once from a dark room into a strong glare of light, lest their eyes be weakened, and permanent injury inflicted upon these organs.

The position in which children sleep requires to be carefully attended to. Sir Charles Bell mentions that the *eneuresis infantum*, with which they are so often affected, frequently arises from lying upon the back, and that it will be removed or prevented by accustoming them to lie on the side. It is also of the greatest importance, that they be kept sufficiently warm. I believe that many infantile diseases arise from the neglect of this precaution. Children have little power of evolving heat; on this account, when delicate they should never be permitted to sleep alone, but made to lie with the nurse, that they may receive warmth from her body.

At whatever period we go to sleep, one fact is certain, that we can never with impunity convert day into night. Even in the most scorching seasons of the year, it is better to travel under the burning sunshine, than in the cool of the evening, when the dews are falling and the air is damp. A case in support of this statement, is given by Valangin in his work on Diet. Two colonels in the French army had a dispute whether it was not most safe to march in the heat of the day, or in the evening. To ascertain this point, they got permission from the commanding officer to put their respective plans into execution. Accordingly, the one with his division marched during the day, although it was in the heat of summer, and rested all night—the other slept in the day-time, and marched during the evening and part of the night. The result was that the first performed a journey of six hundred miles, without losing a single man or horse, while the latter lost most of his horses, and several of his men.

It now becomes a question at what hour we should retire to rest, how long our rest ought to continue, and when it should be broken in the morning. These points I shall briefly discuss, in the order in which they stand.

It is not very easy to ascertain the most appropriate hour for going to bed, as this depends very much upon the habits and occupation of the individual. Laborers and all hard wrought people, who are obliged to get up betimes, require to go to rest early; and in their case, nine o'clock may be the best hour. Those who are not obliged to rise early, may delay the period of retiring to rest for an hour or two longer; and may thus go to bed at ten or eleven. These are the usual periods allotted among the middle ranks of life for this purpose; and it may be laid down as a rule, that to make a custom of remaining up for a later period than eleven must be prejudicial. Those, therefore, who habitually delay going to bed till twelve, or one, or two, are acting in direct opposition to the laws of health, in so far as they are compelled to pass in sleep a portion of the ensuing day, which ought to be appropriated to wakefulness and exertion. Late hours are in every respect hurtful, whether they be employed in study or amusement. A fresh supply of stimulus is thrown upon the mind, which prevents it from sinking into slumber at the proper period, and restlessness, dreaming, and disturbed repose inevitably ensue. Among other things, the eyes are injured, those organs suffering much more from the candle-light, to which they are necessarily exposed, than from the natural light of day.

With regard to the necessary quantity of sleep, so much depends upon age, constitution, and employment, that it is impossible to lay down any fixed rule which will apply to all cases. Jeremy Taylor states that three hours only in the twenty-four should be devoted to sleep. Baxter extends the period to four hours, Wesley to six, Lord Coke and Sir William Jones to seven, and Sir John Sinclair to eight. With the latter I am disposed to coincide. Taking the average of mankind, we shall come as nearly as possible to the truth when we say that nearly one-third part of life ought to be spent in sleep: in some cases, even more may be necessary, and in few, can a much smaller portion be safely dispensed with. When a person in young, strong, and healthy, an hour or two less may be sufficient; but childhood and extreme old age require a still greater portion. No person who passes only eight hours in bed, can be said to waste his time in sleep. If, however, he exceeds this, and is, at the same time, in possession of vigor and youth, ne lays himself open to the charge of slumbering away those hours which should be devoted to some other purpose. According to Georget,' women should sleep a couple of hours longer than men. For the former he allows six or seven hours, for the latter eight or nine. I doubt, however, if the female constitution, generally speaking, requires more sleep than the male; at least it is certain that women endure protracted wakefulness better than men, but whether this may result from custom is a question worthy of being considered.

Barry, in his work on Digestion, has made an ingenious, but somewhat whimsical, calculation on the tendency of sleep to prolong life. He asserts, that the duration of human life may be ascertained by the number of pulsations which the individual is able to perform. Thus, if a man's life extends to 70 years, and his heart throbs 60 times each minute, the whole number of its pulsations will amount to 2,207,520,000 ; but if, by intemperance, or any other cause, he raises the pulse to 75 in the minute, the same number of pulsations would be completed in 56 years, and the duration of life abbreviated 14 years. Arguing from these data, he alleges, that sleep has a tendency to prolong life, as, during its continuance, the pulsations are less numerous than in the waking state. There is a sort of theoretical truth in this statement, but it is liable to be modified by so many circumstances, that its application can never become general. If this were not the case, it would be natural to infer that the length of a man's life would correspond with that of his slumbers; whereas it is well known, that too much sleep dehilitates the frame, and lays the foundation of various diseases, which tend to shorten rather than extend the duration of life.

Those who indulge most in sleep, generally require the least of it. Such are the wealthy and luxurious, who pass nearly the half of their existence in slumber, while the hard-working peasant and mechanic, who would seem, at first sight, to require more than any other class of society, are contented with seven or eight hours of repose—a period brief in proportion to that expended by them in toil, yet sufficiently long for the wants of nature, as is proved by the strength and health which they almost uniformly enjoy.

For reasons already stated, more sleep is requisite in winter than in summer. Were there even no constitutional causes for this difference, we should be disposed to sleep longer in the one than in the other, as some of the circumstances which induce us to sit up late and rise early in summer, are wanting during winter ; and we consequently feel disposed to lie longer in bed during the latter season of the year.

The hour of getting up in the morning is not of less importance than that at which we ought to lie down at night. There can be no doubt that some of the most admirable conducives to health is early rising. ' Let us,' says Solomon, ' go forth into the fields ; let us lodge in the villages ; let us *get up early* to the vineyards ; let us see if the vine flourish—if the tender grape appear—if the pomegranates bud forth.'

Almost all men who have distinguished themselves in science, literature, and the arts, have been early risers. The industrious, the active-minded, the enthusiast in the pursuit of knowledge or gain, are up betimes at their respective occupations ; while the sluggard wastes the most beautiful period of life in pernicious slumber. Homer, Virgil, and Horace are all represented as early risers : the same was the case with Paley, Franklin, Priestly, Parkhurst, and Buffon, the latter of whom ordered his *valet de chambre* to awaken him every morning, and compel him to get up by force if he evinced any reluctance : for this service the valet was rewarded with a crown each day, which recompense he forfeited if he did not oblige his master to get out of bed before the clock struck six. Bishops Jewel and Burnet rose regularly every morning at four o'-clock. Sir Thomas More did the same thing ; and so convinced was he of the beneficial effects of getting up betimes, that, in his ' Utopia,' he represented the inhabitants attending lectures before sunrise. Napoleon was an early riser ; so was Frederick the Great and, Charles XII ; so is the Duke of Wellington ; and so

in truth, is almost every one distinguished for energy and indefatigability of mind.

Every circumstance contributes to render early rising advisable to those who are in the enjoyment of health. There is no time equal in beauty and freshness to the morning, when nature has just parted with the gloomy mantle which night had flung over her, and stands before us like a young bride, from whose aspect the veil which covered her loveliness, has been withdrawn. The whole material world has a vivifying appearance. The husbandman is up at his labour, the forest leaves sparkle with drops of crystal dew, the flowers raise their rejoicing heads towards the sun, the birds pour forth their anthems of gladness ; and the wide face of creation itself seems as if awakened and refreshed from a mighty slumber. All these things, however, are hid from the eyes of the sluggard ; nature, in her most glorious aspect, is, to him, a sealed book ; and while every scene around him is full of beauty, interest, and animation, he alone is passionless and uninspired. Behold him stretched upon his couch of rest ! In vain does the clock proclaim that the reign of day has commenced ! In vain does the morning light stream fiercely in by the chinks of his window, as if to startle him from his repose ! He hears not—he sees not, for blindness and deafness rule over him with despotic sway, and lay a deadening spell upon his faculties. And when he does at length awake—far on in the day—from the torpor of this benumbing sleep, he is not refreshed. He does not start at once into new life—an altered man, with joy in his mind, and vigour in his frame. On the contrary, he is dull, languid, and stupid, as if half recovered from a paroxysm of drunkenness. He yawns, stretches himself, and stalks into the breakfast parlour, to partake in solitude, and without appetite, of his unrefreshing meal—while his eyes are red and gummy, his beard unshorn, his face unwashed, and his clothes disorderly, and ill put on. Uncleanliness and sluggishness generally go hand in hand ; for the obtuseness of mind which disposes a man to waste the most precious hours of existence in debasng sleep, will naturally make him neglect his person.

The character of the early riser is the very reverse of the sloven's. His countenance is ruddy, his eye joyous and serene, and his frame full of vigour and activity. His mind, also, is clear and unclouded, and free from that oppressive languor which weighs like a nightmare upon the spirit of the sluggard. The man who rises betimes, is in the fair way of laying in both health and wealth ; while he who dozes away his existence in unnecessary sleep, will acquire neither. On the contrary, he runs every chance of losing whatever portion of them he may yet be in possession of, and of sinking fast in the grade of society—a bankrupt both in person and in purse.[*]

The most striking instances of the good effects of early rising, are to be found in our peasantry and farmers, whose hale complexions, good appetites, and vigourous persons, are evidences of the benefit derived from this custom, conjoined with labour ; while the wan, unhealthy countenances and enfeebled frames of those who keep late hours, lie long in bed, and pass the night in dissipation, study, or pleasure, are equally con-

* In the will of the late Mr James Sergeant of the borough of Leicester, is the following clause relative to early rising :— ' As my nephews are fond of indulging in bed of a morning, and as I wish them to improve the time while they are young. I direct that they shall prove to the satisfaction of my executors, that have got out of bed in the morning, and either employed themselves in business, or taken exercise in the open air, from five o'clock every morning, from the 5th of April, to the 10th of October, being three hours each day, and from seven o'clock in the morning from the 10th of October to the 5th of April, being two hours every morning for two whole years ; this to be done for some two years during the first seven years, to the satisfaction of my executors, who may excuse them in case of illness, but the task must be made up when they are well, and if they will not do this, they shall not receive any share of my property.'

clusive proofs of the pernicious consequences resulting from an opposite practice.

Early rising, therefore, is highly beneficial ; but care should be taken not to carry it to excess. It can never be healthful to rise till the sun has been for some time above the horizon ; for until this is the case, there is a dampness in the air which must prove injurious to the constitution, especially when it is not naturally very strong. Owing to this, early rising is injurious to most delicate people ; and, in all cases, the heat of the sun should be allowed to have acquired some strength before we think of getting out of doors. No healthy man in the summer, should lie longer in bed than six o'clock. If he does so, he loses the most valuable part of the day, and injures his own constitution. Persons subject to gout, should always go to sleep early, and rise early. The former mitigates the violence of the evening paroxysm, which is always increased by wakefulness ; and the latter lessens the tendency to plethora, which is favoured by long protracted sleep.

It is common in some of the foreign universities to go to bed at eight, and rise at three or four in the morning ; and this plan is recommended by Willich in his 'Lectures on Diet and Regimen.' Sir John Sinclair, in allusion to it, judiciously observes, ' I have no doubt of the superior healthiness, in the winter time, of rising by day-light, and using candle-light at the close of the day, than rising by candle-light, and using it some hours before day-light approaches. It remains

to be ascertained by which system the eyes are least likely to be affected.

Dr Franklin in one of his ingenious Essays, has some fine observations on early rising ; and makes an amusing calculation of the saving that might be made in the city of Paris alone, by using the sunshine instead of candles. This saving he estimates at 96,000,000 of livres, or £4,000,000 sterling. This is mentioned in a satirical vein, but probably there is a great deal of truth in the statement. Indeed, if people were to go sooner to bed, and get up earlier, it is inconceivable what sums might be saved ; but according to the absurd custom of polished society, day is, in a great measure, converted into night, and the order of things reversed in a manner at once capricious and hurtful.

To conclude. The same law which regulates our desire for food, also governs sleep. As we indulge in sleep to moderation or excess, it becomes a blessing or a curse—in the one case recruiting the energies of nature, and diffusing vigour alike over the mind and frame : in the other, debasing the character of man, stupifying his intellect, enfeebling his body, and rendering him useless alike to others and himself. The glutton, the drunkard, and the sloven bear the strictest affinity to each other, both in the violation of nature's laws, and in the consequences thence entailed upon themselves. What in moderation is harmless or beneficial, in excess is a curse ; and sleep carried to the latter extreme, may be pronounced an act of intemperance almost as much as excessive eating or drinking.

THE END.

CONTENTS OF THE PHILOSOPHY OF SLEEP.

INDEX

TO THE PHILOSOPHY OF SLEEP.

———

THE

ANATOMY

OF

DRUNKENNESS.

BY

ROBERT MACNISH,

AUTHOR OF "THE PHILOSOPHY OF SLEEP," AND MEMBER OF THE FACULTY OF PHYSICIANS
AND SURGEONS OF GLASGOW.

FROM THE FIFTH GLASGOW EDITION.

————————

HARTFORD:

WILLIAM ANDRUS.

1842.

ANATOMY OF DRUNKENNESS.

ADVERTISEMENT.

In preparing the present edition of the ANATOMY OF DRUNKENNESS for the press, I have spared no pains to render the work as complete as possible. Some parts have been re-written, some new facts added, and several inaccuracies, which had crept into the former edition, rectified. Altogether, I am in hopes that this impression will be considered an improvement upon its predecessors, and that no fact of any importance has been overlooked or treated more slightly than it deserves.

R. M.

SEPTEMBER 20th, 1834.

CHAPTER I.

PRELIMINARY OBSERVATIONS.

Drunkenness is not, like some other vices, peculiar to modern times. It is handed down to us from 'hoar antiquity ;' and, if the records of the antediluvian era were more complete, we should probably find that it was not unknown to the remotest ages of the world. The cases of Noah and Lot, recorded in the sacred writings, are the earliest of which tradition or history has left any record ; and both occurred in the infancy of society. Indeed, wherever the grape flourished, inebriation prevailed. The formation of wine from this fruit, was among the earliest discoveries of man, and the bad consequences thence resulting, seem to have been almost coeval with the discovery. Those regions whose ungenial latitudes indisposed them to yield the vine, gave birth to other products which served as substititutes ; and the inhabitants rivalled or surpassed those of the south in all kinds of Bacchanalian indulgence—the pleasures of drinking constituting one of the most fertile themes of their poetry, in the same manner as, in other climates, they gave inspiration to the souls of Anacreon and Hafiz.

Drunkenness has varied greatly at different times and among different nations. There can be no doubt that it prevails more in a rude than in a civilized society. This is so much the case, that as men get more refined, the vice will gradually be found to soften down, and assume a less revolting character. Nor can there be a doubt that it prevails to a much greater extent in northern than in southern latitudes.[*] The nature of the climate renders this inevitable, and gives to the human frame its capabilities of withstanding liquor : hence a quantity which scarcely ruffles the frozen current of a Norwegian's blood, would scatter madness

[*] In making this observation, I have only in view the countries north of the equator ; for as we proceed to the south of that line, the vice increases precisely in the same manner as in the opposite direction. To use the words of Montesquieu, ' Go from the equator to our pole, and you will find drunkenness increasing together with the degree of latitude. Go from the same equator to the opposite pole, and you will find drunkenness travelling south, as on this side it travels towards the north.'

and fever into the brain of the Hindoo. Even in Europe, the inhabitants of the south are far less adapted to sustain intoxicating agents than those of the north. Much of this depends upon the coldness of the climate, and much also upon the peculiar physical and moral frame to which that coldness gives rise. The natives of the south are a lively, versatile people ; sanguine in their temperaments, and susceptible, to an extraordinary degree, of every impression. Their minds seem to inherit the brilliancy of their climate, and are rich with sparkling thoughts and beautiful imagery. The northern nations are the reverse of all this. With more intensity of purpose, with greater depth of reasoning powers, and superior solidity of judgment, they are in a great measure destitute of that sportive and creative brilliancy which hangs like a rainbow over the spirits of the south, and clothes them in a perpetual sunshine of delight. The one is chiefly led by the heart, the other by the head. The one possesses the beauty of a flower-garden, the other the sternness of the rock, mixed with its naked hardihood. Upon constitutions so differently organized, it cannot be expected that a given portion of stimulus will operate with equal power. The airy inflamable nature of the first, is easily roused to excitation, and manifests feelings which the second does not experience till he has partaken much more largely of the stimulating cause. On this account, the one may be inebriated, and the other remain comparatively sober upon a similar quantity. In speaking of this subject, it is always to be remembered that a person is not to be considered a drunkard because he consumes a certain portion of liquor ; but because what he does consumes produces certain effects upon his system. The Russian, therefore, may take six glasses a-day, and be as temperate as the Italian who takes four, or the Indian who takes two. But even when this is acceded to, the balance of sobriety will be found in favour of the south: the inhabitants there not only drink less, but are, *bona fide*, more seldom intoxicated than the others. Those who have contrasted London and Paris, may easily verify this fact ; and those who have done the same to the cities of Moscow and Rome, can bear still stronger testimony. Who ever heard of an Englishman sipping *eau sucree*, and treating his friends to a glass of lemonade? Yet such things are common in France; and, of all the practices of that country, they are those most thoroughly visited by the contemptuous malisons of John Bull.

It is a common belief that wine was the only inebriating liquor known to antiquity; but this is a mistake. Tacitus mentions the use of ale or beer as common among the Germans of his time. By the Egyptians, likewise, whose country was ill adapted to the cultivation of the grape, it was employed as a substitute for wine. Ale was common in the middle ages; and Mr Park states that very good beer is made, by the usual process of brewing and malting, in the interior of Africa. The favourite drink of our Saxon ancestors was ale or mead. Those worshippers of Odin were so notoriously addicted to drunkenness, that it was regarded as honourable rather than otherwise; and the man who could withstand the greatest quantity was looked upon with admiration and respect: whence the drunken songs of the Scandinavian scalds; whence the glories of Valhalla, the fancied happiness of whose inhabitants consisted in quaffing draughts from the skulls of their enemies slain in battle. Even ardent spirit, which is generally supposed to be a modern discovery, existed from a very early period. It is said to have been first made by the Arabians in the middle ages, and in all likelihood may lay claim to a still remoter origin. Alcohol was known to the alchymists as early as the middle of the twelfth century, although the process of preparing it was by them, at that time, kept a profound secret. The spirituous liquor called arrack, has been manufactured in the island of Java, as well as in the continent of Hindostan, from time immemorial. Brandy appears to have been known to Galen, who recommends it for the cure of voracious appetite;[*] and its distillation was common in Sicily at the commencement of the fourteenth century. As to wine, it was so common in ancient times as to have a tutelar god appropriated to it: Bacchus and his companion Silenus are as household words in the mouths of all, and constituted most important features of the heathen mythology. We have all heard of the Falernian and Campanian wines, and of the wines of Cyprus and Shiraz. Indeed, there is reason to believe that the ancients were in no respect inferior to the moderns in the excellence of their vinous liquors, whatever they may have been in the variety. Wine was so common in the eastern nations, that Mahomet, foreseeing the baleful effects of its propagation, forbade it to his followers, who, to compensate themselves, had recourse to opium. The Gothic or dark ages seem to have been those in which it was least common: in proof of this it may be mentioned, that in 1298 it was vended as a cordial by the English apothecaries. At the present day it is little drunk, except by the upper classes, in those countries which do not naturally furnish the grape. In those that do, it is so cheap as to come within the reach of even the lowest.[†]

In speaking of drunkenness, it is impossible not to be struck with the physical and moral degradation which it has spread over the world. Wherever intoxicating liquors become general, morality has been found on the decline. They seem to act like the simoom of the desert, and scatter destruction and misery around their path. The ruin of Rome was owing to luxury, of which indulgence in wine was the principal ingredient.

[*] Good's Study of Medicine, vol. i. p. 113, 2d edit.
[†] The quantity of wine raised in France alone is almost incredible. The vineyards in that country are said to occupy five millions of acres, or a twenty-sixth part of the whole territory. Paris alone consumes more than three times the quantity of wine consumed in the British Isles. It is true that much of the wine drank in the French capital is of a weak quality, being used as a substitute for small beer. But after every allowance is made, enough remains to show clearly, if other proofs were wanting, how much use of wine here is restricted by our exorbitant duties. It would be well for the morals of this country if the people abandoned the use of ardent spirits, and were enabled to resort to such wines as the French are in the habit of drinking.

R

Hannibal's army fell less by the arms of Scipio than by the wines of Capua; and the inebriated hero of Macedon after slaying his friend Clytus, and burning the palace of Persepolis, expired at last of a fit of intoxication, in his thirty-third year. A volume might be written in illustration of the evil effects of dissipation; but this is unnecessary to those who look carefully around them, and more especially to those who are conversant with the history of mankind. At the same time, when we speak of drunkenness as occurring in antiquity, it is proper to remark, that there were certain countries in which it was viewed in a much more dishonourable light than by any modern nation. The Nervii refused to drink wine, alleging that it made them cowardly and effeminate: these simple people had no idea of what by our seamen is called *Dutch courage*; they did not feel the necessity of elevating their native valour by an artificial excitement. The ancient Spartans held ebriety in such abhorrence, that, with a view to inspire the rising generation with a due contempt of the vice, it was customary to intoxicate the slaves and exhibit them publicly in this degraded condition. By the Indians, drunkenness is looked upon as a species of insanity; and, in their language, the word *ramgam*, signifying a drunkard, signifies also a madman. Both the ancients and moderns could jest as well as moralize upon this subject. 'There hangs a bottle of wine,' was the derisive exclamation of the Roman soldier, as they pointed to the body of the drunken Bonosus, who, in a fit of despair, suspended himself upon a tree. 'If you wish to have a shoe of durable materials,' exclaims the facetious Matthew Langsberg, 'you should make the upper leather of the mouth of a hard drinker—for that never lets in water.'

If we turn from antiquity to our own times, we shall find little cause to congratulate ourselves upon any improvement. The vice has certainly diminished among the higher orders of society, but there is every reason to fear that, of late, it has made fearful strides among the lower. Thirty or forty years ago, a landlord did not conceive he had done justice to his guests unless he sent them from his table in a state of intoxication. This practice still prevails pretty generally in Ireland and in the highlands of Scotland, but in other parts of the kingdom it is fast giving way: and it is to be hoped that the day is not far distant when greater temperance will extend to these jovial districts, and render their hospitality a little more consonant with prudence and moderation. The increase of drunkenness among the lower classes may be imputed to various causes, and chiefly to the late abandonment of part of the duty on rum and whiskey. This was done with a double motive of benefiting agriculture and commerce, and of driving the 'giant smuggler' from the field. The latter object it has in a great measure failed of effecting. The smuggler still plies his trade to a considerable extent, and brings his commodity to the market with nearly the same certainty of acquiring profit as ever. It would be well if the liquor vended to the poor possessed the qualities of that furnished by the contraband dealer; but, instead of that, it is usually a vile compound of every thing spurious and pestilent, and seems expressly contrived for preying upon the vitals of the unfortunate victims who partake of it. The extent to which adulteration has been carried in all kinds of liquor, is indeed such as to interest every class of society. Wine, for instance, is often impregnated with alum and sugar of lead, the latter dangerous ingredient being resorted to by innkeepers and others, to take away the sour taste so common in bad wines. Even the colour of these liquids is frequently artificial; and the deep rich complexion so greatly admired by persons not in the secrets of the trade, is often caused, or at least heightened, by factitious additions, such as elder-berries, bilberries, red-woods, &c. Alum and sugar of lead are also common in spirituous liquors;

: nd, in any cases, oil of vitriol, turpentine, and other materials equally abominable, are to be found in combination with them. That detestable liquor called British gin, is literally compounded of these ingredients: nor are malt liquors, with their multifarious narcotic additions, less thoroughly sophisticated or less detrimental to the health. From these circumstances, two conclusions must naturally be drawn; viz. that inebriating agents often contain elements of disease foreign to themselves; and that all persons purchasing them should endeavour to ascertain the state of their purity, and employ no dealer whose honour and honesty are not known to be unimpeachable. Liquors, even in their purest state, are too often injurious to the constitution without the admixture of poisons.*

The varieties of wine are so numerous as almost to defy calculation. Mr Brande, in his table, gives a list of no less than forty-four different kinds, and there are others which he has not enumerated. Ardent spirits are fewer in number, and may be mostly comprised under the names of rum, gin, brandy, and whiskey. The first is the prevailing drink over the West Indies, North America, and such cities of Great Britain as are intimately connected with these regions by commerce. The second is extensively used in Holland and Switzerland, the countries which principally furnish it, and has found its way pretty generally over the whole of Europe. The third is chiefly produced in Charente and Languedoc, and is the spirit most commonly found in the south. The fourth is confined in a great measure to Ireland and Scotland, in which latter country the best has always been made. Of malt liquors we have many varieties. Britain, especially England, is the country which furnishes them in greatest perfection They are the natural drinks of Englishmen—the *vinum Anglicorum*, as foreigners have often remarked. Every town of any consequence in the empire has its brewery; and in almost every one is there some difference in the quality of the liquor. Brown stout, London and Scotch porters, Burton, Dorchester, Edinburgh and Alloa ales, are only a few of the endless varieties of these widely-circulated fluids.

Besides wines, ardent spirits, and malt liquors, there are many other agents possessing inebriating properties. Among others, the *Peganum Harmala* or Syrian rue, so often used by the sultan Solyman; the *Hibiscus Saldarissa*, which furnishes the Indian bangue, and from which the *Nepenthes* of the ancients is supposed to have been made; the *Balsac*, or Turkish bangue, found on the shores of the Levant; the *Penang*, or Indian betle; the *Hyoscyamus Niger;* and the *Atropa Belladonna*. In addition to these, and many more, there are opium, tobacco, *Cocculus Indicus*, and the innumerable tribes of liqueurs and ethers, together with other agents of a less potent nature, such as clary, darnel, and saffron. The variety of agents capable of exciting drunkenness is indeed surprising, and in proportion to their number seems the prevalence of that fatal vice to which an improper use of them gives rise.

CHAPTER II.

CAUSES OF DRUNKENNESS.

The causes of drunkenness are so obvious, that few authors have thought it necessary to point them out: we shall merely say a few words upon the subject. There are some persons who will never be drunkards, and others who will be so in spite of all that can be done to prevent them. Some are drunkards by choice, and others by necessity. The former have an innate and constitutional fondness for liquor, and drink *con amore*. Such men are usually of a sanguineous temperament,

* See Accum's Treatise on the Adulteration of Food; Child on Brewing Porter; and Shannon on Brewing and Distillation.

of coarse unintellectual minds, and of low and animal propensities. They have, in general, a certain rigidity of fibre, and a flow of animal spirits which other people are without. They delight in the roar and riot of drinking clubs; and with them, in particular, all the miseries of life may be referred to the bottle.

The drunkard by necessity was never meant by na ture to be dissipated. He is perhaps a person of amiable disposition, whom misfortune has overtaken, and who, instead of bearing up manfully against it, endeavours to drown his sorrows in liquor. It is an excess of sensibility, a partial mental weakness, an absolute misery of the heart, which drives him on. Drunkenness, with him, is a consequence of misfortune; it is a solitary dissipation preying upon him in silence. Such a man frequently dies broken-hearted, even before his excesses have had time to destroy him by their own unassisted agency.

Some become drunkards from excess of indulgence in youth. There are parents who have a common custom of treating their children to wine, punch, and other intoxicating liquors. This, in reality, is regularly bringing them up in an apprenticeship to drunkenness. Others are taught the vice by frequenting drinking clubs and masonic lodges. These are the genuine academies of tippling. Two-thirds of the drunkards we meet with, have been initiated in that love of intemperance and boisterous irregularity which distinguish their future lives. Men who are good singers are very apt to become drunkards, and, in truth, most of them are so, more or less, especially if they have naturally much joviality or warmth of temperament. A fine voice to such men is a fatal accomplishment.

Ebriety prevails to an alarming degree among the lower orders of society. It exists more in towns than in the country, and more among mechanics than husbandmen. Most of the misery to be observed among the working classes spring from this source. No persons are more addicted to the habit, and all its attendant vices than the pampered servants of the great. Innkeepers, musicians, actors, and men who lead a rambling and eccentric life, are exposed to a similar hazard. Husbands sometimes teach their wives to be drunkards by indulging them in toddy and such fluids, every time they themselves sit down to their libations.

Women frequently acquire the vice by drinking porter and ale while nursing. These stimulants are usually recommended to them from well-meant but mistaken motives, by their female attendants. Many fine young women are ruined by this pernicious practice. Their persons become gross, their milk unhealthy, and a foundation is too often laid for future indulgence in liquor.

The frequent use of cordials, such as noyeau, shrub, kirsch-wasser, curacoa, and anissette, sometimes leads to the practice. The active principle of these liqueurs is neither more nor less than ardent spirits.*

Among other causes, may be mentioned the excessive use of spiritous tinctures for the cure of hypochondria and indigestion. Persons who use strong tea, especially green, run the same risk. The latter species is singularly hurtful to the constitution, producing hysteria, heartburn, and general debility of the chylopoetic viscera. Some of these bad effects are relieved for a time by the use of spirits; and what was at first employed as a medicine, soon becomes an essential requisite.

Certain occupations have a tendency to induce drunkenness. Innkeepers, recruiting-sergeants, pugilists, &c., are all exposed in a great degree to temptation in this respect; and intemperance is a vice which may be very often justly charged against them. Commercial travellers, also, taken as a body, are open to the accusation of indulging too freely in the bottle, al-

* Liqueurs often contain narcotic principles; therefore their use is doubly improper.

though I am not aware that they carry it to such excess as to entitle many of them to be ranked as drunkards. 'Well fed, riding from town to town, and walking to the houses of the several tradesmen, they have an employment not only more agreeable, but more conducive to health than almost any other dependant on traffic. But they destroy their constitutions by intemperance; not generally by drunkenness, but by taking more liquor than nature requires. Dining at the traveller's table, each drinks his pint or bottle of wine; he then takes negus or spirit with several of his customers; and at night he must have a glass or two of brandy and water. Few commercial travellers bear the employ for thirty years—the majority not twenty.'*

Some waiters allege that unmarried women, especially if somewhat advanced in life, are more given to liquor than those who are married. This point I am unable from my own observation to decide. Women who indulge in this way, are *solitary* dram-drinkers, and so would men be, had not the arbitrary opinions of the world invested the practice in them with much less moral turpitude than in the opposite sex. Of the two sexes, there can be no doubt that men are much the more addicted to all sorts of intemperance.

Drunkenness appears to be in some measure hereditary. We frequently see it descending from parents to their children. This may undoubtedly often arise from bad example and imitation, but there can be little question that, in many instances at least, it exists as a family predisposition.

Men of genius are often unfortunately addicted to drinking. Nature, as she has gifted them with greater powers than their fellows, seem also to have mingled with their cup of life more bitterness. There is a melancholy which is apt to come like a cloud over the imaginations of such characters. Their minds possess a susceptibility and delicacy of structure which unfit them for the gross atmosphere of human nature; wherefore, high talent has ever been distinguished for sadness and gloom. Genius lives in a world of its own: it is the essence of a superior nature—the loftier imaginings of the mind, clothed with a more spiritual and refined verdure. Few men endowed with such faculties enjoy the ordinary happiness of humanity. The stream of their lives runs harsh and broken. Melancholy thoughts sweep perpetually across their soul; and if these be heightened by misfortune, they are plunged into the deepest misery.

To relieve these feelings, many plans have been adopted. Dr Johnson fled for years to wine under his habitual gloom. He found that the pangs were removed while its immediate influence lasted, but he also found that they returned with double force when that influence passed away. He saw the dangerous precipice on which he stood, and, by an unusual effort of volition, gave it over. In its stead he substituted tea; and to this milder stimulus had recourse in his melancholy. Voltaire and Fontenelle, for the same purpose, used coffee. The excitements of Newton and Hobbes were the fumes of tobacco, while Demosthenes and Haller were sufficiently stimulated by drinking freely of cold water. Such are the differences of constitution.

'As good be melancholy still, as drunken beasts and beggars.' So says old Burton, in his Anatomy of Melancholy, and there are few who will not subscribe to his creed. The same author quaintly, but justly remarks, 'If a drunken man gets a child, it will never, likely, have a good brain.' Dr Darwin, a great authority on all subjects connected with life, says, that he never knew a glutton affected with the gout, who was not at the same time addicted to liquor. He also observes, 'it is remarkable that all the diseases from drinking spirituous or fermented liquors are liable to

* Thackrah on the Effects of the Principal Arts, Trades and Professions, p. 83.

become hereditary, even to the third generation, gradually increasing, if the cause be continued, till the family becomes extinct.'*

We need not endeavour to trace farther the remote causes of drunkenness. A drunkard is rarely able to recall the particular circumstances which made him so. The vice creeps upon him insensibly, and he is involved in its fetters before he is aware. It is enough that we know the proximate cause, and also the certain consequences. One thing is certain, that a man who addicts himself to intemperance, can never be said to be sound in mind or body. The former is a state of partial insanity, while the effects of the liquor remain; and the latter is always more or less diseased in its actions.

CHAPTER III.

PHENOMENA OF DRUNKENNESS.

The consequences of drunkenness are dreadful, but the pleasures of getting drunk are certainly ecstatic. While the illusion lasts, happiness is complete; care and melancholy are thrown to the wind: and Elysium, with all its glories, descends upon the dazzled imagination of the drinker.

Some authors have spoken of the pleasure of being completely drunk; this, however, is not the most exquisite period. The time is when a person is neither 'drunken nor sober, but neighbor to both,' as Bishop Andrews says in his ''Ex—ale—tation of Ale.' The moment is when the ethereal emanations begin to float around the brain—when the soul is commencing to expand its wings and rise from earth—when the tongue feels itself somewhat loosened in the mouth, and breaks the previous taciturnity, if any such existed.

What are the sensations of incipient drunkenness? First, an unusual serenity prevails over the mind, and the soul of the votary is filled with a placid satisfaction. By degrees he is sensible of a soft and not unmusical humming in his ears, at every pause of the conversation. He seems, to himself, to wear his head lighter than usual upon his shoulders. Then a species of obscurity, thinner than the finest mist, passes before his eyes, and makes him see objects rather indistinctly. The lights begin to dance and appear double. A gayety and warmth are felt at the same time about the heart. The imagination is expanded, and filled with a thousand delightful images. He becomes loquacious, and pours forth, in enthusiastic language, the thoughts which are born, as it were, within him.

Now comes a spirit of universal contentment with himself and all the world. He thinks no more of misery; it is dissolved in the bliss of the moment. This is the acme of the fit—the ecstacy is now perfect. As yet the sensorium is in tolerable order; it is only shaken, but the capability of thinking with accuracy still remains. About this time, the drunkard pours out all the secrets of his soul. His qualities, good or bad, come forth without reserve; and now, if at any time, the human heart may be seen into. In a short period, he is seized with a most inordinate propensity to talk nonsense, though he is perfectly conscious of doing so. He also commits many foolish things, knowing them to be foolish. The power of volition, that faculty which keeps the will subordinate to the judgment, seems totally weakened. The most delightful time seems to be that immediately before becoming very talkative. When this takes place, a man turns ridi mirth, though more boisterous, is not so exquisite. At first the intoxication partakes of sentiment, but latterly, it becomes mere animal.

After this the scene thickens. The drunkard's imagination gets disordered with the most grotesque con-

* Botanic Garden.

ceptions. Instead of moderating his drink, he pours it down more rapidly than ever; glass follows glass with reckless energy. His head becomes perfectly giddy. The candles burn blue, or green, or yellow; and where there are perhaps only three on the table, he sees a dozen. According to his temperament, he is amorous, or musical, or quarrelsome. Many possess a most extraordinary wit; and a great flow of spirits is a general attendant. In the latter stages, the speech is thick, and the use of the tongue in a great measure lost. His mouth is half open, and idiotic in the expression; while his eyes are glazed, wavering, and watery. He is apt to fancy that he has offended some one of the company, and is ridiculously profuse with his apologies. Frequently he mistakes one person for another, and imagines that some of those before him are individuals who are, in reality, absent or even dead. The muscular powers are, all along, much affected: this indeed happens before any great change takes place in the mind, and goes on progressively increasing. He can no longer walk with steadiness, but totters from side to side. The limbs become powerless, and inadequate to sustain his weight. He is, however, not always sensible of any deficiency in this respect: and while exciting mirth by his eccentric motions, imagines that he walks with the most perfect steadiness. In attempting to run, he conceives that he passes over the ground with astonishing rapidity. To his distorted eyes, all men, and even inanimate nature itself, seem to be drunken, while he alone is sober. Houses reel from side to side as if they had lost their balance; trees and steeples nod like tipsy Bacchanals; and the very earth seems to slip from under his feet, and leave him walking and floundering upon the air. The last stage of drunkenness is total insensibility. The man tumbles perhaps beneath the table, and is carried away in a state of stupor to his couch. In this condition he is said to be *dead drunk*.

When the drunkard is put to bed, let us suppose that his faculties are not totally absorbed in apoplectic stupor; let us suppose that he still possesses consciousness and feeling, though these are both disordered; then begins 'the tug of war;' then comes the misery which is doomed to succeed his previous raptures. No sooner is his head laid upon the pillow, than it is seized with the strongest throbbing. His heart beats quick and hard against the ribs. A noise like the distant fall of a cascade, or rushing of a river, is heard in his ears: sough—sough—sough, goes the sound. His senses now become more drowned and stupified. A dim recollection of his carousals, like a shadowy and indistinct dream, passes before the mind. He still hears, as in echo, the cries and laughter of his companions. Wild fantastic fancies accumulate thickly around the brain. His giddiness is greater than ever; and he feels as if in a ship tossed upon a heaving sea. At last he drops insensibly into a profound slumber.

In the morning he awakes in a high fever. The whole body is parched; the palms of the hands in particular, are like leather. His head is often violently painful. He feels excessive thirst; while his tongue is white, dry, and stiff. The whole inside of the mouth is likewise hot and constricted, and the throat often sore. Then look at his eyes—how sickly, dull, and languid! The fire, which first lighted them up the evening before, is all gone. A stupor like that of the last stage of drunkenness still clings about them, and they are disagreeably affected by the light. The complexion sustains as great a change: it is no longer flushed with the gayety and excitation, but pale and wayworn, indicating a profound mental and bodily exhaustion. There is probably sickness, and the appetite is totally gone. Even yet the delirium of intoxication has not left him, for his head still rings, his heart still throbs violently; and if he attempt getting up, he stumbles with giddiness. The mind also is sadly depressed, and

the proceedings of the previous night are painfully remembered. He is sorry for his conduct, promises solemnly never again so to commit himself, and calls impatiently for something to quench his thirst. Such are the usual phenomena of a fit of drunkenness.

In the beginning of intoxication we are inclined to sleep, especially if we indulge alone. In companies, the noise and opportunity of conversing prevent this; and when a certain quantity has been drunk, the drowsy tendency wears away. A person who wishes to stand out well, should never talk much. This increases the effects of the liquor, and hurries on intoxication. Hence, every experienced drunkard holds it to be a piece of prudence to keep his tongue under restraint.

The giddiness of intoxication is always greater in darkness than in the light. I know of no rational way by which this can be explained; but, certain it is, the drunkard never so well knows his true condition as when alone and in darkness. Possibly the noise and light distracted the mind, and made the bodily sensations be, for the time, in some measure unfelt.

There are some persons who get sick from drinking even a small quantity; and this sickness is, upon the whole, a favourable circumstance, as it proves an effectual curb upon them, however much they may be disposed to intemperance. In such cases, it will generally be found that the sickness takes place as soon as vertigo makes its appearance: it seems, in reality, to be produced by this sensation. This, however, is a rare circumstance, for though vertigo from ordinary causes has a strong tendency to produce sickness, that arising from drunkenness has seldom this effect. The nausea and sickness sometimes occurring in intoxication, proceed almost always from the surcharged and disordered state of the stomach, and very seldom from the accompanying giddiness.

Intoxication, before it proceeds too far, has a powerful tendency to increase the appetite. Perhaps it would be more correct to say, that inebriating liquors, by stimulating the stomach, have this power. We often see gluttony and drunkenness combined together at the same time. This continues till the last stage, when, from overloading and excess of irritation, the stomach expels its contents by vomiting.

All along, the action of the kidneys is much increased, especially at the commencement of intoxication. When a large quantity of intoxicating fluid has been suddenly taken into the stomach, the usual preliminary symptoms of drunkenness do not appear. An instantaneous stupefaction ensues; and the person is at once knocked down. This cannot be imputed to distention of the cerebral vessels, but to a sudden operation on the nervous branches of the stomach. The brain is thrown into a state of collapse, and many of its functions suspended. In such cases the face is not at first tumid and ruddy, but pale and contracted. The pulse is likewise feeble, and the body cold and powerless. When re-action takes place, these symptoms wear off, and those of sanguineous apoplexy succeed; such as turgid countenance, full but slow pulse, and strong stertorous breathing. The vessels of the brain have now become filled, and there is a strong determination to that organ.

Persons of tender or compassionate minds are particularly subject, during intoxication, to be affected to tears at the sight of any distressing object, or even on hearing an affecting tale. Drunkenness in such characters, may be said to melt the heart, and open up the fountains of sorrow. Their sympathy is often ridiculous, and aroused by the most trifling causes. Those who have a living imagination, combined with this tenderness of heart, sometimes conceives fictitious causes of distress, and weep bitterly at the woe of their own creating.

There are some persons in whom drunkenness calls forth a spirit of piety, or rather of religious hypocrisy, which is both ludicrous and disgusting. They become sentimental over their cups; and, while in a state of debasement most offensive to God and man, they will weep at the wickedness of the human heart, entreat you to eschew swearing and profane company, and have a greater regard for the welfare of your immortal soul. These sanctimonious drunkards seem to consider ehriety as the most venial of offences.

During a paroxysm of drunkenness, the body is much less sensible to external stimuli than at other times: it is particularly capable of resisting cold. Seamen, when absent on shore, are prone to get intoxicated; and they will frequently lie for hours on the highway, even in the depth of winter, without any bad consequences. A drunk man seldom shivers from cold. His frame seems steeled against it, and he holds ont with an apathy which is astonishing. The body is, in like manner, insensible to injuries, such as cuts, bruises, &c. He frequently receives, in fighting, the most severe blows, without seemingly feeling them, and without, in fact, being aware of the matter, till sobered. Persons in intoxication have been known to chop off their fingers, and otherwise disfigure themselves, laughing all the while at the action. But when the paroxysm is off, and the frame weakened, things are changed. External agents are then withstood with little vigour, with even less than in the natural state of the-body. The person shivers on the slightest chill, and is more than usually subject to fevers and all sorts of contagion.

External stimuli frequently break the fit. Men have been instantly sobered by having a bucket of cold water thrown upon them, or by falling into a stream. Strong emotions of the mind produce the same effect, such as the sense of danger, or a piece of good or bad news, suddenly communicated.

There are particular situations and circumstances in which a man can stand liquor better than in others. In the close atmosphere of a large town, he is soon overpowered; and it is here that the genuine drunkard is to be met with in the greatest perfection. In the country, especially in a mountainous district, or on the sea-shore, where the air is cold and piercing, a great quantity may be taken with impunity. The highlanders drink largely of ardent spirits, and they are often intoxicated, yet, among them, there are comparatively few who can be called habitual drunkards. A keen air seems to deaden its effects, and it soon evaporates from their constitutions. Sailors and soldiers who are hard wrought. also consume enormous quantities without injury; porters and all sorts of labourers do the same. With these men exercise is a corrective; but in towns, where no counteracting agency is employed, it acts with irresistible power upon the frame, and soon proves destructive.

A great quantity of liquors may also be taken without inebriating, in certain diseases, such as spasm tetanus, gangrene, and retrocedent gout.

Certain circumstances of constitution make one person naturally more apt to get intoxicated than another. 'Mr Pitt,' says a modern writer, 'would retire in the midst of a warm debate, and enliven his faculties with a couple of bottles of Port. Pitt's constitution enabled him to do this with impunity. He was afflicted with what is called a coldness of stomach; and the quantity of wine that would have closed the oratory of so professed a Bacchanalian as Sheridan, scarcely excited the son of Chatham.'*

All kinds of intoxicating agents act much more rapidly and powerfully upon an empty than a full stomach. In like manner, when the stomach is disordered, and subject to weakness, heartburn, or disease of any kind, ebriety is more rapidly produced than when this organ is sound and healthy.

-- The stomach may get accustomed to a strong stimu-

* Rede's Memoir of the right Hon. George Canning.

lus, and resist it powerfully, while it yields to one much weaker. I have known people who could drink eight or ten glasses of raw spirits at a sitting without feeling them much, become perfectly intoxicated by half the quantity made into toddy. In like manner, he who is in the constant habit of using one spirit,—rum, for instance,—cannot, for the most part, indulge to an equal extent in another, without experiencing more severe effects than if he had partaken of his usual beverage. This happens even when the strength of the two liquors is the same.

The mind exercises a considerable effect upon drunkenness, and may often control it powerfully. When in the company of a superior whom we respect, or of a female in whose presence it would be indelicate to get intoxicated, a much greater portion of liquor may be withstood than in societies where no such restraints operate.

Drunkenness has sometimes a curious effect upon the memory. Actions committed during intoxication may be forgotten on a recovery from this state, and remembered distinctly when the person becomes again intoxicated. Drunkenness has thus an analogy to dreaming, in which state circumstances are occasionally brought to mind which had entirely been forgotten. The same thing may also occur in fevers, wherein even languages with which we were familiar in childhood or youth, but had forgotten, are renewed upon the memory and pass away from it again when the disease which recalled them is removed.

With most people intoxication is a gradual process, and increases progressively as they pour down the liquor; but there are some individuals in whom it takes place suddenly, and without any previous indication of its approach. It is not uncommon to see such persons sit for hours at the bottle without experiencing any thing beyond a moderate elevation of spirits, yet assume all at once the outrage and boisterous irregularity of the most decided drunkenness.

Some drunkards retain their senses after the physical powers are quite exhausted. Others, even when the mind is wrought to a pitch leading to the most absurd actions, preserve a degree of cunning and observation which enables them to elude the tricks which their companions are preparing to play upon them. In such cases, they display great address, and take the first opportunity of retaliating; or, if such does not occur, of slipping out of the room unobserved and getting away. Some, while the whole mind seems locked up in the stupor of forgetfulness, hear all that is going on. No one should ever presume on the intoxicated state of another to talk of him detractingly in his presence. While apparently deprived of all sensation, he may be an attentive listener; and whatever is said, though unheeded at the moment, is not forgotten afterwards, but treasured carefully up in the memory. Much discord and ill-will frequently arise from such imprudence.

There are persons who are exceedingly profuse, and fond of giving away their money, watches, rings, &c., to the company. This peculiarity will never, I believe be found in a miser: avarice is a passion strong under every circumstance. Drinking does not loosen the grasp of the covetous man, or open his heart: he is for ever the same.

The generality of people are apt to talk of their private affairs when intoxicated. They then reveal the most deeply-hidden secrets to their companions. Others have their minds so happily constituted that nothing escapes them. They are, even in their most unguarded moments, secret and close as the grave.

The natural disposition may be better discovered in drunkenness than at any other time. In modern society, life is all a disguise. Almost every man walks in masquerade, and his most intimate friend very often does not know his real character. Many wear smiles constantly upon their cheeks, whose hearts are unprincipled and treacherous. Many with violent tempers have all the external calm and softness of charity itself. Some speak always with sympathy, who, at soul, are full of gall and bitterness. Intoxication tears off the veil, and sets each in his true light, whatever they may be. The combative man will quarrel, the amorous will love, the detractor will abuse his neighbour. I have known exceptions, but they are few in number. At one time they seemed more numerous, but closer observation convinced me that most of those whom I thought drunkenness had libelled, inherited at bottom the genuine dispositions which it brought forth. The exceptions, however, which now and then occur, are sufficiently striking, and point out the injustice of always Judging of a man's real disposition from his drunken moments. To use the words of Addison, ' Not only does this vice betray the hidden faults of a man, and show them in the most odious colours, but often occasions faults to which he is not naturally subject. Wine throws a man out of himself, and infuses qualities into the mind which she is a stranger to in his sober moments.' The well known maxim ' in vino veritas,' therefore, though very generally true, is to be received with some restrictions, although, these I am satisfied, are by no means so numerous, as many authors would have us to belive.

CHAPTER IV

DRUNKENNESS MODIFIED BY TEMPERAMENT.

Under the last head I have described the usual phenomena of intoxication ; but it is necessary to remark that these are apt to be modified by the physical and moral frame of the drinker. Great diversity of opinion exists with regard to the doctrine of the temperaments ; some authors affirming, and others denying their existence. Into this controversy it is needless to enter. All I contend for is, that the bodily and mental constitution of every man is not alike, and that on these peculiarities depend certain differences during a paroxysm of drunkenness.

1. *Sanguineous Drunkard.*—The sanguine temperament seems to feel most intensely the excitement of the bottle. Persons of this stamp have usually a ruddy complexion, thick neck, small head, and strong museular fibre. Their intellect is in general *mediocre*, for great bodily strength and corresponding mental powers are rarely united together. In such people, the animal propensities prevail over the moral and intellectual ones. They are prone to combativeness and sensuality, and are either very good-natured or extremely quarrelsome. All their passions are keen : like the Irish women, they will fight for their friends or with them as occasion requires. They are talkative from the beginning, and, during confirmed intoxication, perfectly obstreporous. It is men of this class who are the heroes of all drunken companies, the patron of masonic lodges, the presidents and getters-up of jovial meetings. With them, eating and drinking are the grand ends of human life. Look at their eyes, how they sparkle at the sight of wine, and how their lips smack and their teeth water in the neighbourhood of a good dinner : they would scent out a banquet in Siberia. When intoxicated, their passions are highly excited : the energies of a hundred minds then seem concentrated into one focus. Their mirth, their anger, their love, their folly, are all equally intense and unquenchable. Such men cannot conceal their feelings. In drunkenness, the veil is removed from them, and their characters stand revealed, as in a glass to the eye of the beholder. The Roderick Random of Smollett had much of this temperament, blended, however, with more intellect than usually belongs to it.

II. *Melancholy-Drunkard.*—Melancholy, in drunkards, sometimes arises from temperament, but more frequently from habitual intoxication or misfortune, Some men are melancholy by nature, but become highly mirthful when they have drunk a considerable quantity. Men of this tone of mind seem to enjoy the bottle more exquisitely than even the sanguineous class. The joyousness which it excites breaks in upon their gloom like sunshine upon darkness. Above all, the sensations, of the moment when mirth begins with its magic to charm away care, are inexpressible. Pleasure falls in showers of fragrance upon their souls ; they are at peace with themselves and all mankind, and enjoy, as it were, a foretaste of paradise. Robert Burns was an example of this variety. His melancholy was constitutional, but heightened by misfortune. The bottle commonly dispelled it, and gave rise to the most delightful images ; sometimes, however, it only aggravated the gloom.

III. *Surly Drunkard.*—Some men are not excited to mirth by intoxication : on the contrary, it renders them gloomy and discontented. Even those who in the sober state are sufficiently gay, become, occasionally thus altered. A great propensity to take offence is a characteristic among persons of this temperament. They are suspicious, and very often mischievous. If at some former period they have had a difference with any of the company, they are sure to revive it, although, probably, it has been long ago cemented on both sides, and even forgotten by the other party. People of this description are very unpleasant companions. They are in general so foul-tongued, quarrelsome, and indecent in conversation, that established clubs of drinkers have made it a practice to exclude them from their society.

IV. *Phlegmatic Drunkard.*—Persons of this temperament are heavy-rolling machines, and, like the above, are not roused to mirth by liquor. Their vital actions are dull and spiritless—the blood in their veins as sluggish as the river Jordan, and their energies stagnant as the Dead Sea. They are altogether a negative sort of beings, with passions too inert to lead them to any thing very good or very bad. They are a species of animated clods, but not thoroughly animated—for the vital fire of feeling has got cooled in penetrating their frozen frames. A new prometheus would require to breathe into their nostrils, to give them the ordinary glow and warmth of humanity. Look at a phlegmatic man—how dead, passionless and uninspired is the expression of his clammy lips and vacant eye ! Speak to him—how cold, slow, and tame is his conversation ! the words come forth as if they were drawn from his mouth with a pair of pincers : and the ideas are as frozen as if concocted in the bowels of Lapland. Liquor produces no effect upon his mental powers ; or, if it does, it is a smothering one. The whole energies of the drink fall on his almost impassive frame. From the first, his drunkenness is stupifying ; he is seized with a kind of lethargy, the white of his eyes turns up, he breathes loud and harshly, and sinks into an apoplectic stupor. Yet all this is perfectly harmless, and wears away without leaving any mark behind it.

Such persons are very apt to be played upon by their companions. There are few men who, in their younger days who have not assisted in shaving the heads and painting the faces of these lethargic drunkards.

V. *Nervous Drunkard.*—This is a very harmless and very tiresome personage. Generally of a weak mind and irritable constitution, he does not become boisterous with mirth, and rarely shows the least glimmering of wit or mental energy. He is talkative and fond of long winded stories, which he tells in a drivelling, silly manner. Never warmed into enthusiasm by liquor he keeps chatting at some ridiculous tale, very much in the way of a garrulous old man in his dotage.*

* The old gentleman who is represented as speaking, in Bun-

VI. *Choleric Drunkard.*—There are a variety of drunkards whom I can only class under the above title. They seem to possess few of the qualities of the other races, and are chiefly distinguished by an uncommon testiness of disposition. They are quick, irritable, and impatient, but withal good at heart, and, when in humour, very pleasant and generous. They are easily put out of temper, but it returns almost immediately. This disposition is very prevalent among Welshmen and Highland lairds. Mountaineers are usually quick tempered: but such men are not the worst or most unpleasant. Sterne is undoubtedly right when he says that more virtue is to be found in warm than cold dispositions. Commodore Trunnion is a marked example of this temperament; and Captain Fluellen, who compelled the *heroic* Pistol to eat the leek, is another.

VII. *Periodical Drunkard.*—There are persons whose temperaments are so peculiarly constituted, that they indulge to excess *periodically*, and are, in the intervals of these indulgences, remarkably sober. This is not a very common case, but I have known more than one instance of it; and a gentleman, distinguished by the power of his eloquence in the senate and at the bar, is said to furnish another. In the cases which I have known, the drunken mania, for it can get no other name, came on three or four times a-year. The persons from a state of complete sobriety, felt the most intense desire for drink; and no power, short of absolute force or confinement, could restrain them from the indulgence. In every case they seemed to be quite aware of the uncontrollable nature of their passion, and proceeded systematically by confining themselves to their room, and procuring a large quantity of ardent spirits. As soon as this was done, they commenced and drank to excess till vomiting ensued, and the stomach absolutely refused to receive another drop of liquor. This state may last a few days or a few weeks according to constitutional strength, or the rapidity with which the libations are poured down. During the continuance of the attack, the individual exhibits such a state of mind as may be looked for from his peculiar temperament; he may be sanguineous, or melancholy, or surly, or phlegmatic, or nervous, or choleric. So soon as the stomach rejects onery thing that is swallowed, and severe sickness comes on, the fit ceases. From that moment recovery takes place, and the former fondness for liquor is succeeded by aversion or disgust. This gains such ascendency over him, that he abstains religiously from it for weeks, or months, or even for a year, as the case may be. During this interval he leads a life of the most exemplary temperance, drinking nothing but cold water, and probably shunning every society where he is likely to be exposed to indulgence. So soon as this period of sobriety has expired, the fit again comes on; and he continues playing the same game for perhaps the better part of a long life. This class of persons I would call periodical drunkards.

These different varieties are sometimes found strongly marked; at other times so blended together that it is not easy to say which predominates. The most agreeable drunkard is he whose temperament lies between the sanguineous and the melancholic. The genuine sanguineous is a sad noisy dog, and so common that every person must have met with him. The naval service furnishes a great many gentlemen of this description. The phlegmatic, I think, is rarer, but both the nervous and the surly are not unusual.

CHAPTER V.

DRUNKENNESS MODIFIED BY THE INEBRIATING AGENT.

Intoxication is not only influenced by temperament, bury's admirable caricature of the 'Long Story,' furnishes one of the best illustrations I have ever seen of this variety. It is worth consulting, both on account of the story-teller, and the effect his tedious garrulity produced upon the company.

but by the nature of the agent which produces it. Thus, ebriety from ardent spirits differs in some particulars from that brought on by opium or malt liquors, such as porter and ale.

I. *Modified by Ardent Spirits.*—Alcohol is the principle of intoxication in all liquors. It is this which gives to wine,* ale, and spirits, their characteristic properties. In the natural state, however, it is so pungent, that it could not be received into the stomach, even in a moderate quantity, without producing death. It can, therefore, only be used in dilution; and in this state we have it, from the strongest ardent spirits, to simple small beer. The first (ardent spirits) being the most concentrated of its combinations, act most rapidly upon the constitution. They are more inflammatory, and intoxicate sooner than any of the others. Swallowed in an overdose, they act almost instantaneously—extinguishing the senses and overcoming the whole body with a sudden stupor. When spirits are swallowed raw, as in the form of a dram, they excite a glow of heat in the throat and stomach, succeeded, in those who are not much accustomed to their use, by a flushing of the countenance, and a copious discharge of tears. They are strongly diuretic.

Persons who indulge too much in spirits rarely get corpulent, unless their indulgence be coupled with good living. Their bodies become emaciated; they get spindle-shanked; their eyes are glazed and hollow; their cheeks fall in; and a premature old age overtakes them. They do not eat so well as their brother drunkards. An insatiable desire for a morning dram makes them early risers, and their breakfast amounts to almost nothing.

The principal varieties of spirits, as already mentioned, are rum, brandy, whiskey, and gin. It is needless to enter into any detail of the history of these fluids. Brandy kills soonest; it takes most rapidly to the head, and, more readily than the others, tinges the face to a crimson or livid hue. Rum is probably the next in point of fatality; and, after that, whiskey and gin. The superior diuretic qualities of the two latter, and the less luscious sources from whence they are procured, may possibly account for such differences. I am at the same time aware that some persons entertain a different idea of the relative danger of these liquors: some, for instance, conceive that gin is more rapidly fatal than any of them; but it is to be remembered, that it, more than any other ardent spirit, is liable to adulteration. That, from this circumstance, more lives may be lost by its use, I do not deny. In speaking of gin, however, and comparing its effects with those of the rest of the class to which it belongs, I must be understood to speak of it in its pure condition, and not in that detestable state of sophistication in which such vast quantities of it are drunk in London and elsewhere. When pure, I have no hesitation in affirming that it is decidedly more wholesome than either brandy or rum; and that the popular belief of its greater tendency to produce dropsy, is quite unfounded.

An experiment has lately been made for the purpose of ascertaining the comparative powers of gin, brandy, and rum upon the human body, which is not less remarkable for the inconsequent conclusions deduced from it, than for the ignorance it displays in confounding dead animal matter with the living fibre. It was made as follows:—

A piece of raw liver was put into a glass of gin, another into a glass of rum, and a third into a glass of brandy. That in the gin was, in a given time, partially decomposed; that in the rum, in the same time, not diminished; and that in the brandy quite dissolved. It was concluded from these results, that rum was the most wholesome spirit of the three, and brandy the

* Alcohol appears to exist in wines, in a very peculiar state of combination. In the Appendix, I have availed myself of Dr Paris's valuable remarks on this subject.

least. The inferences deduced from these premises are not only erroneous, but glaringly absurd ; the premises would even afford grounds for drawing results of the very opposite nature : it might be said, for instance, that though brandy be capable of dissolving dead animal matter, there is no evidence that it can do the same to the living stomach, and that it would in reality prove less hurtful than the others, in so far as it would, more effectually than they, dissolve the food contained in that organ. These experiments, in fact, prove nothing ; and could only have been suggested by one completely ignorant of the functions of the animal economy. There is a power inherent in the vital principle which resists the laws that operate upon dead matter. This is known to every practitioner, and is the reason why the most plausible and recondite speculations of chemistry have come to naught in their trials upon the living frame. The only way to judge of the respective effects of ardent spirits, is by experience and physiological reasoning, both of which inform us that the spirit most powerfully diuretic must rank highest in the scale of safety. Now and then persons are met with on whose frames both gin and whiskey have a much more heating effect than the two other varieties of spirits. This, however, is not common, and when it does occur, can only be referred to some accountable idiosyncrasy of constitution.

II. *Modified by Wines.*—Drunkenness from wines closely resembles that from ardent spirits. It is equally airy and volatile, more especially if the light wines, such as Champagne, Claret, Chambertin, or Volnay, be drunk. On the former, a person may get tipsy several times of a night. The fixed air evolved from it produces a feeling analogous to ebriety, independent of the spirit it contains. Port, Sherry, and Madeira are heavier wines, and have a stronger tendency to excite headache and fever.

The wine-bidder has usually an ominous rotundity of face, and, not unfrequently, of corporation. His nose is well studded over with carbuncles of the claret complexion ; and the red of his cheeks resembles very closely the hue of that wine. The drunkard from ardent spirits is apt to be poor, miserable, emaciated figure, broken in mind and in fortune ; but the votary of the juice of the grape may usually boast the 'paunch well lined with capon,' and calls to recollection the bluff figure of Sir John Falstaff over his potations of sack.*

III. *Modified by Malt Liquors.*—Malt liquors under which title we include all kinds of porter and ales, produce the worst species of drunkenness ; as, in addition to the intoxicating principle, some noxious ingredients are usually added, for the purpose of preserving them and giving them their bitter. The hop of these fluids is highly narcotic, and brewers often add other substances, to heighten its effect, such as hyoscyamus, opium, belladonna, cocculus Indicus, lauro cerasus, &c. Malt liquors, therefore, act in two ways upon the body, partly by the alcohol they contain, and partly by the narcotic principle. In addition to this, the fermentation which they undergo is much less perfect than that of spirits or wine. After being swallowed, this process is carried on in the stomach, by which fixed air is copiously liberated, and the digestion of delicate stomachs materially impaired. Cider, spruce, ginger, and table beers, in consequence of their imperfect fermentation, often produce the same bad effects, long after their first briskness has vanished.

Persons addicted to malt liquors increase enormously

in bulk. They become loaded with fat ; their chin gets double or triple, the eye prominent, and the whole face bloated and stupid. Their circulation is clogged, while the pulse feels like a cord, and is full and laboring, but not quick. During sleep, the breathing is stertorous. Every thing indicates an excess of blood ; and when a pound or two is taken away, immense relief is obtained. The blood, in such cases, is more dark and sizy than in the others. In seven cases out of ten, malt liquor drunkards die of apoplexy or palsy. If they escape this hazard, swelled liver or dropsy carries them off. The abdomen seldom loses its prominency, but the lower extremities get ultimately emaciated. Profuse bleedings frequently ensue from the nose, and save life, by emptying the blood-vessels of the brain.

The drunkenness in question is peculiarly of British growth. The most noted examples of it are to be found in innkeepers and their wives, recruiting sergeants, guards of stage-coaches, &c. The quantity of malt liquors which such persons will consume in a day is prodigious. Seven English pints is quite a common allowance, and not unfrequently twice that quantity is taken without any perceptible effect. Many of the coal-heavers on the Thames think nothing of drinking daily two gallons of porter, especially in the summer season, when they labor under profuse perspiration. A friend has informed me that he knew an instance of one of them having consumed eighteen pints in one day, and he states that there are many such instances.*

The effects of malt liquors on the body, if not so immediately rapid as those of ardent spirits, are more stupifying, more lasting, and less easily removed. The last are particularly prone to produce levity and mirth, but the first have a stunning influence on the brain, and, in a short time, render dull and sluggish the gayest disposition. They also produce sickness and vomiting more readily than either spirits or wine.

Both wine and malt liquors have a greater tendency to swell the body than ardent spirits. They form blood with greater rapidity, and are altogether more nourishing. The most dreadful effects, upon the whole, are brought on by spirits, but drunkenness from malt liquors is the most speedily fatal. The former break down the body by degrees, the latter operate by some instantaneous apoplexy or rapid inflammation.

No one has ever given the respective characters of the malt liquor and ardent spirit drunkard with greater truth than Hogarth, in his Beer Alley and Gin Lane. The first is represented as plump, rubicund, and bloated ; the second as pale, tottering, and emaciated, and dashed over with the aspect of blank despair.

IV. *Modified by Opium.*—The drunkenness produced by opium has also some characteristics which it is necessary to mention. The drug is principally employed by the Mahometans. By their religion, these people are forbidden the use of wine,† and use opium as a substitute. And a delightful substitute it is while the first excitation continues ; for images it occasions in the mind are more exquisite than any produced even by wine.

There is reason to believe that the use of this medicine has, of late years, gained ground in Great Britain. We are told by the 'English Opium-Eater,' whose powerful and interesting ' Confessions' have excited so deep an interest, that the practice exists among the work people at Manchester. Many of our fashionable ladies have recourse to it when troubled with vapours, or low spirits ; some of them even carry it about with them for the purpose. This practice is most perni-

---

* There is reason to believe that the Sack of Shakspeare was Sherry.—'Falstaff. You rogue ! here's *lime* in this Sack too. There is nothing but roguery to be found in villanous man. Yet a coward is worse than a cup of Sack with lime in it.'— Lime, it is well known, is added to the grapes in the manufacture of Sherry. This not only gives the wine what is called its dry quality, but probably acts by neutralizing a portion of the malic or tartaric acid.

* 'It is recorded of a Welsh squire, William Lewis, who died in 1793, that he drank *eight gallons* of ale *per diem*, and weighed forty stones.'—*Wadd's Comments on Corpulency.*

† 'The law of Mahomet which prohibits the drinking of wine, is a law fitted to the climate of Arabia ; and, indeed, before Mahomet's time, water was the common drink of the Arabs. The law which forbade the Carthaginians to drink wine, was also a law of the climate.'—*Montesquieu, Book, xiv. Chap. x.*

cious, and no way different from that of drunkards, who swallow wine and other liquors to drive away care. While the first effects continue, the intended purpose is sufficiently gained, but the melancholy which follows is infinitely greater than can be compensated by the previous exhilaration.

Opium acts differently on different constitutions. While it disposes some to calm, it arouses others to fury.. Whatever passion predominates at the time, it increases; whether it be love, or hatred, or revenge, or benevolence. Lord Kames, in his Sketches of Man, speaks of the fanatical Faquirs, who, when excited by this drug, have been known, with poisoned daggers, to assail and butcher every European whom they could overcome. In the century before last, one of this nation attacked a body of Dutch sailors, and murdered seventeen of them in one minute. The Malays are strongly addicted to opium. When violently aroused by it, they sometimes perform what is called *Running-a-Muck*, which consists in rushing out in a state of phrensied excitement, heightened by fanaticism, and murdering every one who comes in their way. The Turkish commanders are well aware of the powers of this drug in inspiring an artificial courage; and frequently give it to their men when they put them on any enterprise of great danger.

Some minds are rendered melancholy by opium. Its usual effect, however, is to give rise to lively and happy sensations. The late Duchess of Gordon is said to have used it freely, previous to appearing in great parties, where she wished to shine by the gayety of her conversation and brilliancy of her wit. A celebrated pleader at the Scotch bar is reported to do the same thing, and always with a happy effect.

In this country opium is much used, but seldom with the view of producing intoxication. Some, indeed, deny that it can do so, strictly speaking. If by intoxication is meant a state precisely similar to that from over-indulgence in vinous or spiritous liquors, they are undoubtedly right; but drunkenness merits a wider latitude of signification. The ecstacies of opium are much more entrancing than those of wine. There is more poetry in its visions—more mental aggrandizement—more range of imagination. Wine, in common with it, invigorates the animal powers and propensities, but opium, in a more peculiar manner, strengthens those proper to man, and gives, for a period amounting to hours, a higher tone to the intellectual faculties. It inspires the mind with a thousand delightful images, lifts the soul from earth, and casts a halo of poetic thought and feeling over the spirits of the most unimaginative. Under its influence, the mind wears no longer that blank passionless aspect which, even in gifted natures, it is apt to assume. On the contrary, it is clothed with beauty 'as with a garment,' and colours every thought that passes through it with the hues of wonder and romance. Such are the feelings which the luxurious and opulent mussulman seeks to enjoy. To stir up the languid current of his mind, satiated with excess of pleasure and rendered sluggish by indolence, he has recourse to that remedy which his own genial climate produces in greatest perfection. Seated perhaps amid the luxuries of Oriental splendour—with fountains bubbling around, and the citron shading him with its canopy, and scattering perfume on all sides—he lets loose the reins of an imagination conversant from infancy with every thing gorgeous and magnificent. The veil which shades the world of fancy is withdrawn, and the wonders lying behind it exposed to view; he sees palaces and temples in the clouds; or the Paradise of Mahomet, with its houris and bowers of amaranth, may stand revealed to his excited senses. Every thing is steeped in poetic exaggeration. The zephyrs seem converted into aerial music, the trees bear golden fruit, the rose blushes with unaccustomed beauty and perfume. Earth, in a word, is brought nearer to the sky,

and becomes one vast Eden of pleasure. Such are the first effects of opium; but in proportion as they are great, so is the depression which succeeds them. Languor and exhaustion invariably come after; to remove which, the drug is again had recourse to, and becomes almost an essential of existence.

Opium retains at all times its power of exciting the imagination, provided sufficient doses are taken. But, when it has been continued so long as to bring disease upon the constitution, the pleasurable feelings wear away, and are succeeded by others of a very different kind. Instead of disposing the mind to be happy, it now acts upon it like the spell of a demon, and calls up phantoms of horror and disgust. The fancy is still as powerful as ever, but it is turned in another direction. Formerly it clothed all objects with the light of heaven; now it invests them with the attributes of hell. Goblins, spectres, and every kind of distempered vision haunt the mind, peopling it with dreary and revolting imagery. The sleep is no longer cheered with its former sights of happiness. Frightful dreams usurp their place, till, at last, the person becomes the victim of an almost perpetual misery.* Nor is this confined to the mind alone, for the body suffers in an equal degree. Emaciation, loss of appetite, sickness, vomiting, and a total disorganization of the digestive functions, as well as of the mental powers, are sure to ensue, and never fail to terminate in death, if the evil habit which brings them on is continued.

Opium resembles the other agents of intoxication in this, that the fondness for it increases with use, and that at last, it becomes nearly essential for bodily comfort and peace of mind. The quantity which may be taken varies exceedingly, and depends wholly upon age, constitution, and habit. A single drop of laudanum has been known to kill a new-born child; and four grains of solid opium have destroyed an adult. Certain diseases such as fevers, phrensies, &c., facilitate the action of opium upon the system; others, such as diarrhœa, cramp, &c., resist it; and a quantity which would destroy life in the former, would have little perceptible effect in the latter. By habit, enormous quantities of the drug may be taken with comparative impunity. There are many persons in this country who make a practice of swallowing half an ounce of laudanum night and morning, and some will even take from one to two drachms daily of solid opium. The Teriakis, or opium-eaters of Constantinople, will sometimes swallow a hundred grains at a single dose. Nay, it is confidently affirmed that some of them will take at once three drachms in the morning, and repeat the same dose at night, with no other effect than a pleasing exhilaration of spirits. The 'English Opium-Eater' himself, furnishes one of the most extraordinary instances on record of the power of habit in bringing the body to withstand this drug. He took daily *eight thousand drops* of laudanum, containing *three hundred and twenty grains* of opium. This enormous quantity

* The following description, by a modern traveller, of a scene witnessed by him in the East, gives a lively picture of the effects of this drug:—

'There is a decoction of the head and seeds of the poppy, which they call Cóquenar, for the sale of which there are taverns in every quarter of the town, similar to our coffee-houses. It is extremely amusing to visit these houses, and to observe carefully those who resort there for the purpose of drinking it, both before they have taken the dose, before it begins to operate, and while it is operating. On entering the tavern, they are dejected and languishing: soon after they have taken two or three cups of this beverage, they are peevish, and as it were enraged; every thing displeases them. They find fault with every thing, and quarrel with one another, but in the course of its operation they make it up again;—and, each one giving himself up to his predominant passion, the lover speaks sweet things to his idol—another, half asleep, laughs in his sleeps—a third talks big and blusters—a fourth tells ridiculous stories. In a word, a person would believe himself to be really in a mad-house. A kind of lethargy and stupidity succeed to this disorder y gayety; but the Persians, far from treating it as it deserves, call it an ecstacy, and maintain that there is something exquisite and heavenly in this state.'—*Chardin.*

he reduced suddenly, and without any considerable effort, to *one thousand drops*, or *forty grains*. 'Instantaneously,' says he, ' and as if by magic, the cloud of profoundest melancholy which rested upon my brain, like some black vapours which I have seen roll away from the summits of the mountains, drew of in one day—passed off with its murky banners, as simultaneously as a ship that has been stranded, and is floated off by the spring-tide.'

The circumstance of the body being brought by degrees to withstand a great quantity of opium is not solitary, but exists as a general rule with regard to all stimulants and narcotics. A person who is in the habit of drinking ale, wine, or spirits, will take much more with impunity than one who is not; and the faculty of withstanding these agents goes on strengthening till it acquires a certain point, after which it becomes weakened. When this takes place, their is either organic disease or general debility. A confirmed drunkard, whose constitution has suffered from indulgence, can not take so much liquor, without feeling it, as one who is in the habit of taking his glass, but whose strength is yet unimpaired. It is, I suspect, the same, though probably in a less degree, with regard to opium.

Mithridates, king of Pontus, affords an instance of the effects of habit in enabling the body to withstand poisons : and on the same principle, we find that physicians and nurses who are much exposed to infection, are less liable than those persons whose frames are not similarly fortified.

Opium resembles wine, spirit, and ales, in effecting the brain and disposing to apoplexy. Taken in an over-dose, it is fatal in from six to twenty-four hours, according to the quantity swallowed, and the constitution, habits, &c., of the persons submitted to its operation. The following are the principal symptoms of poisoning from opium. Giddiness succeeded by stupor; insensibility to light, while the eyes are closed, and the pupil immoveable, and sometimes dilated. The pulse is generally small and feeble, but, occasionally, slow and full, as in common apoplexy. The breathing at first is scarcely perceptible, but is apt to become stertorous. Foam sometimes issues from the mouth : in other cases there is vomiting. The countenance is cadaverous and pale or livid. A narcotic odour is often perceptible in the breath. The skin is cold, and the body exceedingly relaxed; now and then it is convulsed. By being struck shaken, or excited any way, the person sometimes recovers for a short period from his stupor, and stares wildly around him, but only to relapse into lethargy. At last death ensues, but shortly before this event, a deceitful show of animation occasionally makes its appearance, and may impose upon superficial observers.

I extract the following interesting case of opium-eating from a London paper :—

'An inquest was held at Walpole lately, on the body of Rebecca Eason, aged five years, who had been diseased from her birth, was unable to walk or articulate, and from her size, did not appear to be more than *five weeks* old. The mother had for many years been in the habit of taking opium in large quantities, (nearly a quarter of an ounce a day ;*) and, it is supposed, had entailed a disease on her child which caused its death ; it was reduced to a mere skeleton, and had been in that state from birth. Verdict ; ' Died by the visitation of God ; but from the great quantity of opium taken by the mother during her pregnancy of the said child, and of sucking it, she had greatly injured its health.' It appeared that the mother of the deceased had had five children ; that she began to take opium after the birth and weaning of her first child, which was and is remarkably healthy ; and that the other children have all lingered and died in the same emaciated state as the

. * Equal to nearly three thousand drops of laudanum.

child who was the subject of this investigation. The mother is under thirty : she was severely censured by the coroner for indulging in so pernicious a practice.'

V. *Modified by Tobacco.*—A variety of drunkenness is excited by tobacco. This luxury was introduced into Europe from the new world, in 1559, by a Spanish gentleman, named Hernandez de Toledo, who brought a small quantity into Spain and Portugal. From thence, by the agency of the French ambassador at Lisbon, it found its way to Paris, where it was used in the form of powder by Catherine de Medicis, the abandoned instigator of the massacre of the Protestants on St. Bartholomew's day. This woman, therefore, may be considered the inventor of snuff, as well as the contriver of that most atrocious transaction. It then came under the patronage of the Cardinal Santa Crocé, the Pope's nuncio, who, returning from his embassy at the Spanish and Portuguese courts, carried the plant to his own country, and thus acquired a fame little inferior to that which, at another period, he had won by piously bringing a portion of the *real* cross from the Holy Land. It was received with general enthusiasm in the Papal States, and hardly less favorably in England, into which it was introduced by Sir Walter Raleigh, in 1585. It was not, however, without opposition that it gained a footing either in this country or in the rest of Europe. Its principal opponents were the priests, the physicians, and the sovereign princes ; by the former, its use was declared sinful ; and in 1624, Pope Urban VIII. published a bull, excommunicating all persons found guilty of taking snuff when in church. This bull was renewed in 1690 by Pope Innocent ; and about twenty-nine years afterwards, the Sultan Amurath IV. made smoking a capital offence, on the ground of its producing infertility. For a long time smoking was forbidden in Russia, under the pain of having the nose cut off : and in some parts of Switzerland, it was likewise made a subject of public prosecution—the public regulations of the Canton of Berne, in 1661, placing the prohibition of smoking in the list of the ten commandments, immediately under that against adultery. Nay, that British Solomon James I. did not think it beneath the royal dignity to take up his pen upon the subject. He accordingly, in 1603, published his famous 'Counterblaste to Tobacco,' in which the following remarkable passage occurs :—' It is a custom loathsome to the eye, hateful to the nose, harmful to the brain, dangerous to the lungs, and, in the black stinking fume thereof, nearest resembling the horrible Stygian smoke of the pit that is bottomless.'* But notwithstanding this regal and sacerdotal wrath, the plant extended itself far and wide, and is at this moment the most universal luxury in existence.

The effects of tobacco are considerably different from those of any other inebriating agent. Instead of quickening, it lowers the pulse, and, when used to excess, produces languor, depression of the system, giddiness, confusion of ideas, violent pain in the stomach, vomiting, convulsions, and even death. Its essential oil is so intensely powerful, that two or three drops inserted into a raw wound, would prove almost instantly fatal.* Mr Barrow, in his travels, speaks of the use

* ' Tobacco,' King James farther observes, ' is the lively image and pattern of hell, for it hath, by allusion, in it all the parts and vices of the world, whereby hell may be gained ; to wit, first, it is a smoke ; so are all the vanities of this world. Secondly, it delightest them that take it ; so do all the pleasures of the world delight the men of the world. Thirdly, it maketh men *drunken* and light in the head ; so do all the vanities of the world, men are drunken therewith. Fourthly, he that taketh tobacco cannot leave it ; it doth bewitch him ; even so the pleasures of the world make men loath to leave them ; they are, for the most part, enchanted with them. And, farther, besides all this, it is like hell in the very substance of it, for it is a stinking loathsome thing, and so is hell.' And, moreover, his majesty declares, that ' were he to invite the devil to a dinner, he should have three dishes ; first, a pig ; second, a poll of ling and mustard ; and, third, a pipe of tobacco for digestion.'

† It appears from Mr. Brodie's experiments, that the essential

made by the Hottentots of this plant, for the purpose of destroying snakes. 'A Hottentot,' says he, 'applied some of it from the short end of his wooden tobacco pipe to the mouth of a snake while darting out his tongue. The effect was as instantaneous as an electric shock ; with a convulsive motion that was momentary, the snake half untwisted itself, and never stirred more ; and the muscles were so contracted, that the whole animal felt hard and rigid, as if dried in the sun.' When used in moderation, tobacco has a soothing effect upon the mind, disposing to placid enjoyment, and mellowing every passion into repose. Its effects, therefore, are inebriating ; and those who habitually indulge in it may with propriety be denominated drunkards. In whatever form it is used, it produces sickness, stupor, bewilderment, and staggering, in those unaccustomed to its use. There is no form in which it can be taken that is not decidedly injurious and disgusting. The whole, from snuffing to plugging, are at once so utterly uncleanly and unnatural, that it is incredible in what manner they ever insinuated themselves into civilized society. A vast quantity of valuable time is wasted by the votaries of tobacco, especially by the smokers ; and that the devotees of snuff are not greatly behind in this respect, will be shown by the following singular calculation of Lord Stanhope :—

' Every professed, inveterate, incurable snuff-taker,' says his Lordship, ' at a moderate computation, takes one pinch in ten minutes. Every pinch, with the agreeable ceremony of blowing and wiping the nose, and other incidental circumstances, consumes a minute and a half. One minute and a half out of every ten, allowing sixteen hours to a snuff-taking day, amounts to two hours and twenty-four minutes out of every natural day, or one day out of ten. One day out of every ten amounts to thirty-six days and a half in a year. Hence, if we suppose the practice to be persisted in forty years, two entire years of the snuff-taker's life will be dedicated to tickling his nose and two more to blowing it. The expense of snuff, snuff-boxes, and handkerchiefs, will be the subject of a second essay, in which it will appear that this luxury encroaches as much on the income of the snuff-taker as it does on his time ; and that by proper application of the time and money thus lost to the public, a fund might be constituted for the discharge of the national debt.'

But this is not the worst of snuffing, for though a moderate quantity taken now and then, may do no harm, yet, in the extent to which habitual snuffers carry it, it is positively pernicious. The membrane which lines the nose gets thickened, the olfactory nerves blunted, and the sense of smell consequently impaired. Nor is this all, for, by the strong inspirations which are made when the powder is drawn up, some of the latter is pretty sure to escape into the stomach. This organ is thence directly subjected to a powerful medicine, which not only acts as a narcotic, but produces heartburn and every other symptom of indigestion. It is generally believed that Napoleon owed his death to the morbid state of his stomach produced by excessive snuffing. Snuffing has also a strong tendency to give a determination to the head, and on this account piethoric subjects should be the very last ever to enter upon the habit. If it were attended with no other inconvenience, the black loathsome discharge from the nose, and swelling and rubicundity of this organ, with other circumstances equally disagreeable, ought to deter every man from becoming a snuffer.

The smoker, while engaged at *his* occupation, is even a happier man than the snuffer. An air of peculiar satisfaction beams upon his countenance ; and as he puffs

forth volumes of fragrance, he seems to dwell in an atmosphere of contented happiness. His illusions have not the elevated and magnificent character of those brought on by opium or wine. There is nothing of Raphael or Michael Angelo in their composition—nothing of the Roman or Venitian schools—nothing of Milton's sublimity, or Ariosto's dazzling romance ; but there is something equally delightful, and in its way, equally perfect. His visions stand in the same relation to those of opium or wine, as the Dutch pictures of Ostade to the Italian ones of Paul Veronese—as Washington Irving to Lord Byron—or as Izaak Walton to Froissart. There is an air of delightful homeliness about them. He does not let his imagination run riot in the clouds, but restrains it to the lower sphere of earth, and meditates delightfully in this less elevated region. If his fancy be unusually brilliant, or somewhat heated by previous drinking, he may see thousands of strange forms floating in the tobacco smoke. He may people it, according to his temperament, with agreeable or revolting images—with flowers and gems springing up, as in dreams before him—or with reptiles, serpents, and the whole host of *diablerie,* skimming, like motes in the sunshine, amid its curling wreaths.

This all that can be said in favour of smoking, and quite enough to render the habit too common to leave any hope of its suppression, either by the weapons of ridicule, or the more summary plan of the Sultan Amurath. In no sense, except as affording a temporary gratification, can it be justified or defended. It pollutes the breath, blackens the teeth, wastes the saliva which is required for digestion, and injures the complexion. In addition to this, it is apt to produce dyspepsia, and other disorders of the stomach ; and in corpulent subjects, it disposes to apoplexy. At the present moment, smoking is fashionable, and crowds of young men are to be seen at all hours walking the streets with cigars in their mouths, annoying the passengers. They seem to consider it manly to be able to smoke a certain number, without reflecting that there is scarcely an old woman in the country who would not beat them to naught with their own weapons, and that they would gain no sort of honour were they able to outsmoke all the burgomasters of Amsterdam. As the practice, however, seems more resorted to by these young gentlemen for the sake of effect, and of exhibiting a little of the *haut ton*, than for any thing else, it is likely soon to die a natural death among them ; particularly as jockeys and porters have lately taken the field in the same way, being determined that no class of the community shall enjoy the exclusive monopoly of street smoking.

The observations made upon the effects of snuffing and smoking, apply in a still stronger degree to chewing. This is the worst way for the health in which tobacco can be used. The waste of saliva is greater than even in smoking, and the derangements of the digestive organs proportionably severe. All confirmed chewers are more than usually subject to dyspepsia and hypochondriasis : and many of them are afflicted with liver complaint, brought on by their imprudent habit.

The most innocent, and at the same time most disgusting way of using tobacco, is plugging, which consists in inserting a short roll of the plant in the nostril, and allowing it to remain there so long as the person feels disposed. Fortunately this habit is as rare as it is abominable ; and it is to be hoped that it will never become common in Great Britain.

I have observed, that persons who are much addicted to liquor have an inordinate liking to tobacco in all its different forms : and it is remarkable that in the early stages of ebriety almost every man is desirous of having a pinch of snuff. This last fact it is not easy to explain, but the former may be accounted for by that incessant

---

oil of tobacco operates very differently from the infusion. The former acts instantly on the heart, suspending its action, even while the animal continues to inspire, and destroying life by producing syncope. The latter appears to operate solely on the brain, leaving the circulation unaffected.

craving after excitement which cling to the system of the confirmed drunkard.

From several of the foregoing circumstances, we are justified in considering tobacco closely allied to intoxicating liquor, and its confirmed votaries as a species of drunkards. At least, it is certain that when used to excess, it gives birth to many of the corporeal and mental manifestations of ebriety.

VI. *Modified by Nitrous Oxide.*—The drunkenness, if it merit that name, from inhaling nitrous oxide, is likewise of a character widely differing from intoxication in general. This gas was discovered by Dr Priestley, but its peculiar effects upon the human body were first perceived in 1799, by Sir Humphrey Davy, who, in the following year, published a very elaborate account of its nature and properties, interspersed with details by some of the most eminent literary and scientific characters of the sensations they experienced on receiving it into their lungs.

According to these statements, on breathing the gas the pulse is accelerated, and a feeling of heat and expansion pervades the chest. The most vivid and highly pleasurable ideas pass, at the same time, through the mind ; and the imagination is exalted to a pitch of entrancing ecstasy. The hearing is rendered more acute, the face is flushed, and the body seems so light that the person conceives himself capable of rising up and mounting into the air. Some assume theatrical attitudes ; others laugh immoderately, and stamp upon the ground. There is an universal increase of muscular power, attended with the most exquisite delight. In a few cases there are melancholy, giddiness, and indistinct vision but generally the feelings are those of perfect pleasure. After these strange effects have ceased, no debility ensues, like that which commonly follows high excitement. On the contrary, the mind is strong and collected, and the body unusually vigorous for some hours after the operation.

At the time of the discovery of the effects of nitrous oxide strong hopes were excited that it might prove useful in various diseases. These, unfortunately have not been realized. Even the alleged properties of the gas have now fallen into some discredit. That it has produced remarkable effects cannot be denied, but there is much reason for thinking that, in many cases, these were in a great measure brought about by the influence of imagination. Philosophers seem to be divided on this point and their conflicting testimonies it is not easy to reconcile. Having tried the experiment of inhaling the gas myself, and having seen it tried upon others, I have no doubt that there is much truth in the reports generally published of its properties, although in many cases, imagination has made these appear greater than they really are. The intoxication which it produces is entirely one *sui generis*, and differs so much from that produced by other agents, that it can hardly be looked upon as the same thing.

The effects of nitrous oxide upon myself, though considerable, were not so striking as I have seen upon others. The principal feelings produced, were giddiness and violent beating in the head, such as occur in the acme of drunkenness. There was also a strong propensity to laugh : it occurs to me, however, that in my own case, and probably in some others, the risible tendency might be controlled by a strong effort of volition, in the same way as in most cases of drunkenness, were the effort imperatively requisite. Altogether I experienced nearly the sensations of highly excited ebriety. ' There was the same seeming lightness and expansion of the head, the same mirthfulness of spirit, and the same inordinate propensity to do foolish things, knowing them to be foolish, as occur in drunkenness in general. I was perfectly aware what I was about, and could, I am persuaded, with some effort, have subjected the whimsies of fancy to the sober dictates of

judgment. In a word, the gas produced precisely a temporary paroxysm of drunkenness, and such a determination of blood upwards as rendered the complexion livid, and left behind some degree of headache. Such are the effects upon myself, but with most people, there is a total unconsciousness of the part they are acting. They perform the most extravagant pranks, and on recovering their self-possession are totally ignorant of the circumstance. Sometimes the gas has an opposite effect, and the person instantly drops down insensible, as if struck by lightning : he recovers, however, immediately. Those who wish to know more of this curious subject, should read Sir H. Davy's work, but, above all, they should try the gas upon themselves. In the mean time I shall lay before the reader the details, in their own words, of the sensations experienced by Messrs Edgeworth and Coleridge, and by Dr Kinglake.

MR EDGEWORTH'S CASE.—' My first sensation was an universal and considerable tremor. I then perceived some giddiness in my head, and a violent dizziness in my sight ; these sensations by degrees subsided, and I felt a great propensity to bite through the wooden mouth-piece, or the tube of the bag through which I inspired the air. After I had breathed all the air that was in the bag, I eagerly wished for more. I then felt a strong propensity to laugh, and did burst into a violent fit of laughter, and capered about the room without having the power of restraining myself. By degrees, these feelings subsided, except the tremor, which lasted for an hour after I had breathed the air, and I felt a weakness in my knees. The principal feeling through the whole of the time, or what I should call the characteristical part of the effect, was a total difficulty of restraining my feelings, both corporeal and mental, or, in other words, not having any command of myself.'

MR COLERIDGE'S CASE.—'The first time I inspired the nitrous oxide, I felt an highly pleasurable sensation of warmth over my whole frame, resembling that which I once remember to have experienced after returning from a walk in the snow into a warm room. The only motion which I felt inclined to make, was that of laughing at those who were looking at me. My eyes felt distended, and, towards the last, my heart beat as if it were leaping up and down. On removing the mouthpiece, the whole sensation went off almost instantly.

'The second time, I felt the same pleasurable sensation of warmth, but not, I think, in quite so great a degree. I wished to know what effect it would have on my impressions : I fixed my eye on some trees in the distance, but I did not find any other effect, except that they became dimmer and dimmer, and looked at last as if I had seen them through tears. My heart beat more violently than the first time. This was after a hearty dinner.

'The third time, I was more violently acted on than in the two former. Towards the last, I could not avoid, nor indeed felt any wish to avoid, beating the ground with my feet ; and, after the mouth-piece was removed, I remained for a few seconds motionless, in great ecstacy.

'The fourth time was immediately after breakfast. The first few inspirations affected me so little, that I thought Mr Davy had given me atmospheric air ; but soon felt the warmth beginning about my chest, and spreading upward and downward, so that I could feel its progress over my whole frame. My heart did not beat so violently ; my sensations were highly pleasurable, not so intense or apparently local, but of more unmingled pleasure than I had ever before experienced.'

DR KINGLAKE'S CASE.—'My first inspiration of it was limited to four quarts, diluted with an equal quantity of atmospheric air. After a few inspirations, a sense of additional freedom and power (call it energy, if you please) agreeably pervaded the region of the lungs ; this was quickly succeeded by an almost delirious but highly pleasurable sensation in the brain, which was soon diffused over the whole frame, imparting to the muscular power at once an increased disposition and tone for action ; but the mental effect of the excitement was such as to absorb in a sort of intoxicating placidity and delight, volition, or rather the power of voluntary motion. These effects were in a greater or less degree protracted during about five minutes, when the former state returned, with the difference however of feeling more cheerful and alert, for several hours after.

'It seemed also to have had the farther effect of reviving rheumatic irritations in the shoulder and knee-joints, which had not been previously felt for many months. No perceptible change was induced in the pulse, either at or subsequent to the time of inhaling the gas.

'The effects produced by a second trial of its powers, were more extensive, and concentrated on the brain. In this instance, nearly six quarts undiluted, were accurately and fully inhaled. As on the former occasion, it immediately proved agreeably respirable, but before the whole quantity was quite exhausted, its agency was exerted so strongly on the brain, as progressively to suspend the senses of seeing, hearing, feeling, and ultimately the power of volition itself. At this period, the pulse was much augmented both in force and frequency ; slight convulsive twitches of muscles of the arms were also induced ; no painful sensation, nausea, or languor, however, either preceded, accompanied or followed this state, nor did a minute elapse before the brain rallied, and resumed its wonted faculties, when a sense of glowing warmth extended over the system, was speedily succeeded by a re-instatement of the equilibrium of health.

'The more permanent effects were (as in the first experiment) an invigorated feel of vital power, improved spirits, transient irritations in different parts, but not so characteristically rheumatic as in the former instance.

'Among the circumstances most worthy of regard in considering the properties and administration of this powerful aerial agent, may be ranked, the fact of its being contrary to the prevailing opinion, both respirable, and salutary ; that it impresses the brain and system at large with a more or less strong and durable degree of pleasurable sensation ; that unlike the effect of other violently exciting agents, no sensible exhaustion or diminution of vital power accrues from the exertions of its stimulant property ; that its most excessive operation even, is neither permanently nor transiently debilitating ; and finally, that it fairly promises, under judicious application, to prove an extremely efficient remedy, as well in the vast tribe of diseases originating from deficient irritability and sensibility, as in those proceeding from morbid associations, and modifications of those vital principles.'*

CHAPTER VI.

ENUMERATION OF THE LESS COMMON INTOXICATING AGENTS.

In this chapter, I shall content myself with the enumeration of a few of the less common intoxicating agents. To detail all the productions of nature which have the power of inebriating, would be an endless and uninteresting topic.

Hemlock.—A powerful narcotic, producing giddiness, elevation of spirits, and other symptoms of ebriety. It was by an effusion of the leaf of this plant that Socrates was poisoned.

Leopard's-bane.—(*Arnica montana.*)—Properties analogous to those of hemlock and other narcotics.

* The doses in these experiments, were from five to seven quarts

Bangue.—This is the leaf of a species of wild hemp, growing on the shores of Turkey, and of the Grecian Archipelago. It possesses many of the properties of opium, and is used by the poorer classes of Mussulmen as a substitute for this drug. Before being used, it is dried, and the excissated leaves are either chewed entire, or reduced into a fine powder, and made into pills. Its effects are to elevate the spirits, dispel melancholy, and give increased energy to the corporeal faculties—followed by languor both of body and mind.

Hop.—Similar in its effects to opium, only inferior in degree. Used in porter brewing.

Wolf's-bane.—(*Aconitum napellus.*)—A most deadly narcotic, producing, in small doses, the usual symptoms of ebriety, such as giddiness, elevation of spirits, &c. When taken to excess it is inevitably fatal.

Cocculus Indicus.—The intoxicating powers of this berry are considerable. It is used by the brewers to increase the strength of porter and ales ; and is sometimes thrown into ponds for the purpose of intoxicating the fishes, but they may thereby be more easily caught.

Foxglove.—(*Digitalis.*)—Likewise a powerful narcotic, and capable of producing many of the symptoms of drunkenness. It has the peculiar effect of lowering, instead of raising the pulse.

Nightshade.—(*Belladonna.*)—This is one of the most virulent narcotics we possess. Like opium, hop, and cocculus Indicus, it is used by brewers to augment the intoxicating properties of malt liquors. 'The Scots,' says Buchanan, 'mixed a quantity of the juice of the belladonna with the bread and drink with which, by their truce, they were bound to supply the Danes, which so intoxicated them, that the Scots killed the greater part of Sweno's army.'

'Some children ate, in a garden, the fruit of the belladonna, (*deadly nightshade.*) Shortly after, they had burning fever, with convulsions, and very strong palpitations of the heart ; they lost their senses, and became completely delirious : one of them, four years of age, died the next day : the stomach contained some berries of the belladonna crushed, and some seeds ; it exhibited three ulcers ; the heart was livid, and the pericardium without serosity.'*

'One child ate four ripe berries of the belladonna, another ate six. Both one and the other were guilty of extravagancies which astonished the mother ; their pupils were dilated ; their countenances no longer remained the same ; they had a cheerful delirium, accompanied with fever. The physician being called in, found them in a state of great agitation, talking at random, running, jumping, laughing sardonically ; their countenances purple, and pulse hurried. He administered to each of them half a grain of emetic tartar and a drachm of glauber salt, in four or five ounces of water : they had copious evacuations during seven or eight hours, and the symptoms disappeared.'†

Henbane.—(*Hyoscyamus.*)—Similar in its properties to nightshade and opium. The intoxicating properties of hyoscyamus appear to have been known from a very early period. It was with this plant that the Assassin Prince, commonly called the 'Old Man of the Mountain,' inebriated his followers preparatory to installing them into his service. The following eloquent passage from a modern writer will prove interesting :—

'There was at Alamoot, and also at Masiat, in Syria, a delicious garden, encompassed with lofty walls, adorned with trees and flowers of every kind—with murmuring brooks and translucent lakes—with bowers of roses and trellises of the vine—airy halls and splendid kiosks, furnished with carpets of Persia and silks of Byzantium. Beautiful maidens and blooming boys were the inhabitants of this delicious spot, which resounded with the melody of birds, the murmur of

* Journal Générale de Médecine, liv. xxiv. p. 224.
† Gazette de Santé. 11 Thermidor, an xv. p. 908

streams, and the tones and voices of instruments—all respired contentment and pleasure. When the chief had noticed any youth to be distinguished for strength and resolution, he invited him to a banquet, where he placed him beside himself, conversed with him on the happiness reserved for the faithful, and contrived to administer to him an intoxicating draught, prepared from the *hyoscyamus*. While insensible, he was conveyed to the garden of delight, and there awakened by the application of vinegar. On opening his eyes, all Paradise met his view ; the black-eyed and blue-robed houris surrounded him, obedient to his wishes ; sweet music filled his ears ; the richest viands were served up in the most costly vessels, and the choicest wines sparkled in golden cups. The fortunate youth believed himself really in the Paradise of the Prophet, and the language of his attendants confirmed the delusion. When he had had his filled enjoyment, and nature was yielding to exhaustion, the opiate was again administered, and the sleeper transported back to the side of the chief, to whom he communicated what had passed, and who assured him of the truth and reality of all he had experienced, telling him such was the bliss reserved for the obedient servants of the Imaum, and enjoining, at the same time, the strictest secrecy. Ever after, the rapturous vision possessed the imagination of the deluded enthusiast, and he panted for the hour when death, received in obeying the commands of his superior, should dismiss him to the bowers of Paradise.'*

Palm Wine.—This is prepared from the juice which exudes from the palm tree. Its properties are very inebriating ; and it is an amusing fact to witness the stupor and giddiness into which the lizards frequenting these trees are thrown, by partaking of the juice which yields it. They exhibit all the usual phenomena of intoxication.

Camphor.—The intoxicating properties of camphor are considerable. It elevates the spirits, increases voluntary motion, and gives rise to vertigo ; and these effects, as in the case of all narcotics, are succeeded by drowsiness, lassitude, and general depression. In large doses, syncope, convulsions, delirium, and even death, take place. It is sometimes used as a substitute for opium in cases of delirium, where, from particular circumstances, the latter either cannot be taken, or does not produce its usual effects. The common belief, however, of camphor being an antidote to this medicine, is quite unfounded. It neither decomposes opium, nor prevents it from acting poisonously upon the system : but, in consequence of its stimulating properties, it may be advantageously given in small doses to remove the stupor and coma produced by opium.

Saffron.—This aromatic possesses moderate intoxicating properties. Taken in sufficient doses, it accelerates the pulse, produces giddiness, raises the spirits, and gives rise to paroxysms of laughter. In a word, it exhibits many of the phenomena occasioned by overindulgence in liquors, only in a very inferior degree.

Darnel.—Possesses slight intoxicating properties.

Clary.—Possesses slight intoxicating properties.

Carbonic Acid.—Carbonic acid partially inebriates, as is seen in drinking ginger beer, Champagne, or even soda water, in which no alcoholic principle exists.

Ethers.—Ethers, when taken in quantity, give rise to a species of intoxication, which resembles that from ardent spirits in all respects, except in being more fugacious.

Intense Cold.—Intense cold produces giddiness, thickness of speech, confusion of ideas, and other symptoms of drunkenness. Captain Parry speaks of the effects so produced upon two young gentlemen who were exposed to an extremely low temperature. 'They looked wild,' says he, ' spoke thick and indistinctly, and it was impossible to draw from them a

* Von Hammer's Hist. of the Assassins.

rational answer to any of our questions. After being on board for a short time, the mental faculties appeared gradually to return, aud it was not till then that a looker-on could easily persuade himself that they had not been drinking too freely.'

CHAPTER VII.

DIFFERENCES IN THE ACTION OF OPIUM AND ALCOHOL.

The *modus operandi* of opium upon the body is considerably different from that of alcohol. The latter intoxicates chiefly by acting *directly* upon the nerves, the former by acting *secondarily* upon them, through the medium of absorption. This is easily proved by injecting a quantity of each into the cellular tissue of any animal, and comparing the effects with those produced when either is received into the stomach. M. Orfila* details some interesting experiments which he made upon dogs. In applying the watery extract of opium to them in the first manner, (by injection into the cellular tissue,) immediate stupor, convulsions, and debility ensue, and proved fatal in an hour or two. When, on the contrary, even a larger quantity was introduced into the stomach of the animal, it survived ten, twelve, or eighteen hours, although the œsophagus was purposely tied to prevent vomiting. The operation of alcohol was the reverse of this; for, when injected into the cellular substance, the effects were slight ; but when carried into the stomach, they were powerful and almost instantaneous. This proves that opium acts chiefly by being taken up by the absorbents, as this is done much more rapidly by the drug being directly applied to a raw surface than in the stomach, where the various secretions and processes of digestion retard its absorption. Besides, alcohol taken in quantity produces instant stupefaction. It is no sooner swallowed than the person drops down insensible. Here is no time for absorption ; the whole energies of the spirit are exerted against the nervous system. The same rapid privation of power never occurs after swallowing opium. There is always an interval, and generally one of some extent, between the swallowing and the stupor which succeeds. Another proof that opium acts in this manner, is the circumstance of its being much more speedily fatal than alcohol, when injected into the bloodvessels. Three or four grains in solution, forced into the carotid artery of a dog, will kill him in a few minutes. Alcohol, used in the same manner, would not bring on death for several hours.

In addition it may be stated, that a species of drunkenness is produced by inhaling the gas of intoxicating liquors. Those employed in bottling spirits from the cask, feel it frequently with great severity. This proves that there is a close sympathy between the nerves of the nose and lungs, and those of the stomach. From all these circumstances, it is pretty evident that intoxication from spirits is produced more by the direct action of the fluid upon the nerves of the latter organ, than by absorption.

Mr Brodie supposes that there is no absorption whatever of alcohol, and supports his views with a number of striking facts.* This, however, is a length to

* Toxiologi Générale.

† The following are the grounds on which he supports his doctrine :—' 1. In experiments where animals have been killed by the injection of spirits into the stomach, I have found this organ to bear the marks of great inflammation, but never any preternatural appearances whatever in the brain. 2. The effects of spirits taken into the stomach, in the last experiment, were so instantaneous, that it appears impossible that absorption should have taken place before they were produced. 3. A person who is intoxicated frequently becomes suddenly sober after vomiting. 4. In the experiments which I have just related, I mixed tincture of rhubarb with the spirits, knowing, from the experiments of Mr Home and Mr William Brande, that this (*rhubarb*) when absorbed into the circulation, was readily separated from the blood by the kidneys; and that very small quantities might be

which I cannot go. I am inclined to think that though such absorption is not necessary to produce drunkenness, it generally takes place to a greater or lesser degree ; nor can I conceive any reason why alcohol may not be taken into the circulation as well as any other fluid. My reasons for supposing that it is absorbed are the following :—1. The blood, breath, and perspiration of a confirmed drunkard differ from those of a sober man ; the former being darker, and the two latter strongly impregnated with a spiritous odour. 2. The perspiration of the wine-drinker is often of the hue of his favourité liquor ; after a debauch on Port, Burgundy, or Claret, it is not uncommon to see the shirt or sheets in which he lies, tinted to a rosy colour by the moisture which exudes from his body. 2. Madder, mercury, and sulphur, are received into the circulation unchanged ; the former dyeing the bones, and the others exhaling through the pores of the skin, so as to communicate their peculiar odours to the person, and even discolour coins and other metallic substances in his pockets. The first of these reasons is a direct proof of absorption : the second shows, that as wine is received into the circulation, and passes throught it, alcohol may do the same ; and the third furnishes collateral evidence of other agents exhibiting this phenomenon as well as spiritous liquors. The doctrine of absorption is supported by Dr Trotter,* who conceives that alcohol de-oxygenizes the blood, and causes it to give out an unusual portion of hydrogen gas. The quantity of this gas in the bodies of drunkards is so great, that many have attempted to explain from it the circumstances of *Spontaneous Combustion,* by which it is alleged, the human frame has been sometimes destroyed, by being burned to ashes.

CHAPTER VIII.

PHYSIOLOGY OF DRUNKENNESS.

In administering medicines, the practitioner has a natural desire to learn the means by which they produce their effects upon the body. Thus, he is not contented with knowing that squill acts as a diuretic, and that mercury increases the secretion of the bile. He inquires by what process they do so ; and understands that the first excites into increased action the secretory arteries of the kidneys, and the last the secretory veins of the liver. In like manner, he does not rest satisfied with the trite knowledge that wines, and spirits, and ales, produce intoxication: he extends his researches beyond this point, and is naturally anxious to ascertain by what peculiar action of the system these agents give rise to so extraordinary an effect.

All the agents of which we have spoken, with the exception of tobacco, whose action from the first is decidedly sedative, operate partly by stimulating the frame. They cause the heart to throb more vigorously, and the blood to circulate freer, while, at the same time, they exert a peculiar action upon the nervous system. The nature of this action, it is probable, will never be satisfactorily explained. If mere stimulation were all that was wanted, drunkenness ought to be present in many cases where it is never met with. It, or more properly speaking, its symptoms, ought to exist in inflammatory fever, and after violent exercise, such as running or hard walking. Inebriating agents, therefore, with few exceptions, have a twofold action. They both act by increasing the circulation, and by influencing the nerves ; and the latter operation, there can be no doubt, is the more important of the two. Having stated this general fact, it will be better to consider the cause of each individual symptom in detail.

detected in the urine by the addition of potash.; but though I never failed to find urine in the bladder, I never detected rhubarb in it.'—*Phil. Trans. of the Roy. Soc. of Lond.* 1811. part I. p. 178.
—.* Essay on Drunkenness.

I. *Vertigo.*—This is partly produced by the occular delusions under which the drunkard labours, but it is principally owing to other causes ; as it is actually greater when the eyes are shut than when they are open—these causes, by the exclusion of light, being unaccountably increased. Vertigo, from intoxication, is far less liable to produce sickness and vomiting than from any other cause ; and when it does produce them, it is to a very inconsiderable degree. These symptoms, in ninety-nine cases out of a hundred, arise from the disordered state of the stomach, and not, as we have elsewhere mentioned, from the accompanying giddiness. There are, indeed, a certain class of subjects who vomit and become pale, as soon as vertigo comes over them, but such are few in number compared with those whose stomachs are unaffected by this sensation. In swinging, smoking, sailing at sea, on turning rapidly round, sickness and vomiting are apt to occur ; and there seems no doubt that they proceed in a great measure from the vertigo brought on by these actions. The giddiness of drunkenness, therefore, as it very rarely sickens, must be presumed to have some characters peculiar to itself. In this, as well as in some other affections, it seems to be the consequence of a close sympathy between the brain and nerves of the stomach ; and whatever affects the latter organ, or any other viscus sympathizing with it, may bring it on equally with inebriating agents : calculi in the ureters or biliary ducts are illustrations of this fact. In intoxication, the giddiness is more strongly marked, because the powers both of body and mind are temporarily impaired, and the sensorium so disordered as to be unable to regulate the conduct.

A degree of vertigo may be produced by loading the stomach too rapidly and copiously after a long fast. Common food, in this instance, amounts to a strong stimulus in consequence of the state of the stomach, in which there was an unnatural want of excitement. This organ was in a state of torpor ; and a stimulus which, in ordinary circumstances, would hardly have been felt, proves, in reality, highly exciting. For the same reason, objects have an unnatural luminousness when a person is suddenly brought from intense darkness to a brilliant light.

II. *Double Vision.*—The double vision which occurs in drunkenness may be readily accounted for by the influence of increased circulation in the brain upon the nerves of sight. In frenzy, and various fevers, the same phenomenon occurs. Every nerve is supplied with vessels ; and it is conceivable that any unusual impulse of blood into the optics may so far affect that pair as to derange their actions. Whence, they convey false impressions to the brain,-which is itself too much thrown off its just equilibrium to remedy, even if that under any circumstances were possible, the distorted images of the retina. The refraction of light in the tears, which are secreted more copiously than usual during intoxication, may also assist in multiplying objects to the eye.

III. *Staggering and Stammering.*—These symptoms are, in like manner, to be explained from the disordered state of the brain and nervous system. When the organ of sensation is affected, it is impossible that parts whose actions depend upon it can perform their functions well. The nervous fluid is probably carried to the muscles in a broken and irregular current, and the filaments which are scattered over the body are themselves directly stunned and paralyzed ; hence, the insensibility to pain, and other external impressions. This insensibility extends everywhere, even to the organs of diglutition and speech. The utterance is thick and indistinct, indicating a loss of power in the lingual nerves which give action to the tongue ; and the same want of energy seems to prevail in the gustatory branches which give it tase.

IV. *Heat and Flushing.*—These result from the strong determination of blood to the surface of the body. This reddens and tumefies the face and eyes, and excites an universal glow of heat. Blood is the cause of animal heat, and the more it is determined to any part, the greater is the quantity of caloric evolved therefrom.

V *Ringing in the Ears.*—This is accounted for by the generally increased action within the head, and more particularly by the throbbing of the internal carotid arteries which run in the immediate neighbourhood of the ears.

VI. *Elevation of Spirits.*—The mental pleasure of intoxication is not easily explained on physiological principles. We feel a delight in being rocked gently, in swinging on a chair, or in being tickled. These undoubtedly act upon the nerves, but in what manner, it would be idle to attempt investigating. Intoxicating agents no doubt do the same thing. The mental manifestations produced by their influence depend almost entirely upon the nerves, and are, unlike the corporeal ones, in a great measure independent of vascular excitement. The power of exciting the feelings inherent in these principles, can only be accounted for by supposing a most intimate relation to subsist between the body and the mind. The brain, through the medium of its nervous branches, is the source of all this excitement. These branches receive the impressions and convey them to their fountain-head, whence they are showered like sparkling rain-drops over the mind, in a thousand fantastic varieties. No bodily affection ever influences the mind but through the remote or proximate agency of this organ. It sits enthroned in the citadel of thought, and, though material itself, acts with wizard power both upon matter and spirit. No other texture has the same pervading principle. If the lungs be diseased, we have expectoration and cough; if the liver, jaundice or dropsy; if the stomach, indigestion; but when the brain is affected, we have not merely many bodily symptoms, but severe affections of the mind; nor are such affections ever produced by any organ but through the agency of the brain. It therefore acts in a double capacity upon the frame, being both the source of the corporeal feelings, and of the mental manifestations. Admitting this truth, there can be little difficulty in apprehending why intoxication produces so powerful a mental influence. This must proceed from a resistless impulse being given to the brain, by virtue of the peculiar action of inebriating agents upon the nerves. That organ of the mind is suddenly endowed with increased energy. Not only does the blood circulate through it more rapidly, but an action, *sui generis,* is given to its whole substance. Mere increase of circulation, as we have already stated, is not sufficient: there must be some other principle at work upon its texture; and it is this principle, whatever it may be, which is the main cause of drunkenness. At first, ebriety has a soothing effect, and falls over the spirit like the hum of bees, or the distant murmur of a cascade. Then to these soft dreams of Elysium succeed a state of maddening energy and excitement in the brain. The thoughts which emanate from its prolific tabernacle, are more fervid and original than ever—they rush out with augmented copiousness, and sparkle over the understanding like the aurora borealis, or the eccentric scintillations of light upon a summer cloud. In a word, the organ is excited to a high, but not a diseased action, for this is coupled with pain, and, instead of pleasurable, produces afflicting ideas. But its energies, like those of any other part, are apt to be over-excited. When this takes place, the balance is broken; the mind gets tumultuous and disordered, and the ideas inconsistent, wavering, and absurd. Then come the torpor and exhaustion subsequent on such excessive stimulus. The person falls into drowsiness or stupor, and his mind, as well as his body, is followed by languor corresponding to the previous excitation.

Such is a slight and unsatisfactory attempt to eluci-

date some of the more prominent phenomena of drunkenness. Some are omitted as being too obvious to require explanation, and others have been elsewhere cursorily accounted for in differents parts of the word.

CHAPTER IX

METHOD OF CURING THE FIT OF DRUNKENNESS.

1. *From Liquors.*—Generally speaking, there is no remedy for drunkenness equal to vomiting. The sooner the stomach is emptied of its contents the better, and this may, in most cases, be accomplished by drinking freely of tepid water, and tickling the fauces. On more obstinate occasions, powerful emetics will be necessary. The best for the purpose, are ten grains of sulphate of copper, half a drachm of sulphate of zinc, or five grains of tartar emetic. Either of these should be dissolved in a small quantity of tepid water, and instantly swallowed. Should this treatment fail in effecting vomiting, and dangerous symptoms supervene, the stomach pump should be employed. Cold applications to the head are likewise useful. In all cases, the head ought to be well elevated, and the neckcloth removed, that there may be no impediment to the circulation. Where there is total insensibility, where the pulse is slow and full, the pupils dilated, the face flushed, and the breathing stertorous, it becomes a question whether blooding might be useful. Darwin* and Trotter speak discouragingly of the practice. As a general rule I think it is bad; and that many persons who would have recovered, if left to themselves, have lost their lives by being prematurely bled. In all cases it should be done cautiously, and not for a considerable time. Vomiting and other means should invariably be first had recourse to, and if they fail, and nature is unable of her own power to overcome the stupor, blooding may be tried. In this respect, liquors differ from opium the insensibility from which is benefitted by abstraction of blood.

There is one variety of drunkenness in which both blooding and cold are inadmissible. This is when a person is struck down, as it were, by drinking suddenly a great quantity of ardent spirits. Here he is overcome by an instantaneous stupor: his countenance is ghastly and pale, his pulse feeble, and his body cold, While these symptoms continue, there is no remedy but vomiting. When, however, they wear off, and are succeeded, as they usually are by flushing, heat, and general excitement, the case is changed, and must be treated as any other where such symptoms exist.

The acetate of ammonia is said to possess singular properties in restoring from intoxication. This fact was ascertained by M. Masurer, a French chemist. According to him, from twenty to thirty drops in a glass of water, will, in most cases, relieve the patient from the sense of giddiness and oppression of the brain; or, if that quantity should be insufficient, half the same may be again given in eight or ten minutes after. In some csses the remedy will occasion nausea or vomiting, which, however, will be salutary to the patient, as the state of the brain is much aggravated by the load on the stomach and subsequent indigestion. It is also farther stated that the value of this medicine is greatly enhanced from its not occasioning that heat of the stomach and subsequent inflammation which are apt to be produced by pure ammonia. Whether it possesses all the virtues attributed to it, I cannot say from personal observation, having never had occasion to use it in any case which came under my management; but I think it at least promises to be useful, and is, at all events,

---

* Zoonomia.

worthy of a trial. I must mention, however, that the acetate of ammonia is seldom to be procured in the highly concentrated state in which it is used by M. Masurer. Owing to the great difficulty of crystallizing it, it is rarely seen except in the fluid state, in which condition it is recommended by the French chemist. The form in which it is almost always used in this country is that of the Aq. Acet. Ammon. or Spirit of Mindererus, in doses of half an ounce or an ounce, but whether in this shape it would be equally effectual in obviating the effects of drunkenness, remains to be seen.

Mr Broomley of Deptford recommends a draught composed of two drachms of Aq. Ammon. Aromat. in two ounces of water, is an effectual remedy in drunkenness.

The carbonate of ammonia might be used with a good effect. M. Dupuy, director to the veterinary school at Toulouse, tried a curious experiment with this medicine upon a horse. Having previously intoxicated the animal by injecting a demiletre of alcohol into the jugular vein, he injected five grains of the carbonate of ammonia, dissolved in an ounce of water, into the same vein, when the effects of the alcohol immediately ceased.

We have already mentioned that the excitement of drunkenness is succeeded by universal languor. In the first stage, the drunkard is full of energy, and capable of withstanding vigorously all external influences. In the second, there is general torpor and exhaustion, and he is more than usually subject to every impression, whether of cold or contagion. Persons are often picked up half dead in the second stage. The stimulus of intoxication had enabled them to endure the chill of the atmosphere, but the succeeding weakness left them more susceptible than before of its severity. In this state the body will not sustain any farther abstraction of stimuli ; and blooding and cold would be highly injurious. Vomiting is here equally necessary, as in all other instances ; but the person must be kept in a warm temperature, and cherished with light and nourishing food—with soups, if such can be procured, and even with negus, if the protrastration of strength is very great.

A paroxysm of *periodical* drunkenness may be sometimes shortened by putting such small quantities of tartar emetic into the liquor which the person indulges in, as to bring on nausea. This, however, must be done with secrecy and caution.

It may here be mentioned, though not with a view of recommending the practice, that the vegetable acids have a strong effect both in counteracting and removing drunkenness. To illustrate this fact, the following circumstance may be mentioned :—About twenty years ago, an English regiment was stationed in Glasgow, the men of which, as is common in all regiments, became enamoured of whiskey. This liquor, to which they gave the whimsical denomination of *white ale*, was new to them—being nearly unknown in England : and they soon indulged in it to such an extent, as to attract the censure of their officers. Being obliged to be at quarters by a certain hour, they found out the plan of sobering themselves by drinking large quantities of vinegar, perhaps a gill or two at a draught. This, except in very bad cases, had the desired effect, and enabled them to enter the barrack-court, or appear on parade, in a state of tolerable sobriety. The power of the vegetable acids in resisting intoxication, is well shown in the case of cold punch—a larger portion of which can be withstood than of either grog or toddy, even when the quantity of spirit is precisely the same.

There is nothing which has so strong a tendency to dispel the effects of a debauch as hard exercise especially if the air be cold. Aperients and diaphoretics are also extremel useful for the same purpose.

For some days after drinking too much, the food

should be light and unirritating, consisting principally of vegetables. Animal food is apt to heat the body, and dispose it to inflammatory complaints.*

II. *From Opium.*—When a dangerous quantity of opium has been taken, the treatment, in the first instance is the same as with regard to spirits, or any other intoxicating fluid. Immediate vomiting, by the administration of similar emetics, is to be attempted, and when it has taken place, it should be encouraged by warm drinks till there is reason to believe that the stomach has been freed of the poison. These drinks, however, should not be given before vomiting is produced, for, in the event of their failing to excite it, they remain upon the stomach, and thus dissolve the opium and promote its absorption. But when vomiting occurs from the action of the emetics, it will in all probability be encouraged by warm drinks, and the stomach thus more effectually cleared of the poison. Large quantities of a strong infusion of coffee ought then to be given, or the vegetable acids, such as vinegar or lemon-juice, mixed with water. These serve to mitigate the bad consequences which often follow, even after the opium has been brought completely up. If the person show signs of apoplexy, more especially if he be of a plethoric habit, the jugular vein, or temporal artery should be opened, and a considerable quantity of blood taken away. Indeed, it may be laid down as a general rule, that as soon as the poison is rejected, the patient ought to be bled, and the operation should be repeated according to circumstances. Every means must be used to arouse him from stupor. He must be moved about, if possible, from room to room, hartshorn applied to his nostrils, and all plans adopted to prevent him from sinking into lethargy. For this purpose, camphor, assafœtida, or musk, might be administered with advantage. It is also a good practice to sponge the body well with cold water ; and the effusion of cold water on the head and over the body, is still more effectual. In cases where vomiting cannot be brought about by the ordinary means, M. Orfila suggests that one or two grains of tartar emetic, dissolved in an ounce or two of water, might be injected into the veins. In desperate cases, the stomach pump must be had recourse to. Purgatives are latterly necessary.

Many practitioners consider vinegar and the other vegetable acids antidotes to opium. This opinion M. Orfila has most satisfactorily shown to be erroneous. In a series of well-conducted and conclusive experiments made by him, it appears that the vegetable acids aggravate the symptoms of poisoning by opium, whenever they are not vomited. They hurry them on more rapidly, render them more violent, produce death at an earlier period, and give rise to an inflammation of the stomach—an event which hardly ever occurs when they are not employed. These effects, it would appear, are partly produced by their power of dissolving opium, which they do better than the mere unassisted fluids of the stomach ; consequently the absorption is more energetic. The only time when acids can be of any use, is after the person has brought up the poison by vomiting. They then mitigate the subsequent symptoms, and promote recovery ; but if they be swallowed before vomiting takes place, and if this act cannot by any means be brought about, they aggravate the disorder,

* In speaking of the treatment, it is necesary to guard against confounding other affections with drunkenness :—' There is a species of delirium that often attends the accession of *typhus fever*, from contagion, that I have known to be mistaken for ebriety. Among seamen and soldiers, whose habits of intoxication are common, it will sometimes require nice discernment to decide ; for the vacant stare in the countenance, the look of idiotism, incoherent speech, faltering voice, and tottering walk, are so alike in both cases, that the naval and military surgeon ought at all times to be very cautious how he gives up a man to punishment, under these suspicious circumstances. Nay, the appearances of his having come from a tavern, with even the effluvium of liquor about him, are signs not always to be trusted ; for these haunts of seamen and soldiers are often the sources of infection. —*Trotter.*

S

and death ensues more rapidly than if they had not been taken.

Coffee has likewise a good effect when taken after the opium is got off the stomach; but it differs from the acids in this, that it does not, under any circumstances, increase the danger. While the opium is still unremoved, the coffee may be considered merely inert; and it is, therefore, a matter of indifference whether at this time it be taken or not. Afterwards, however, it produces the same beneficial effects as lemonade, tartaric acid, or vinegar. According to Orfila, the infusion is more powerful as an antidote than the decoction. Drunkenness or poisoning from the other narcotics, such as hemlock, belladonna, aconite, hyoscyamus, &c., is treated precisely in the same manner as that from opium.

III. *From Tobacco.*—If a person feel giddy or languid from the use of this luxury, he should lay himself down on his back, exposed to a current of cool air. Should this fail of reviving him, let him either swallow twenty or thirty drops of hartshorn, mixed with a glass of cold water, or an ounce of vinegar moderately diluted. When tobacco has been received into the stomach, so as to produce dangerous symptoms, a powerful emetic must immediately be given, and vomiting encouraged by copious drinks, till the poison is brought up. After this, vinegar ought to be freely exhibited, and lethargy prevented by the external and internal use of stimuli. If apoplectic symptoms appear, blooding must be had recourse to. The same rule applies here, with regard to acids, as in the case of opium. They should never be given till the stomach is thoroughly liberated of its contents by previous vomiting.

Accidents happen oftener with tobacco than is commonly supposed. Severe languor, retching, and convulsive attacks sometimes ensue from the application of ointment made with this plant, for the cure of the ring-worm; and Santeuil, the celebrated French poet, lost his life in consequence of having unknowingly drunk a glass of wine, into which had been put some Spanish snuff.

IV. *From Nitrous Oxide.* Though the inhalation of this gas is seldom attended with any risk, yet, in very plethoric habits, there might be a determination of blood to the head, sufficient to produce apoplexy. If a person therefore becomes after the experiment, convulsed, stupified, and livid in the countenance, and if these symptons do not soon wear away, some means must be adopted for their removal. In general, a free exposure to fresh air, and dashing cold water over the face, will be quite sufficient; but if the affection is so obstinate as to resist this plan, it will then be necessary to draw some blood from the arm, or, what is still better, from the jugular vein. When, in delicate subjects, hysteria and other nervous symptoms are produced, blooding is not necessary; all that is requisite to be done being the application of cold water to the brow or temples, and of hartshorn to the nostrils. In obstinate cases, twenty or thirty drops of the latter in a glass of water, may be administered with advantage.

CHAPTER X.

PATHOLOGY OF DRUNKENNESS.

The evil consequences of drinking, both in a physical and moral point of view, seem to have been known from the most remote antiquity. They are expressly mentioned in Scripture; nor can there be a doubt that the Homeric fiction of the companions of Ulysses being turned into swine by the enchanted cup of Circe, plainly implied the bestial degradation into which men bring themselves by coming under the dominion of so detestable habit. Having mentioned these circumstances in favour of the accuracy of ancient knowledge, we shall simply proceed to detail the effects of drunkenness so far as the medical practitioner is professionally interested in knowing them. The moral consequences belong more properly to the legislator and divine, and do not require to be here particularly considered.

I. *State of the Liver.*—One of the most common consequences of drunkenness is acute inflammation. This may affect any organ, but its attacks are principally confined to the brain, the stomach, and the liver. It is unnecessary to enter into any detail of its nature and treatment. These are precisely the same as when it proceeds from any other cause. The inflammation of drunkenness is, in a great majority of cases, chronic; and the viscus which, in nine cases out of ten, suffers, is the liver.

Liquors, from the earliest ages, have been known to affect this organ. Probably the story of Prometheus stealing fire from heaven and animating clay, alluded to the effects of wine upon the human body; and the punishment of having his liver devoured by a vulture may be supposed to refer to the consequences which men draw upon themselves, by over-indulgence—this organ becoming thereby highly diseased. Man is not the only animal so affected. Swine who are fed on the refuse of breweries, have their livers enlarged in the same manner. Their other viscera become also indurated, and their flesh so tough, that unless killed early, they are unfit to be eaten. Some fowl-dealers in London are said to mix gin with the food of the birds, by which means they are fattened, and their livers swelled to a great size. The French manage to enlarge this organ in geese, by piercing it shortly after the creatures are fledged.[*]

Neither malt liquors nor wine have so rapid and decided an effect upon the liver as ardent spirits. Indeed, it is alleged, although I cannot go this length, that the wine that is *perfectly pure* does not affect the liver; and the fact of our continental neighbours being much less troubled with hepatic complaints than the wine-drinkers among ourselves, gives some countenance to the allegation; for it is well known that to suit the British market, the vinous liquors used in this country are sophisticated with brandy. In wine that is perfectly pure the alcohol exists in such a state of chemical combination, as greatly to modify its effects upon the system. In the wine generally to be met with, much of it exists mechanically or uncombined, and all this portion of spirit acts precisely in the same manner as if separately used.[†]

The liver is a viscus which, in confirmed topers, never escapes; and it withstands disease better than any other vital part, except, perhaps, the spleen. Sometimes, by a slow chronic action, it is enlarged to double its usual size, and totally disorganized, and yet the person suffers comparatively little. The disease frequently arises in tropical climates, from warmth and other natural causes, but an excess in spirituous liquors is more frequently the cause than is generally imagined.

The consequences which follow chronic inflammation of the liver, are very extensive. The bile, in general, is not secreted in due quantity or quality, consequently digestion is defective, the bowels, from want of their usual stimulus, become torpid. The person gets jaundiced, his skin becoming yellow, dry, and rough, and the white of his eyes discoloured. As the enlargement goes on, the free passage of blood in the veins is impeded, and their extremities throw out lymph: this accumulating, forms dropsy, a disease with which a great proportion of drunkards are ultimately more or less affected.

The jaundice of drunkenness is not an original dis-

---

[*] 'They have a custom of fostering a liver complaint in their geese, which encourages its growth to the enormous weight of some pounds; and this diseased viscus is considered a great delicacy.'—*Matthew's Diary of an invalid.*

[†] Vide Appendix No. 1.

ease, but merely a symptom of the one under consideration A very slight cause will often bring it on; it is, consequently, not always dangerous. Dropsy is, for the most part, also symptomatic of diseased liver, but sometimes, more especially in dram-drinkers, it arises from general debility of the system. In the former case, effusion always takes place in the cavity of the abdomen. In the latter, there is general anasarca throughout the body, usually coupled with more or less topical affection. In every instance, dropsy, whether general or local, is a very dangerous disease.

II. *State of the Stomach, &c.*—Like the liver, the stomach is more subject to chronic than acute inflammation. It is also apt to get indurated, from long-continued, slow action going on within its substance. This disease is extremely insidious, frequently proceeding great lengths before it is discovered. The organ is often thickened to half an inch, or even an inch; and its different tunics so matted together that they cannot be separated. The pyloric orifice becomes, in many cases, contracted. The cardiac may suffer the same disorganization, and so may the œsophagus; but these are less common, and, it must be admitted, more rapidly fatal. When the stomach is much thickened, it may sometimes be felt like a hard ball below the left ribs. At this point there is also a dull uneasy pain, which is augmented upon pressure.

Indigestion or spasm may arise from a mere imperfect action of this organ, without any disease of its structure: but when organic derangement takes place, they are constant attendants. In the latter case it is extremely difficult for any food to remain on the stomach; it is speedily vomited. What little is retained undergoes a painful fermentation, which produces sickness and heartburn. There is, at the same time, much obstinacy in the bowels, and the body becomes emaciated.

This disease, though generally produced by dissipation, originates sometimes from other causes, and affects the soberest people. Whenever the stomach is neglected, when acidity is allowed to become habitual, or indigestible food too much made use of, the foundation may be laid for slow inflammation, terminating in schirrus and all its bad consequences.

Vomiting of bilious matter in the mornings, is a very common circumstance among all classes of drunkards. But there is another kind of vomiting, much more dangerous, to which they are subject; and that is when inflammation of the villous coat of the stomach takes place. In such a state there is not much acute pain, but rather a dull feeling of uneasiness over the abdomen, attended with the throwing up of a dark, crude matter, resembling coffee grounds. I have seen two cases in which the vomiting stopped suddenly, in consequence of metastasis to the head. In these, the affection soon proved fatal, the persons being seized with indistinctness of vision, low delirium, and general want of muscular power: the action of the kidneys was also totally suspended for three days before death. On examination, *post mortem*, there was effusion in the ventricles of the brain, besides extensive inflammation along the inner surface of the upper portion of the alimentary canal.

Bilious complaints, which were formerly in a great measure unknown to the common people, are now exceedingly common among them, and proceed in a great measure from the indulgence in ardent spirits to which that class of society is so much addicted.

There is nothing more indicative of health, than a good appetite for breakfast; but confirmed topers, from the depraved state of their stomachs, lose all relish for this meal.

Persons of this description are generally of a costive habit of body, but a debauch, with those who are constitutionally sober is, for the most part, followed by more or less diarrhœa.

In the latter stages of a drunkard's life, though he has still the relish for liquor as strongly as ever, he no longer enjoys his former power of withstanding it. This proceeds from general weakness of the system, and more particularly of the stomach. This organ gets debilitated, and soon gives way, while the person is intoxicated much easier, and often vomits what he has swallowed. His appetite likewise fails; and, to restore it, he has recourse to various bitters, which only aggravate the matter, especially as they are in most cases taken under the medium of ardent spirits. Bitters are often dangerous remedies. When used moderately, and in cases of weak digestion from natural causes, they frequently produce the best effects; but a long continuance of them is invariably injurious. There is a narcotic principle residing in most bitters, which physicians have too much overlooked. It destroys the sensibility of the stomach, determines to the head, and predisposes to apoplexy and palsy. This was the effects of the famous Portland powder,* so celebrated many years ago for the cure of gout; and similar consequences will, in the long run, follow bitters as they are commonly administered. Persons addicted to intemperance, have an inordinate liking for these substances; let them be ever so nauseous, they are swallowed greedily, especially if dissolved in spirits. Their fondness for purl, herb-ale, and other pernicious morning drinks, is equally striking.

There is nothing more characteristic of a tippler than an indifference to tea, and beverages of a like nature. When a woman exhibits this quality, we may reasonably suspect her of indulging in liquor. If drunkards partake of tea, they usually saturate it largely with ardent spirits. The unadulterated fluid is too weak a stimulus for unnatural appetites.

III. *State of the Brain.*—Inflammation of this organ is often a consequence of intemperance. It may fol low immediately after a debauch, or it may arise secondarily from an excess of irritation being applied to the body during the stage of debility. Even an abstraction of stimulus, as by applying too much cold to the head, may bring it on in this latter state.

Dr Armstrong, in his lectures, speaks of a chronic inflammation of the brain and its membranes, proceeding, among other causes, from the free use of strong wines and liquors. According to him, it is much more common after, than before, forty years of age, although he has seen several instances occurring in young persons. The brain gets diseased, the diameter of the vessels being diminished, while their coats are thickened and less transparent than usual. In some places they swell out and assume a varicose appearance. The organ itself has no longer the same delicate and elastic texture, becoming either unnaturally hard, or of a morbid softness. Slight effusions in the various cavities are apt to take place. Under these cirunmstances, there is a strong risk of apoplexy. To this structure is to be ascribed the mental debasement, the loss of memory, and gradual extinction of the intellectual powers. I believe that the brains of all confirmed drunkards exhibit more or less of the above appearances.

IV. *State of the Kidneys.*—During intoxication the action of the kidneys is always much increased; and this is a favourable circumstance, as, more than any thing else, it carries off the bad effects of drinking. The kidney, however, in confirmed drunkards, is apt to become permanently diseased, and secrets its accustomed fluid with unusual activity, not only in the moments of drunkenness, when such an increase is useful, but at all periods, even when the persons abstains from every sort of indulgence. The disease called diabetes

* The Portland Powder consisted of equal parts of the roots of round birthwort and gentian, of the leaves of germander and ground pine, and of the tops of the lesser centaury, all dried. Drs Cullen, Darwin, and Murray of Gottingen, with many other eminent physicians, bear testimony to the pernicious effects of this compound.

is thus produced, which consists in a morbid increase of the secretion, accompanied with a diseased state of the ___ of the kidneys. This affection is mostly fatal texture

V. *State of the Bladder.*—Drunkenness affects this organ in common with almost every other; hence it is subject to paralysis, spasm, induration, &c., and to all bad consequences thence resulting—such as pain, incontinence, and retention of urine.

VI. *State of the Blood and Breath.*—The blood of a professed drunkard, as already stated, differs from that of a sober man. It is more dark, and approaches to the character of venous. The ruddy tint of those carbuncles which are apt to form upon the face, is no proof to the contrary, as the blood which supplies them crimsoned by exposure to the air, on the same principle as that by which the blood in the pulmonary arteries receives purification by the process of breathing. The blood of a malt-liquor drinker is not merely darker, but also more thick and sizy than in other cases, owing, no doubt, to the very nutritious nature of his habitual beverage.

The breath of a drunkard is disgustingly bad, and has always a spiritous odour. This is partly owing to the stomach, which communicates the flavour of its customary contents to respiration; and partly, also, there can be little doubt, to the absorption of the liquor by the blood, through the medium of the lacteals.

VII. *State of the Perspiration.*—The perspiration of a confirmed drunkard is as offensive as his breath, and has often a strong spiritous odour. I have met with two instances, the one in a Claret, the other in a Port drinker, in which the moisture which exuded from their bodies had a ruddy complexion, similar to that of the wine on which they had committed their debauch.

VIII. *State of the Eyes, &c.*—The eyes may be affected with acute or chronic inflammation. Almost all drunkards have the latter more or less. Their eyes are red and watery, and have an expression so peculiar, that the cause can never be mistaken. This, and a certain want of firmness about the lips, which are loose, gross, and sensual, betray at once the topor. Drunkenness impairs vision. The delicacy of the retina is probably affected; and it is evident, that, from long-continued inflammation, the tunica adnata which covers the cornea must lose its original clearness and transparency.

Most drunkards have a constant tenderness and redness of the nostrils. This, I conceive, arises from the state of the stomach and œsophagus. The same membrane which lines them is prolonged upwards to the nose and mouth, and carries thus far its irritability.

There is no organ which so rapidly betrays the Bacchanalian propensities of its owner as the nose. It not only becomes red and fiery, like that of Bardolph,* but acquires a general increase of size—displaying upon its surface various small pimples, either wholly of a deep crimson hue, or tipped with yellow, in consequence of an accumulation of viscid matter within them. The rest of the face often presents the same carbuncled appearance.

I have remarked that drunkards who have a foul, livid, and pimpled face, are less subject to liver com-

* 'Falstaff. Thou art our admiral: thou bearest the lanthorn in the poop; but 'tis in the *nose* of thee: thou art the knight of the burning lamp.
'Bardolph. Why, Sir John, my face does you no harm.
'Falstaff. No, I'll be sworn! I make as good use of it as many a man doth of a death's head or a memento mori. I never see thy face but I think of hell-fire.'—'When thou rann'st up Gads-hill in the night to catch my horse, if I did not think thou hadst been an *ignis fatuus*, or a ball of wildfire, there's no purchase in money. O! thou art a perpetual triumph—an everlasting bonfire light: thou hast saved me a thousand marks in links and torches, walking with me in the night betwixt tavern and tavern; but the Sack thou hast drunk me would have bought me lights as good cheap, at the dearest chandler's in Europe. I have maintained that salamander of yours with fire any time this two and thirty years—heaven reward me for it!'

plaint than those who are free from such eruptions. In this case the determination of blood to the surface of the body seems to prevent that fluid from being directed so forcibly to the viscera as it otherwise would be. The same fact is sometimes observed in sober persons who are troubled with hepatic affection. While there is a copious rush upon the face or body, they are comparatively well, but no sooner does it go in than they are annoyed by the liver getting into disorder.

IX. *State of the Skin.*—The skin of a drunkard, especially if he be advanced in life, has seldom the appearance of health. It is apt to become either livid or jaundiced in its complexion, and feels rough and scaly. There is a disease spoken of by Dr Darwin, under the title of *Psora Ebriorum*, which is peculiar to people of this description. 'Elderly people,' says he, 'who have been much addicted to spiritous drinks, as beer, wine, or alcohol, are liable to an eruption all over their bodies; which is attended with very afflicting itching, and which they probably propagate from one part of their bodies to another with their own nails by scratching themselves.' I have met with several cases of this disease, which is only one of the many forms of morbid action, which the skin is apt to assume in drunkards.

X. *State of the Hair.*—The hair of drunkards is generally dry, slow of growth, and liable to come out; they are consequently more subject to baldness than other people. At the same time, it would be exceedingly unjust to suspect any one, whose hair was of this description, of indulgence in liquors, for we frequently find in the soberest persons that the hairs are arid, few in number, and prone to decay. Baldness with such persons is merely a local affection, but in drunkards it is constitutional, and proceeds from that general defect of vital energy which pervades their whole system.

XI. *Inflammations.*—Drunkards are exceedingly subject to all kinds of inflammation, both from the direct excitement of the liquor, and from their often remaining out in a state of intoxication, exposed to cold and damp. Hence inflammatory affections of the lungs, intestine, bladder, kidneys, brain, &c., arising from these sources. Rheumatism is often traced to the neglect and exposure of a fit of drunkenness.

XII. *Gout.*—Gout is the offspring of gluttony, drunkenness, or sensuality, or of them all put together. It occurs most frequently with the wine-bibber. A very slight cause may bring it on when hereditary predisposition exists; but in other circumstances considerable excess will be required before it makes its appearance. It is one of the most afflicting consequences of intemperance, and seems to have been known as such from an early age—mention being made of it by Hippocrates, Aretæus, and Galen. Among the Roman ladies gout was very prevalent during the latter times of the empire; and, at the present day, there are few noblemen who have it not to hand down to their offspring as a portion of their heritage.

XIII. *Tremors.*—A general tremor is an attendant upon almost all drunkards. This proceeds from nervous irritability. Even those who are habitually temperate, have a quivering in their hands next morning, if they indulge over night in a debauch. While it lasts, a person cannot hold any thing without shaking, neither can he write steadily. Among those who have long devoted themselves to the mysteries of Silenus, this amounts to a species of palsy, affecting the whole body, and even the ï , with a sort of paralytic trembling. On awaking from sleep, they frequently feel it so strongly, as to seem in the cold fit of an ague, being neither able to walk steadily, nor articulate distinctly. It is singular that the very cause of this distemper should be employed for its cure. When the confirmed drunkard awakes with tremor, he immediately swallows a dram: the most violent shaking is quieted by this means. The opium-eater has recourse to the same method : to remove the agitation produced by one dose of opium, he takes another. This, in both cases, is only adding fuel to the fire—the tremors coming on at shorter intervals, and larger doses being required for their removal.

Drunkards are more subject than any other class of people to apoplexy and palsy.

XIV. *Palpitation of the Heart.*—This is a very distressing consequence of drunkenness, producing difficult breathing, and such a determination to the head as often brings on giddiness. Drunkards are apt to feel it as they step out of bed, and the vertigo is frequently so great as to make them stumble. There are some sober persons who are much annoyed by this affection. In them it may arise from spasmodic action of the fibres of the heart, nervous irritability, or organic disease, such as aneurism, or angina pectoris.

XV. *Hysteria.*—Female drunkards are very subject to hysterical affections. There is a delicacy of fibre in women, and a susceptibility of mind, which makes them feel more acutely than the other sex all external influences. Hence their whole system is often violently affected with hysterics and other varieties of nervous weakness. These affections are not always traced to their true cause, which is often neither more nor less than dram-drinking. When a woman's nose becomes crimsoned at the point, her eyes somewhat red, and more watery than before,' and her lips full and less firm and intellectual in their expression, we may suspect that something wrong is going on.

XVI. *Epilepsy.*—Drunkenness may bring on epilepsy, or falling sickness, and may excite it into action in those who have the disease from other causes. Many persons cannot get slightly intoxicated without having an epileptic or other convulsive attack. These fits generally arise in the early stages before drunkenness has got to a height. If they do not occur early the individual will probably escape them altogether for the time.

XVII. *Sterility.*—This is a state to which confirmed drunkards are very subject.' The children of such persons are, in general, neither numerous nor healthy. From the general defect of vital power in the parental system they are apt to be puny and emaciated, and more than ordinarily liable to inherit all the diseases of those from whom they are sprung. On this account, the chances of long life are much diminished among the children of such parents. In proof of this, it is only necessary to remark, that according to the London bills of mortality one-half of the children born in the metropolis die before attaining their third year ; while of the children of the Society of Friends, a class remarkable for sobriety and regularity of all kinds one-half actually attain the age of forty-seven years. Much of this difference, doubtless, originates in the superior degree of comfort, and correct general habits of the Quakers, which incline them to bestow every care in the rearing of their offspring, and put it in their power to obtain the means of combating disease ; but the mainspring of this superior comfort and regularity is doubtless temperance—a virtue which this class of people possess in an eminent degree.

XVIII. *Emaciation.*—Emaciation is peculiarly characteristic of the spirit drinker. He wears away, before his time, into the 'lean and slippered pantaloon' spoken of by Shakspeare in his 'Stages of Human life.' All drunkards, however, if they live long enough, become emaciated. The eyes get hollow, the cheeks fall in, and wrinkles soon furrow the countenance with the marks of age. The fat is absorbed from every part, and the rounded plumpness which formerly characterized the body soon wears away. The whole form gets lank and debilitated. There is a want of due

warmth, and the hand is usually covered with a chill clammy perspiration.

The occurrence of emaciation is not to be wondered at in persons who are much addicted to ardent spirits, for alcohol, besides being possessed of no nutritive properties, prevents the due chymification of the food, and consequently deteriorates the quality, besides diminishing the quantity of the chyle. The principle of nutrition being thus affected, the person becomes emaciated as a natural consequence.

XIX. *Corpulency.*—Malt liquor and wine drinkers are, for the most part, corpulent, a state of body which rarely attends the spirit drinker, unless he be, at the same time, a *bon vivant*. Both wines and malt liquors are more nourishing than spirits. Under their use, the blood becomes, as it were, enriched, and an universal deposition of fat takes place throughout the system. The omentum and muscles of the belly are, in a particular manner, loaded with this secretion ; whence the abdominal protuberance so remarkable in persons who indulge themselves in wines and ales. As the abdomen is the part which becomes most enlarged, so is it that which longest retains its enlargement. It seldom parts with it, indeed, even in the last stages, when the rest of the body is in the state of emaciation. There can be no doubt that the parts which first lose their corpulency are the lower extremities. Nothing is more common than to see a pair of spindle-shanks tottering under the weight of an enormous corporation, to which they seem attached more like artificial appendages, than natural members. The next parts which give way are the shoulders. They fall flat, and lose their former firmness and rotundity of organization. After this, the whole body becomes loose, flabby, and enelastic ; and five years do as much to the constitution as fifteen would have done under a system of strict temperance and sobriety. The worst system that can befall a corpulent man, is the decline of his lower extremities.* So long as they continue firm, and correspondent with the rest of the body, it is a proof that there is still vigor remaining ; but when they gradually get attenuated, while other parts retain their original fullness, there can be no sign more sure that his constitution is breaking down, and that he will never again enjoy his wonted strength.

XX. *Premature Old Age.*—Drunkenness has a dreadful effect in anticipating the effects of age. It causes time to pace on with giant strides—chases youth from the constitution of its victims—and clothes them prematurely with the gray garniture of years. How often do we see the sunken eye, the shrivelled cheek, the feeble, tottering step, and hoary head, in men who have scarcely entered into the autumn of their existence. To witness this distressing picture, we have only to walk out early in the mornings, and see those gaunt, melancholy shadows of mortality, betaking themselves to the gin-shops, as to the altar of some dreadful demon, and quaffing the poisoned cup to his honor, as the Carthaginians propitiated the deity of their worship, by flinging their children into the fire which burned within his brazen image. Most of these unhappy persons are young, or middle-aged men ; and though some drunkards attain a green old age, they are few in number compared with those who sink untimely into the grave ere the days of their youth have well passed by.†

* This circumstance has not escaped the observation of Shakspeare ;—' Chief Justice, Do you set down your name in the scroll of youth that are written down old, with all the characters of age ! Have you not a moist eye, a dry hand, and a yellow cheek, a white beard, a *decreasing* leg, an increasing belly ? Is not your voice broken, your wind short, your chin double, your wit single, and every part of you blasted with antiquity ; and will you yet call yourself young ? Fie, fie, fie, Sir John !'

† ' Let nobody tell me that there are numbers who, though they live most irregularly, attain, in health, and spirits, those remote periods of life attained by the most sober ; for this argument being grounded on a case full of uncertainty and hazard, and which, besides, so seldom occurs as to look more like a mi-

Nothing is more common than to see a man of fifty as hoary, emaciated, and wrinkled, as if he stood on the borders of fourscore.

The effect of intemperance in shortening life is strikingly exemplified in the contrast afforded by other classes of society to the Quakers, a set of people of whom I must again speak favorably. It appears from accurate calculation, that in London only one person in forty attains the age of four-score, while among Quakers, whose sobriety is proverbial, and who have long set themselves against the use of ardent spirits, not less than one in ten reaches that age—a most striking difference, and one which carries its own inference along with it.

It is remarked by an eminent practitioner, that of more than a hundred men in a glass manufactory, three drank nothing but water, and these three appeared to be of their proper age, while the rest who indulged in strong drinks seemed ten or twelve years olders than they proved to be. This is conclusive.*

XXI. *Ulcers.*—Ulcers often break out on the bodies of drunkards. Sometimes they are fiery and irritable, but in general they possess an indolent character. Of whatever kind they may be, they are always aggravated in such constitutions. A slight cause gives rise to them; and a cut or bruise which, in health, would have healed in a few days, frequently degenerates into a foul sloughy sore. When drunkards are affected with scrofula, scurvy, or any cutaneous disease whatever, they always, *cæteris paribus,* suffer more than other people.

XXII. *Melancholy.*—Though drunkards over their cups are the happiest of mankind, yet, in their solitary hours, they are the most wretched. Gnawing care, heightened perhaps by remorse, preys upon their conscience. While sober, they are distressed both in body and mind, and fly to the bowl to drown their misery in oblivion. Those, especially, whom hard fate drove to this desperate remedy, feel the pangs of low spirits with seven-fold force. The weapon they employ to drive away care is turned upon themselves. Every time it is used, it becomes less capable of scaring the fiend of melancholy, and more effectual in wounding him that uses it.

All drunkards are apt to become peevish and discontented with the world. They turn enemies to the established order of things, and, instead of looking to themselves, absurdly blame the government as the origin of their misfortunes.

XXIII. *Madness.*—This terrible infliction often proceeds from drunkenness. When there is hereditary predisposition, indulgence in liquor is more apt to call it into action than when there is none. The mind and body act reciprocally upon one another; and when the one is injured the other must suffer more or less. In intemperance, the structure of the brain is no longer the same as in health; and the mind, that immortal part of man, whose manifestations depend upon this organ, suffers a corresponding injury.

Intoxication may effect the mind in two ways. A person, after excessive indulgence in liquor, may be seized with delirium, and run into a state of violent outrage and madness. In this case the disease comes suddenly on: the man is fierce and intractable, and requires a strait jacket to keep him in order. Some

racle than the work of nature, men should not suffer themselves to be thereby persuaded to live irregularly, nature having been too liberal to those who did so without suffering by it; a favour which very few have any right to expect.'—*Carnaro on Health.*

* 'The workmen in provision stores have large allowances of whiskey bound to them in their engagements. These are served out to them daily by their employers, for the purpose of urging them, by excitement, to extraordinary exertion. And what is the effect of this murderous system? The men are ruined, scarcely one of them being capable of work beyond fifty years of age, though none but the most able-bodied men can enter such employment.'—[Beecher's Sermons on Intemperance, with an Introductory Essay by John Edgar. This is an excellent little work, which I cordially recommend to the perusal of the reader.

never get drunk without being insanely outrageous: they attack, without distinction, all who come in their way, foam at the mouth, and lose all sense of danger. This fit either goes off in a few hours, or degenerates into a confirmed attack of lunacy. More generally, however, the madness of intoxication is of another character, partaking of the contrast of idiotism, into which state the mind resolves itself, in consequence of a long-continued falling off in the intellectual powers.

Drunkenness, according to the reports of Bethlehem Hospital, and other similar institutions for the insane, is one of the most common causes of lunacy. In support of this fact, it may be mentioned that of two hundred and eighty-six lunatics now in the Richmond Asylum, Dublin, one half owe their madness to drinking; and there are few but must have witnessed the wreck of the most powerful minds by this destructive habit. It has a more deplorable effect upon posterity than any other practice, for it entails, not only bodily disease upon the innocent offspring, but also the more afflicting diseases of the mind. Madness of late years has been greatly on the increase among the lower classes, and can only be referred to the alarming progress of drunkenness, which prevails now to a much greater extent among the poor than ever it did at any former period.*

XXIV. *Delirium Tremens.*—Both the symptoms and treatment of this affection require to be mentioned, because, unlike the diseases already enumerated, it invariably originates in the abuse of stimuli, and is cured in a manner peculiar to itself.

Those who indulge in spirits, especially raw, are most subject to delirium tremens, although wine, malt liquor, opium, and even ether, may give rise to it, if used in immoderate quantities. The sudden cessation of drinking in a confirmed toper, or a course of violent or long protracted intemperance may equally occasion the disease. A man, for instance, of the former description, breaks his leg, or is seized with some complaint, which compels him to abandon his potations. This man in consequence of such abstinence is attacked with delirium tremens. In another man, it is induced by a long course of tippling, or by a hard drinking-bout of several days' continuance.

The disease generally comes on with lassitude, loss of appetite, and frequent exacerbations of cold. The pulse is weak and quick, and the body covered with a chilly moisture. The countenance is pale, there are usually tremors of the limbs, anxiety, and a total disrelish for the common amusements of life. Then succeed retching, vomiting, and much oppression at the pit of the stomach, with sometimes slimy stools. When the person sleeps, which is but seldom, he frequently starts in the utmost terror, having his imagination haunted by frightful dreams. To the first coldness, glows of heat succeed, and the slightest renewed agitation of body or mind, sends out a profuse perspiration. The tongue is dry and furred. Every object appears unnatural and hideous. There is a constant dread of being haunted by spectres. Black or luminous bodies seem to float before the person: he conceives that vermin and all sorts of impure things are crawling upon him, and is constantly endeavouring to pick them off. His ideas are wholly confined to himself and his own affairs, of which he entertains the most disordered notions. He imagines that he is away from home, forgets those who are around him, frequently abuses his attendants, and is irritated beyond measure by the slightest contradiction. Calculations, buildings, and other fantastic schemes often occupy his mind; and a belief that

* It has been considered unnecessary to enter into any detail of the nature and treatment of the foregoing diseases, because they may originate from many other causes besides drunkenness; and when they do arise from this source, they acquire no peculiarity of character. Their treatment is also precisely the same as in ordinary cases—it being always understood, that the bad habit which brought them on must be abandoned before any good can result from medicine. The disease, however, which follows is different, and requires particular consideration.

every person is confederated to ruin him, is commonly entertained. Towards morning there is often much sickness and sometimes vomiting. This state generally lasts from four to ten days, and goes off after a refreshing sleep; but sometimes, either from the original violence of the disease, or from improper treatment, it proves fatal.

Such, in nine cases out of ten, is the character of delirium tremens. Sometimes, however, the symptoms vary, and instead of a weak there is a full pulse; instead of the face being pallid, it is flushed, and the eyes fiery; instead of a cold clammy skin, the surface is hot and dry. This state only occurs in vigorous plethoric subjects. A habitually sober man who has thoughtlessly rushed into a debauch, is more likely to be attacked in this manner than a professed drunkard. Indeed, I never met with an instance of the latter having this modification of the disease.

When the patient perishes from delirium tremens, he is generally carried off in convulsions. There is another termination which the disease sometimes assumes: it may run into madness or confirmed idiotism. Indeed, when it continues much beyond the time mentioned, there is danger of the mind becoming permanently alienated.

Subsultus, low delirium, very cold skin, short disturbed sleep, contracted pupil, strabismus, rapid intermittent pulse, and frequent vomiting, are indications of great danger. When the patient is affected with subsultus from which he recovers in terror, the danger is extreme.

In treating delirium tremens, particular attention must be paid to the nature of the disease, and constitution of the patient. In the first mentioned, and by far the most frequent variety, blooding, which some physicians foolishly recommend, is most pernicious. I have known more than one instance where life was destroyed by this practice. As there is generally much gastric irritation, as is indicated by the foul tongue, black and viscid evacuations and irritable state of the stomach, I commence the treatment by administering a smart dose of calomel. As soon as this has operated, I direct tepid water strongly impregnated with salt, to be dashed over the body, and the patient immediately thereafter to be well dried and put to bed. I then administer laudanum in doses of from forty to sixty drops, according to circumstances, combining with each dose from six to twelve grains of the carbonate of ammonia: this I repeat every now and then till sleep is procured. It may sometimes be necessary to give such doses every two hours, or even every hour, for twelve or twenty successive hours, before the effect is produced. The black drop in doses proportioned to its strength, which is more than three times that of laudanum, may be used as a substitute for the latter; the acetate or muriate of morphia in doses of a quarter or half a grain, is also a good medicine, having less tendency to produce stupor or headache than laudanum, and therefore preferable in cases where the patient is of a plethoric habit of body. It must be admitted, however, that their effects are less to be depended upon than those of laudanum, which, in all common cases will, I believe, be found the best remedy. The great object of the treatment is to soothe the apprehensions of the patient, and procure him rest. So soon as a sound sleep takes place there is generally a crisis, and the disease begins to give way; but till this occurs it is impossible to arrest its progress and effect a cure. A moderate quantity of wine will be necessary, especially if he has been a confirmed drinker, and labours under much weakness. Perhaps the best way of administering wine is along with the laudanum, the latter being dropped into the wine. Where wine cannot be had, porter may be advantageously given in combination with laudanum. The principal means, indeed, after the first purging, are opium, wine, ammonia, and tepid effusions: the latter may be tried two,

three, or four times in the twenty-four hours, as occasion requires, The mind is, at the same time, to be soothed in the gentlest manner, the whimsical ideas of the patient to be humoured, and his fancies indulged as far as possible. All kinds of restraint or contradiction are most hurtful. Some recommend blisters to the head, but these are, in every case, injurious. So soon as all the symptoms of the disease have disappeared some purgative should be administered, but during its progress we must rely almost wholly upon stimulants. To cure, by means of stimuli, a complaint which arose from an over-indulgence in such agents, is apparently paradoxical; but experience confirms the propriety of the practice where, *a priori*, we might expect the contrary.

In the second variety of the disease, the same objections do not apply to blood-letting as in the first, but even there, great caution is necessary, especially if the disease has gone on for any length of time, if the pulse is quick and feeble or the tongue foul. At first, general blooding will often have an excellent effect, but should we not be called till after this stage it will prove a hazardous experiment. Local blooding will then sometimes be serviceable where general blooding could not be safely attempted. The patient should be purged well with calomel, have his head shaved, and kept cool with wet cloths, and sinapisms applied to his feet. When the bowels are well evacuated, and no symptoms of coma exist, opiates must be given as in the first variety, but in smaller and less frequently repeated doses.

Much yet remains to be known with regard to the pathology of delirium tremens. I believe that physicians have committed a dangerous error, in considering these two varieties as modifications of the same disease. In my opinion they are distinct affections and ought to be known under different names. This cannot be better shown than in the conflicting opinions with regard to the real nature of the disease. Dr Clutterbuck, having apparently the second variety in his eye, conceives that delirium tremens arises from congestion or inflammation of the brain; while Dr Ryan, referring to the first, considers it a nervous affection, originating in that species of excitement often accompanying debility. It is very evident, that such different conditions require different curative means. The genuine delirium tremens is that described under the first variety, and I agree with Dr Ryan in the view he takes of the character of this singular disease.

GENERAL REMARKS.—Such are the principal diseases brought on by drunkenness. There are still several others which have not been enumerated—nor is there any affection incident to either the body or mind which the voice does not aggravate into double activity, The number of persons who die in consequence of complaints so produced, is much greater than unprofessional people imagine. This fact is well known to medical men, who are aware that many of the cases they are called upon to attend, originate in liquor, although very often the circumstance is totally unknown either to the patient or his friends. This is particularly the case with regard to affections of the liver, stomach, and other viscera concerned in digestion. Dr Willan, in his reports of the diseases of London, states his conviction that considerably more than one-eight of all the deaths which take place in persons above twenty years old, happen prematurely through excess in drinking spirits. Nor are the moral consequences less striking: Mr Poynter, for three years Under-Sheriff of London and Westminster, made the following declaration before a committee of the House of Commons :—'I have long been in the habit of hearing criminals refer all their misery to drinking, so that I now almost cease to ask them the cause of their ruin. This evil lies at the root of all other evils of this city and elsewhere. Nearly all the convicts for murder with whom I have conversed, have admitted themselves to have been under the influence of liquor at the time of the act.' ' By due observation for nearly twenty years,' says the great Judge Hales, ' I have found that if the murders and manslaughters, the burglaries and robberies, and riots and tumults, and adulteries, fornications, rapes, and other great enormities, they have happened in that time, were divided into five parts, four of them have been the issues and product of excessive drinking—of tavern and ale-house meetings.' According to the *Caledonian Mercury* of October 26, 1829, no fewer than ninety males, and one hundred and thirty *females*, in a state of intoxication, were brought to the different police watch-houses of Edinburgh, in the course of the week—being the greatest number for many years. Nor is Glasgow, in this respect, a whit better than Edinburgh. On March 1, 1830, of forty-five cases brought before the police magistrate in Glasgow, forty were for drunkenness ; and it is correctly ascertained that more than nine thousand cases of drunkenness are annually brought before the police, from this city and suburbs— a frightful picture of vice. In the ingenuous Introductory Essay attached to the Rev Dr Beecher's sermons on Intemperance, the following passage occurs, and I think, instead of exaggerating it rather underrates the number of drunkards in the quarter alluded to. ' Supposing that one-half of the eighteen hundred licensed houses for the sale of spirits which are in that city, send forth each a drunken man every day, there are, in Glasgow, one hundred drunken men, day after day, spreading around them beggary, and wretchedness, and crime !' Had the author given to each licensed house, one drunkard, on an average, I do not think he would have overstepped the bounds of truth. As it is, what a picture of demoralization and wretchedness does it not exhibit !

CHAPTER XI.

SLEEP OF DRUNKARDS.

To enter at large upon the subject of sleep would require a volume. At present I shall only consider it so far as it is modified by drunkenness.

The drunkard seldom knows the delicious and refreshing slumbers of the temperate man. He is restless, and tosses in bed for an hour or two before falling asleep. Even then, his rest is not comfortable. He awakes frequently during night, and each time his mouth is dry, his skin parched, and his head, for the most part, painful and throbbing. These symptoms from the irritable state of his constitution, occur even when he goes soberly to bed ; but if he lie down heated with liquor, he feels them with double force. Most persons who fall asleep in a state of intoxication, have much headach, exhaustion and general fever, on awaking. Some constitutions are lulled to rest by liquors, and others rendered excessively restless ; but the first are no gainers by the difference, as they suffer abundantly afterwards. Phlegmatic drunkards drop into slumber more readily than the others : their sleep is, in reality a sort of apopletic stupor.

I. *Dreams.*—Dreams may be readily supposed to be common, from the deranged manifestations of the stomach and brain which occur in intoxication. They are usually of a painful nature, and leave a gloomy impression upon the mind. In general, they are less palpable to the understanding than those which occur in soberness. They come like painful grotesque conceptions across the imagination ; and though this faculty can embody nothing into shape, meaning, or consistence, it is yet haunted with melancholy ideas. These visions depend much on the mental constitution of the person, and are modified by his habitual tone of thinking. It is, how-

ever, to be remarked, that while the waking thoughts of the drunkard are full of sprightly images, those of his sleep are usually tinged with a shade of perplexing melancholy.

II. *Nightmare.*—Drunkards are more afflicted than other people with this disorder, in so far as they are equally subject to all the ordinary causes, and liable to others from which sober people are exempted. Intoxication is fertile in producing reveries and dreams, those playthings of the fancy ; and it may also give rise to such a distortion of idea, as to call up incubus, and all its frightful accompaniments.

III. *Sleep-walking.* — Somnambulism is another affection to which drunkards are more liable than their neighbours. I apprehend that the slumber is never profound when this takes place, and that, in drunkenness in particular, it may occur in a state of very imperfect sleep. Drunkards, even when consciousness is not quite abolished, frequently leave their beds and walk about the room. They know perfectly well what they are about, and recollect it afterwards. but if questioned, either at the moment or at any future period, they are totally unable to give any reason for their conduct. Sometimes after getting up, they stand a little time and endeavour to account for rising, then go again deliberately to bed. There is often, in the behaviour of these individuals, a strange mixture of folly and rationality. , Persons half tipsy have been known to arise and go out of doors in their night-dress, being all the while sensible of what they were doing, and aware of its absurdity. The drunken somnambulism has not always this character. Sometimes the reflecting faculties are so absorbed in slumber, that the person has no consciousness of what he does. From drinking, the affection is always more dangerous than from any other cause, as the muscles have no longer their former strength and are unable to support the person in his hazardous expeditions. If he gets upon a house-top, he does not balance himself properly, from giddiness ; he is consequently liable to falls and accidents of every kind. It is considered, with justice, dangerous to awaken a sleepwalker In a drunken fit, there is less risk than under other circumstances, the mind being so far confused by intoxication, as to be, in some measure, insensible to the shock.

IV. *Sleep-talking.*—For the same reason that drunkards are peculiarly prone to somnambulism are they subject to sleep-talking, which is merely a modification of the other. The imagination, being vehemently excited by the drunken dream, embodies itself often in speech, which however is, in almost every case, extremely incoherent, and wants the rationality sometimes possessed by the conversation of sleep-talkers under other circumstances.

CHAPTER XII.

SPONTANEOUS COMBUSTION OF DRUNKARDS.

Whether such a quantity of hydrogen may accumulate in the bodies of drunkards as to sustain combustion, is not easy to determine. This subject is, indeed, one which has never been satisfactorily investigated ; and, notwithstanding the cases brought forward in support of the doctrine, the general opinion seems to be, that the whole is fable, or at least so much involved in obscurity as to afford no just grounds for belief. The principal information on this point is in the *Journal de Physique,* in an article by Pierre Aime Lair, a copy of which was published in the sixth volume of the *Philosophical Transactions,* by Mr. Alexander Tilloch. A number of cases are there given : and it is not a little singular that the whole of them are those of women in advanced life. When we consider that writers like Vicq d'Azyr, Le Cat, Maffei, Jacobæus, Rolli, Bianchini, and Mason Good, have given their testimony in support of such facts, it requires some effort to believe them unfounded in truth. At the same time, in perusing the case themselves, it is difficult to divest the mind of an idea that some misstatement or other exists, either as to their alleged cause or their actual nature—and that their relaters have been led into an unintentional misrepresentation· The most curious fact connected with this subject is, that the combustion appears seldom to be sufficiently strong to inflame combustible substances with which it comes in contact, such as woollen or cotton, while it destroys the body, which in other circumstances is hardly combustible at all.* Sometimes the body is consumed by an open flame flickering over it—at other times there is merely a smothered heat or fire, without any visible flame. It is farther alleged that water, instead of allaying, aggravates the combustion. This species of burning, indeed, is perfectly *sui generis*, and bears no resemblance to any species of combustion with which we are acquainted. In most cases it breaks out spontaneously, although it may be occasioned by a candle, a fire, or a stroke of lightning ; but in every case it is wholly peculiar to itself. M. Fodere remarks, that hydrogen gas is developed in certain cases of disease, even in the living body ; and he seems inclined to join with M. Mere in attributing what is called spontaneous combustion, to the united action of hydrogen and electricity in the first instance, favoured by the accumulation of animal oil, and the impregnation of spiritous liquors. In the present state of our knowledge, it is needless to hazard any conjectures upon this mysterious subject. The best way is to give a case or two, and let the reader judge for himself.

CASE OF MARY CLUES.—'This woman, aged fifty, was much addicted to intoxication. Her propensity to this vice had increased after the death of her husband, which happened a year and a half before : for about a year, scarcely a day had passed in the course of which she did not drink at least half a pint of rum or aniseed water. Her health gradually declined, and about the beginning of February she was attacked by the jaundice and confined to her bed. Though she was incapable of much action, and not in a condition to work, she still continued her old habit of drinking every day, and smoking a pipe of tobacco. The bed in which she lay stood parallel to the chimney of the apartment, at the distance from it of about three feet. On Saturday morning, the 1st of March, she fell on the floor, and her extreme weakness having prevented her from getting up, she remained in that state till some one entered and put her to bed. The following night she wished to be left alone : a woman quitted her at half past eleven, and, according to custom, shut the door and locked it. She had put on the fire two large pieces of coal, and placed a light in a candlestick on a chair at the head of the bed. At half past five in the morning, smoke was seen issuing through the window, and the door being speedily broken open, some flames which were in the room were soon extinguished. Between the bed and the chimney were found the remains of the unfortunate Clues ; one leg and a thigh were still entire, but there remained nothing of the skin, the muscles, and the viscera. The bones of the cranium, the breast, the spine,

* 'At a period when criminals were condemned to expiate their crimes in the flames, it is well known what a large quantity of combustible materials was required for burning their bodies. A baker's boy named Renaud being several years ago condemned to be burned at Caen, two large cart loads of fagots were required to consume the body ; and at the end of more than ten hours some remains were still visible. In this country, the extreme incombustibility of the human body was exemplified in the case of Mrs King, who, having been murdered by a foreigner, was afterwards burned by him ; but in the execution of this plan he was engaged for several weeks, and, after all, did not succeed in its completion.'—*Paris and Fonblanque's Medical Jurisprudence.*

and the upper extremities, were entirely calcined, and covered with a whitish efflorescence. The people were much surprised that the furniture had sustained so little injury. The side of the bed which was next the chimney had suffered most ; the wood of it was slightly burned, but the feather-bed, the clothes, and covering were safe. I entered the apartment about two hours after it had been opened, and observed that the walls and every thing in it were blackened ; that it was filled with a very disagreeable vapour ; but that nothing except the body exhibited any very strong traces of fire.'

This case first appeared in the *Annual Register* for 1773, and is a fair specimen of the cases collected in the *Journal de Physique.* There is no evidence that the combustion was spontaneous, as it may have been occasioned either by lightning, or by contact with the fire. The only circumstance which militates against the latter supposition, is the very trifling degree of burning that was found in the apartment.

CASE OF GRACE PITT.—'Grace Pitt, the wife of a fishmonger in the Parish of St. Clement, Ipswich, aged about sixty, had contracted a habit, which she continued for several years, of coming down every night from her bed-room, half-dressed, to smoke a pipe. On the night of the 9th of April, 1744, she got up from her bed as usual. Her daughter, who slept with her, did not perceive she was absent till next morning when she awoke, soon after which she put on her clothes, and going down into the kitchen, found her mother stretched out on the right side, with her head near the grate*; the body extended on the hearth, with the legs on the floor, which was of deal, having the appearance of a log of wood, consumed by a fire without apparent flame. On beholding this spectacle, the girl ran in great haste and poured over her mother's body some water contained in two large vessels in order to extinguish the fire ; while the fœtid odour and smoke which exhaled from the body, almost suffocated some of the neighbours who had hastened to the girl's assistance. The trunk was in some measure incinerated, and resembled a heap of coals covered with white ashes. The head, the arms, the legs, and the thighs, had also participated in the burning. This woman, it is said, had drunk a large quantity of spiritous liquors in consequence of being overjoyed to hear that one of her daughters had returned from Gibraltar. There was no fire in the grate, and the candle had burned entirely out in the socket of the candlestick, which was close to her. Besides, there were found near the consumed body, the clothes of a child and a paper screen, which had sustained no injury by the fire. The dress of this woman consisted of a cotton gown.'

This case is to be found in the *Transactions of the Royal Society of London,* and is one of the most decided, and 'least equivocal instances of this species of combustion to be met with. It was mentioned at the time in all the journals, and was the subject of much speculation and remark. The reality of its occurrence was attested by many witnesses, and three several accounts of it, by different hands, all nearly coincide.

CASE OF DON GIO MARIA BERTHOLI.—'Having spent the day in travelling about the country, he arrived in the evening at the house of his brother-in-law. He immediately requested to be shown to his destined apartment, where he had a handkerchief placed between his shirt and shoulders ; and, being left alone, betook himself to his devotions. A few minutes had scarcely elapsed when an extraordinary noise was heard in the chamber, and the cries of the unfortunate man were particularly distinguished : the people of the house, hastily entering the room, found him extended on the floor, and surrounded by a light flame, which receded (*a mesure*) as they approached, and finally vanished. On the following morning, the patient was examined by Mr Battaglia, who found the integuments of the right arm almost entirely detached, and pendant from the flesh; from the shoulders to the thighs, the integuments were equally injured ; and on the right hand, the part most injured, mortification had already commenced, which, notwithstanding immediate scarification, rapidly extended itself. The patient complained of burning thirst, was horribly convulsed, and was exhausted by continual vomiting, accompanied by fever and delirium. On the fourth day, after two hours of comatose insensibility, he expired. During the whole period of his sufferings, it was impossible to trace any symptomatic affection. A short time previous to his death, M. Battlaglia observed with astonishment that putrefaction had made so much progress ; the body already exhaled an insufferable odour ; worms crawled from it on the bed, and the nails had become detached from the left hand.

'The account given by the unhappy patient was, that he felt a stroke like the blow of a cudgel on the right hand, and at the same time he saw a lambent flame attach itself to his shirt, which was immediately reduced to ashes, his wristbands, at the same time, being utterly untouched. The handkerchief which, as before mentioned, was placed between his shoulders and his shirt, was entire, and free from any traces of burning ; his breeches were equally uninjured, but though not a hair of his head was burned, his coif was totally consumed. The weather, on the night of the accident, was calm, and the air very pure ; no empyreumatic or bituminous odour was perceived in the room, which was also free from smoke ; there was no vestige of fire, except that the lamp which had been full of oil, was found dry, and the wick reduced to a cinder.'

This case is from the work of Foderé, and is given as abridged by Paris and Fonblanque, in their excellent treatise on Medical Jurisprudence. It occurred in 1776, and is one of the best authenticated to be met with. I am not aware that the subject of it was a drunkard; but if he were not, and if the facts be really true, we must conclude that spontaneous combustion may occur in sober persons as well as in drunkards.

CASE OF MADAME MILLET.—'Having,' says Le Cat, 'spent several months at Rheims, in the years 1724 and 1725, I lodged at the house of Sieur Millet, whose wife got intoxicated every day. The domestic economy of the family was managed by a pretty young girl, which I must not omit to remark, in order that all the circumstances which accompanied the fact I am about to relate, may be better understood. This woman was found consumed on the 20th of February, 1725, at the distance of a foot and a half from the hearth in her kitchen. A part of the head only, with a portion of the lower extremities, and a few of the vertebræ, had escaped combustion. A foot and a half of the flooring under the body had been consumed, but a kneading trough and a powdering tub, which were very near the body, sustained no injury. M. Chriteen, a surgeon, examined the remains of the body, with every judicial formality. Jean Millet, the husband, being interrogated by the judges who instituted the inquiry into the affair, declared, that about eight in the evening, on the 19th of February, he had retired to rest with his wife who not being able to sleep, went into the kitchen, where he thought she was warming herself; that, having fallen asleep, he was awakened about two o'clock by an infectious odour, and that, having run to the kitchen, he found the remains of his wife in the state described in the report of the physicians and surgeons. The judges, having no suspicion of the real cause of this event prosecuted the affair with the utmost dilligence. It was very unfortunate for Millet that he had a handsome servant-maid, for neither his probity nor innocence were able to save him from the suspicion of having got rid of his wife by a concerted plot, and of having arranged the rest of the circumstances in such a manner as to give it the appearance of an accident. He experienced, therefore, the whole severity of the

law ; and though, by an appeal to a superior and very enlightened court, which discovered the cause of the combustion, he came off victorious, he suffering so much from uneasiness of mind, that he was obliged to pass the remainder of his days in an hospital.'

The above case has a peculiar importance attached to it, for it shows that, in consequence of combustion, possibly spontaneous, persons have been accused of murder. Forderé, in his work, alludes to several cases of this kind.

Some chemists have attempted to account for this kind of combustion, by the formation of phosphuretted hydrogen in the body. This gas, as is well known, inflames on exposure to the air ; nor can there be a doubt that if a sufficient quantity were generated, the body might be easily enough consumed. If such an accumulation can be proved ever to take place, there is an end to conjecture ; and we have before us a cause sufficiently potent to account for the burning. Altogether I am inclined to think, that although most of the related cases rest on vague report, and are unsupported by such proofs as would warrant us in placing much reliance upon them, yet sufficient evidence nevertheless exists, to show that such a phenomenon as spontaneous combustion has actually taken place, although doubtless the number of cases has been much exaggerated. Dr Mason Good, justly observes, 'There may be some difficulty in giving credit to so marvellous a diathesis · yet, examples of its existence, and of its leading to a migratory and fatal combustion are so numerous, and so well authenticated, and press upon us from so many different countries and eras, that it would be absurd to withhold our assent.' 'It can no longer be doubted,' says Dr Gordon Smith, ' that persons have retired to their chambers in the usual manner, and in place of the individual, a few cinders, and perhaps part of his bones, were found.' Inflammable eructations are said to occur occasionally in northern latitudes, when the body has been exposed to intense cold after excessive indulgence in spirituous liquors; and the case of a Bohemian peasant is narrated, who lost his life in consequence of a column of ignited inflammable air issuing from his mouth, and baffling extinction. This case, as well as others of the same kind, is alleged to have arisen from phosphuretted hydrogen, generated by some chemical combination of alcohol and animal substances in the stomach. What truth there may be in these relations I do not pretend to say. They wear unquestionably the aspect of a fiction ; and are, notwithstanding, repeated from so many quarters, that it is nearly as difficult to doubt them altogether as to give them our entire belief. There is one thing, however, which may be safely denied ; and that is the fact of drunkards having been blown up in consequence of their breath or eructations catching fire from the application of a lighted candle. These tales are principally of American extraction ; and seem elaborated by that propensity for the marvellous for which our transatlantic brethren have, of late years, been distinguished.

Upon the whole, this subject is extremely obscure, and has never been satisfactorily treated by any writer. Sufficient evidence appears to me to exist in support of the occurrence, but any information as to the remote or proximate cause of this singular malady, is as yet exceedingly defective and unsatisfactory.

In a memoir lately read before the Académie des Sciences, the following are stated to be the chief circumstances connected with spontaneous combustion :

'1. The greater part of the persons who have fallen victims to it, have made an immoderate use of alcoholic liquors. 2. The combustion is almost always general, but sometimes is only partial. 3. It is much rarer among men than among women, and they are principally old women. There is but one case of the combustion of a girl seventeen years of age, and that was only partial. 4. The body and the viscera are invariably burnt, while the feet, the hands, and the top of the skull almost always escape combustion. 5. Although it requires several fagots to burn a common corpse, incineration takes place in these spontaneous combustions without any effect on the most combustible matters in the neighborhood. In an extraordinary instance of a double combustion operating upon two persons in one room, neither the apartment nor the furniture was burnt. 6. It has not been at all proved that the presence of an inflamed body is necessary to develope spontaneous human combustions. 7. Water, so far from extinguishing the flame, seems to give it more activity; and when the flame has disappeared, secret combustion goes on. 8. Spontaneous combustions are more frequent in winter than in summer. 9. General combustions are not susceptible of cure, only partial. 10. Those who undergo spontaneous combustions are the prey of a very strong internal heat. 11. The combustion bursts out all at once, and consumes the body in a few hours. 12. The parts of the body not attacked are struck with mortification. 13. In persons who have been attacked with spontaneous combustion, a putrid degeneracy takes place which soon leads to gangrene.'

In this singular malady medicine is of no avail. The combustion is kept up by causes apparently beyond the reach of remedy, and in almost every case, life is extinct before the phenomenon is perceived.

CHAPTER XIII.

DRUNKENNESS JUDICIALLY CONSIDERED.

Not only does the drunkard draw down upon himself many diseases, both of body and mind, but if, in his intoxication, he commit any crime or misdemeanor, he becomes, like other subjects, amenable to the pains of law. In this respect, he is worse off than sober persons, for drunkenness, far from palliating, is held to aggravate every offence: the law does not regard it as any extenuation of crime. 'A drunkard,' says Sir Edward Coke, 'who is *voluntarius demon*, hath no privilege thereby; but what hurt or ill soever he doeth, his drunkenness doth aggravate it.' In the case of the King *versus* Maclauchlin, March, 1737, the plea of drunkenness, set up in mitigation of punishment, was not allowed by the court. Sir George Mackenzie says he never found it sustained, and that in a case of murder it was repelled—Spott *versus* Douglass, 1667. Sir Matthew Hales, c. 4. is clear against the validity of the defence, and all agree that '*levis et modica ebrietas non excusat nec minuit delictum.*' It is a maxim in legal practice, that 'those who presume to commit crimes when drunk, must submit to punishment when sober.' This state of the law is not peculiar to modern times. In ancient Greece it was decreed by Pittacus, that 'he who committed a crime when intoxicated, should receive a double punishment,' *viz.* one for the crime itself, and the other for the ebriety which prompted him to commit it. The Athenians not only punished offences done in drunkenness with increased severity, but, by an enactment of Solon, inebriation in a magistrate was made capital. The Roman law was in some measure, an exception, and admitted ebriety as a plea for any misdeeds committed under its influence: *per vinum delapsis capitalis pœna remittitur.* Notwithstanding this tenderness to offences by drunkards, the Romans, at one period, were inconsistent enough to punish the vice itself with death, if found occurring in a woman. By two acts passed in the reign of James I., drunkenness was punishable with a fine, and, failing payment, with sitting publicly for six hours in the stocks; 4 Jac. I. c. 5, and 21 Jac. I. c. 7. By the first of these acts, Justices of the Peace may proceed against drunkards at the Sessions,

by way of indictment: and this act remained in operation till the 10th of October, 1828, at which time, by the act of the 9 Geo. IV. c. 61, § 35, the law for the suppression of drunkenness was repealed, without providing any punishment for offenders in this respect. Previous to this period, the ecclesiastical courts could take cognizance of the offence, and punish it accordingly. As the law stands at present, therefore drunkenness, *per se*, is not punishable, but acts of violence committed under its influence are held to be aggravated rather than otherwise; nor can the person bring it forward as an extenuation of any folly or misdemeanor which he may chance to commit. In proof of this, it may be stated, that a bond signed in a fit of intoxication, holds in law, and is perfectly binding, unless it can be shown that the person who signed it was inebriated by the collusion or contrivance of those to whom the bond was given. A judge or magistrate found drunk *upon the bench*, is liable to removal from his office; and decisions pronounced by him in that state are held to be null and void. Such persons cannot, while acting *ex officio*, claim the benefit of the repeal in the ancient law—their offence being in itself an outrage on justice, and, therefore, a misdemeanor. Even in blasphemy, uttered in a state of ebriety, the defence goes for nothing, as is manifest from the following case, given in Maclaurin's Arguments and Decisions, p. 731.

'Nov. 22, 1694. Patrick Kinninmouth, of that Ilk, was brought to trial for blasphemy and adultery. The indictment alleged, he had affirmed Christ was a bastard. And that he had said, 'If any woman had God on one side, and Christ on the other, he would stow [cut] the lugs [ears] out of her head in spite of them both.' He pleaded chiefly that he was drunk or mad when he uttered these expressions, if he did utter them. The court found the libel relevant to infer the pains libelled, *i. e.* death; and found the defence, that the pannel was furious or distracted in his wits relevant: but repelled the alledgance of fury or distraction arising *from drunkenness.*'

It thus appears that the laws both of Scotland and England agree in considering drunkenness no palliation of crime, but rather the reverse; and it is well that it is so, seeing that ebriety could be easily counterfeited, and made a cloak for the commission of atrocious offences. By the laws, drunkenness is looked upon as criminal, and this being the case, they could not consistently allow one crime to mitigate the penalties due to another.

There is only one case where drunkenness can ever be alleged in mitigation of punishment—that is, where it has induced 'a state of mind perfectly akin to insanity.' It is, in fact, one of the common causes of that disease. The partition line between intoxication and insanity, may hence become a subject of discussion.

'William M'Donough was indicted and tried for the murder of his wife, before the supreme court of the State of Massachusetts, in November, 1817. It appeared in testimony, that several years previous he had received a severe injury of the head; that although relieved of this, yet its effects were such as occasionally to render him insane. At these periods he complained greatly of his head. The use of spiritous liquors immediately induced a return of the paroxysms, and in one of them, thus induced he murdered his wife. He was with great propriety found guilty. The *voluntary* use of a stimulus which, he was fully aware, would disorder his mind, fully placed him under the power of the law.'[*]

'In the state of New-York, we have a statue which places the property of habitual drunkards under the care of the chancellor, in the same manner as that of lunatics. The overseer of the poor in each town may, when they discover a person to be an habitual drunkard, apply to the chancellor for the exercise of his power

* Beck on Medical Jurisprudence.

and jurisdiction. And in certain cases, when the person considers himself aggrieved, it may be investigated by six freeholders, whether he is actually what he is described to be, and their declaration is, *prima facie*, evidence of the fact.'* [This act was passed March 16, 1821.]

'In Rydgway *v.* Darwin, Lord Eldon cites a case where a commission of lunacy was supported against a person, who, when sober, was a very sensible man, but being in a constant state of intoxication, he was incapable of managing his property.'†

CHAPTER XIV.

METHOD OF CURING THE HABIT OF DRUNKENNESS.

To remove the habit of drunkenness from any one in whom it has been long established, is a task of peculiar difficulty. We have not only to contend against the cravings of the body, but against those of the mind; and in struggling with both, we are, in reality, carrying on a combat with nature herself. The system no longer performs its functions in the usual manner; and to restore these functions to their previous tone of action, is more difficult than it would be to give them an action altogether the reverse of nature and of health.

The first step to be adopted, is the discontinuance of all liquors or substances which have the power of intoxicating. The only question is—should they be dropped at once, or by degrees? Dr Trotter, in his Essay on Drunkenness, has entered into a long train of argument, to prove that, in all cases, they ought to be given up *instanter.* He contends, that, being in themselves injurious, their sudden discontinuance cannot possibly be attended with harm. But his reasonings on this point, though ingenious, are not conclusive. A dark unwholesome dungeon is a bad thing, but it has been remarked, that those who have been long confined to such a place, have become sick if suddenly exposed to the light and pure air, on recovering their liberty: had this been done by degrees, no evil effects would have ensued. A removal from an unhealthy climate (to which years had habituated a man) to a healthy one, has sometimes been attended with similar consequences. Even old ulcers cannot always be quickly healed up with safety. Inebriation becomes, as it were, a second

* Beck on Medical Jurisprudence.
† Collinson on Lunacy.
‡ The laws against intoxication are enforced with great rigour in Sweden. Whoever is seen drunk, is fined, for the first offence, three dollars; for the second, six, for the third and fourth, a still larger sum, and is also deprived of the right of voting at elections, and of being appointed a representative. He is, besides, publicly exposed in the parish church on the following Sunday. If the same individual is found committing the same offence a fifth time, he is shut up in a house of correction, and condemned to six months' hard labour; and if he is again guilty, of a twelvemonths' punishment of a similar description. If the offence has been committed in public, such as at a fair, an auction, &c., the fine is doubled; and if the offender has made his appearance in a church, the punishment is still more severe. Whoever is convicted of having induced another to intoxicate himself, is fined three dollars, which sum is doubled if the person is a minor. An ecclesiastic who falls into this offence loses his benefice: if it is a layman who occupies any considerable post, his functions are suspended, and perhaps he is dismissed. Drunkenness is never admitted as an excuse for any crime; and whoever dies when drunk is buried ignominiously, and deprived of the prayers of the church. It is forbidden to give and more explicitly to sell, any spirituous liquors to students, workmen, servants, apprentices, and private soldiers. Whoever is observed drunk in the streets, or making a noise in a tavern, is sure to be taken to prison and detained till sober, without, however, being on that account exempted from the fines. Half of these fines goes to the informers, (who are generally police officers,) the other half to the poor. If the delinquent has no money, he is kept in prison until some one pays for him, or until he has worked out his enlargement. Twice a year these ordinances are read aloud from the pulpit by the clergy; and every tavern-keeper is bound under the penalty of a heavy fine, to have a copy of them hung up in the principal rooms of his house.'— *Schubert's Travels in Sweden.*

nature, and is not to be rapidly changed with impunity, more than other natures. Spurzheim* advances the same opinion. 'Drunkards,' says he, 'cannot leave off their bad habits suddenly, without injuring their health.' Dr Darwin speaks in like terms of the injurious effects of too sudden a change; and for these, and other reasons about to be detailed, I am disposed, upon the whole, to coincide with them.

If we consider attentively the system of man, we will be satisfied that it accommodates itself to various states of action. It will perform a healthy action, of which there is only one state, or a diseased action, of which there are a hundred. The former is uniform, and homogeneous. It may be raised or lowered, according to the state of the circulation, but its nature is ever the same: when that changes—when it assumes new characters—it is no longer the action of health, but of disease. The latter may be multiplied to infinity, and varies with a thousand circumstances; such as the organ which is affected, and the substance which is taken. Now, drunkenness in the long run, is one of those diseased actions. The system no longer acts with its original purity: it is operated upon by a fictitious excitement, and, in the course of time, assumes a state quite foreign to its original constitution—an action which, however unhealthy, becomes, ultimately, in some measure, natural. When we use opium for a long time, we cannot immediately get rid of it, because it has given rise to a false action in the system—which would suffer a sudden disorder if deprived of its accustomed stimulus. To illustrate this, it may be mentioned, that when Abbas the Great published an edict to prohibit the use of coquenar, (the juice of boiled poppies,) on account of its dismal effects on the constitution, a great mortality followed, which was only stopped at last by restoring the use of the prohibited beverage. Disease, under such circumstances, triumphs over health, and has established so strong a hold upon the body, that it is dislodged with difficulty by its lawful possessor. When we wish to get rid of opium, or any other narcotic to which we are accustomed, we must do so by degrees, and let the healthy action gradually expel the diseased one. Place spirits or wine in the situation of opium, and the results will be the same. For these reasons, I am inclined to think, that, in many cases at least, it would be improper and dangerous to remove intoxicating liquors all at once from the drunkard. Such a proceeding seems at variance with the established actions of the human body, and as injudicious as unphilosophical.

I do not, however, mean to say, that there are no cases in which it would be necessary to drop liquors all at once. When much bodily vigour remains—when the morning cravings for the bottle are not irresistible, nor the appetite altogether broken, the person should give over his bad habits instantly. This is a state of incipient drunkenness. He has not yet acquired the constitution of a confirmed sot, and the sooner he ceases the better. The immediate abandonment of drinking may also, in general, take place when there is any organic disease, such as enlarged liver, dropsy, or schirrus stomach. Under these circumstances, the sacrifice is much less than at a previous period, as the frame has, in a great measure, lost its power of withstanding liquors, and the relish for them is also considerably lessened. But even then, the sudden deprivation of the accustomed stimulus has been known to produce dangerous exhaustion; and it has been found necessary to give it again, though in more moderate quantities. Those drunkards who have no particular disease, unless a tremor and loss of appetite be so denominated, require to be deprived of the bottle by degrees. Their system would be apt to fall into a state of torpor if it were suddenly taken away, and various mental diseases, such as melancholy, madness, and de-

* View of the Elementary Principles of Education.

lirium tremens, might even be the result. With such persons, however, it must be acknowledged that there is very great difficulty in getting their potations diminished. Few have fortitude to submit to any reduction. There is, as the period of the accustomed indulgence arrives, an oppression and faintness at the *præcordia,* which human nature can scarcely endure, together with a gnawing desire, infinitely more insatiable than the longings of a pregnant woman.

To prove the intensity of the desire for the bottle, and the difficulty, often insurmountable, of overcoming it, I extract the following interesting and highly characteristic anecdote from a recent publication :—‘ A gentleman of very amiable dispositions, and justly popular, contracted habits of intemperance : his friends argued, implored, remonstrated ; at last he put an end to all importunity in this manner :—To a friend who was addressing him in the following strain—‘ Dear Sir George, your family are in the utmost distress on account of this unfortunate habit.; they perceive that business is neglected ; your moral influence is gone ; your health is ruined ; and, depend upon it, the coats of your stomach will soon give way, and then a change will come too late.’ The poor victim, deeply convinced of the hopelessness of his case, replied thus :—‘ My good friend, your remarks are just ; they are, indeed, too true ; but I can no longer resist temptation : if a bottle of brandy stood at one hand, and the pit of hell yawned at the other, and if I were convinced I would be pushed in as sure as I took one glass, I could not refrain. You are very kind. I ought to be grateful for so many kind good friends, but you may spare yourselves the trouble of trying to reform me : the thing is impossible.’ ’

The observation of almost every man must have furnished him with cases not less striking than the above. I could relate many such which have occurred in my own practice, but shall at present content myself with one. I was lately consulted by a young gentleman of fortune from the north of England. He was aged twenty-six, and was one of the most lamentable instances of the resistless tyranny of this wretched habit that can possibly be imagined. Every morning, before breakfast, he drank a bottle of brandy : another he consumed between breakfast and dinner ; and a third shortly before going to bed. Independently of this, he indulged in wine and whatever liquor came within his reach. Even during the hours usually appropriated to sleep, the same system was pursued—brandy being placed at the bed side for his use in the night-time. To this destructive vice he had been addicted since his sixteenth year and it had gone on increasing from day to day, till it had acquired its then alarming and almost incredible magnitude. In vain did he try to resist the insidious poison. With the perfect consciousness that he was rapidly destroying himself, and with every desire to struggle against the insatiable cravings of his diseased appetite, he found it utterly impossible to offer the slightest opposition to them. Intolerable sickness, faintings, and tremors, followed every attempt to abandon his potations ; and had they been taken suddenly away from him, it cannot be doubted that delirium tremens and death would have been the result.

There are many persons that cannot be called drunkards, who, nevertheless, indulge pretty freely in the bottle, though after reasonable intervals. Such persons usually possess abundance of health, and resist intoxication powerfully. Here the stomach and system in general lose their irritability, in the same way as in confirmed topers, but this is more from torpor than from weakness. The springs of life become less delicate ; the pivots on which they move get, as it were, clogged, and, though existence goes on with vigour, it is not the bounding and elastic vigour of perfect health. This proceeds, not from debility but from torpor ; the mus-

colar fibre becoming, like the hands of a labouring man hardened and blunted in its sensibilities. Such are the effects brought on by a *frequent* use of inebriating agents, but an *excessive* use in every case gives rise to weakness. This the system can only escape by a proper interval being allowed to elapse between our indulgences. But if dose be heaped on dose, before it has time to rally from former exhaustion, it becomes more and more debilitated ; the blood ceases to circulate with its wonted force ; the secretions get defective, and the tone of the living fibre daily enfeebled. A debauch fevers the system, and no man can stand a perpetual succession of fevers without injuring himself, and at last destroying life.

Drunkenness, in the long run changes its character. The sensations of the confirmed tippler, when intoxicated, are nothing, in point of pleasure, to those of the habitually temperate man, in the same condition. We drink at first for the serenity which is diffused over the mind, and not from any positive love we bear to the liquor. But, in the course of time, the influence of the latter, in producing gay images, is deadened. It is then chiefly a mere animal fondness for drink which actuates us. We like the taste of it, as a child likes sweetmeats ; and the stomach, for a series of years, has been so accustomed to an unnatural stimulus, that it cannot perform its functions properly without it. In such a case, it may readily be believed that liquor could not be suddenly removed with safety.

The habit will sometimes be checked by operating skilfully upon the mind. If the person has a feeling heart, much may be done by representing to him the state of misery into which he will plunge himself, his family, and his friends. Some men by a strong effort, have given up liquors at once, in consequence of such representations.

Some drunkards have attempted to cure themselves by the assumption of voluntary oaths. They go before a magistrate, and swear that, for a certain period, they shall not taste liquors of any kind ; and it is but just to state, that these oaths are sometimes strictly enough kept They are, however, much oftener broken—the physical cravings for the bottle prevailing over whatever religious obligation may have been entered into. Such a proceeding is as absurd as it is immoral, and never answer the purpose of effecting any thing like a radical cure ; for, although the person abides by his solemn engagement, it is only to resume his old habits more inveterately than ever, the moment it expires.

Many men become drunkards from family broils. They find no comfort at home, and gladly seek for it out of doors. In such cases, it will be almost impossible to break the habit. The domestic sympathies and affections, which oppose a barrier to dissipation, and wean away the mind from the bottle, have here no room to act. When the mother of a family becomes addicted to liquor, the case is very afflicting. Home instead of being the seat of comfort and order, becomes a species of Pandemonium : the social circle is broken up, and all its happiness destroyed. In this case there is no remedy but the removal of the drunkard. A feeling of perversity has been known to effect a cure among the fair sex. A man of Philadelphia, who was afflicted with a drunken wife, put a cask of rum in her way, in the charitable hope that she would drink herself to death. She suspected the scheme, and, from a mere principle of contradiction, abstained in all time coming, from any sort of indulgence in the bottle. I may mention another American anecdote of a person reclaimed from drunkenness, by means not less singular. A man in Maryland, notoriously addicted to this vice, hearing an uproar in his kitchen one evening, felt the curiosity to step without noise to the door, to know what was the matter, when he beheld his servants indulging in the most unbounded roar of laughter at a couple of his negro boys, who were mimicking himself in his drunken fits, showing how he reeled and staggered—how he looked and nodded, and hiccupped and tumbled. The picture which these children of nature drew of him, and which had filled the rest with so much merriment, struck him so forcibly, that he became a perfectly sober man, to the unspeakable joy of his wife and children.

Man is very much the creature of habit. By drinking regularly at certain times, he feels the longing for liquor at the stated return of those periods—as after dinner, or immediately before going to bed, or whatever the period may be. He even feels it in certain companies, or in a particular tavern at which he is in the habit of taking his libations. We have all heard the story of the man who could never pass an inn on the roadside without entering it and taking a glass, and who, when, after a violent effort, he succeeded in getting beyond the spot, straightway returned to reward himself with a bumper for his resolution. It is a good rule for drunkards to break all such habits. Let the frequenter of drinking clubs, masonic lodges, and other Bacchanalian assemblages, leave off attending these places; and if he must drink, let him do so at home, where there is every likelihood his potations will be less liberal. Let him also forswear the society of boon companions, either in his own habitation or in theirs. Let him, if he can manage it, remove from the place of his usual residence, and go somewhere else. Let him also take abundance of exercise, court the society of intellectual and sober persons, and turn his attention to reading, or gardening, or sailing, or whatever other amusement he has a fancy for. By following this advice rigidly, he will get rid of that baleful habit which haunts him like his shadow, and intrudes itself by day and by night into the sanctuary of his thoughts. And if he refuses to lay aside the Circean cup, let him refleet that Disease waits upon his steps—that Dropsy, Palsy, Emaciation, Poverty, and Idiotism, followed by the pale phantom, Death, pursue him like attendant spirits, and claim him as their prey.

Sometimes an attack of disease has the effect of sobering drunkards for the rest of their lives. I knew a gentleman who had apoplexy in consequence of dissipation. He fortunately recovered, but the danger which he had escaped made such an impression upon his mind, that he never, till his dying day, tasted any liquor stronger than simple water. Many persons, after such changes, become remarkably lean; but this is not an unhealthy emaciation. Their mental powers also suffer a very material improvement—the intellect becoming more powerful, and the moral feelings more soft and refined.

In a small treatise on Naval Discipline, lately published, the following whimsical and ingenious mode of punishing drunken seamen is recommended :—' Separate for one month every man who was found drunk, from the rest of the crew : mark his clothes ' drunkard ;' give him six-water grog, or, if beer, mixed one-half water ; let them dine when the crew had finished ; employ them in every dirty and disgraceful work, &c. This had such a salutary effect, that in less than six months not a drunken man was to be found in the ship. The same system was introduced by the writer into every ship on board which he subsequently served. When first lieutenant of the Victory and Diomede, the beneficial consequences were acknowledged—the culprits were heard to say that they would rather receive six dozen lashes at the gangway, and be done with it, than be put into the ' drunken mess' (for so it was named) for a month.'

Those persons who have been for many years in the habit of indulging largely in drink, and to whom it has become an *elixir vitæ* indispensable to their happiness, cannot be suddenly deprived of it. This should be done by slow degrees, and must be the result of conviction.

If the quantity be forcibly diminished against the person's will, no good can be done ; he will only seize the first opportunity to remunerate himself for what he has been deprived of, and proceed to greater excesses than before. If his mind can be brought, by calm reflection, to submit to the decrease, much may be accomplished in the way of reformation. Many difficulties undoubtedly attend this gradual process, and no ordinary strength of mind is required for its completion. It is, however, less dangerous than the method recommended by Dr Trotter, and ultimately much more effectual. Even although his plan were free of hazard, its effects are not likely to be lasting. The unnatural action, to which long intemperance had given rise, clings to the system with pertinacious adherence. The remembrance of liquor, like a delightful vision, still attaches itself to the drunkard's mind ; and he longs with insufferable ardour, to feel once more the ecstacies to which it gave birth. This is the consequence of a too rapid separation. Had the sympathies of nature been gradually operated upon, there would have been less violence, and the longings had a better chance of wearing insensibly away.

Among the great authorities for acting in this manner, may be mentioned the celebrated Dr Pitcairn. In attempting to break the habit in a Highland chieftain, one of his patients, he exacted a promise that the latter would every day drop as much sealing-wax into his glass as would receive the impression of his seal. He did so, and as the wax accumulated, the capacity of the glass diminished, an1, consequently, the quantity of whiskey it was capable of containing. By this plan he was cured of his bad habit altogether. In mentioning such a whimsical proceeding, I do not mean particularly to recommend it for adoption ; although I am satisfied that the principle on which its eccentric contriver proceeded was substantially correct.

A strong argument against too sudden a change is afforded in the case of food. I have remarked that persons who are in the daily habit of eating animal food feel a sense of weakness about the stomach if they suddenly discontinue it, and live for a few days entirely upon vegetables. This I have experienced personally, in various trials made for the purpose ; and every person in health, and accustomed to good living, will, I am persuaded, feel the same thing. The stomach, from want of stimulus, loses its tone ; the craving for animal food is strong and incessant ; and, if it be resisted, heart-burn, water-brash, and other forms of indigestion, are sure to ensue. In such a case vegetables arc loathed as intolerably insipid, and even bread is looked upon with disrelish and aversion. It is precisely the same with liquors. Their sudden discontinuance, where they have been long made use of, is almost sure to produce the same, and even worse consequences to the individual.

I cannot give any directions with regard to the regimen of a reformed drunkard. This will depend upon different circumstances, such as age, constitution, diseases, and manner of living. It may be laid down as a general rule, that it ought to be as little heating as possible. , A milk or vegetable diet will commonly be preferable to every other. But there are cases in which food of a richer quality is requisite, as when there is much emaciation and debility. Here it may even be necessary to give a moderate quantity of wine. In gout, likewise, too great a change of living is not always salutary, more especially in advanced years, where there is weakness of the digestive organs, brought on by the disease. In old age, wine is often useful to sustain the system, more especially when sinking by the process of natural decay. The older a person is, the greater the inconvenience of abstaining all at once from liquors, and the more slowly ought they to be taken away. I cannot bring myself to believe that a man who for half a century has drunk freely, can suddenly discontinue this ancient habit without a certain degree of risk; the idea is opposed to all that we know of the bodily and mental functions.

In attempting to cure the habit of drunkenness, opium may sometimes be used with advantage. By giving it in moderate quantities, the liquor which the person is in the habit of taking, may be diminished to a considerable extent, and he may thus be enabled to leave them off altogether. There is only one risk, and it is this—that he may become as confirmed a votary of opium as he was before of strong liquors. Of two evils, however, we should always choose the least: and it is certain that however perniciously opium may act upon the system, its moral effects and its power of injuring reputation are decidedly less formidable than those of the ordinary intoxicating agents.

The following anecdote has been communicated to me by the late Mr Alexander Balfour, (author of " Contemplation,' ' Weeds and Wildflowers,' and other ingenious works,) and exhibts a mode of curing dram-drinking equally novel and effective:

About the middle of last century, in a provincial town on the east coast of Scotland, where smuggling was common, it was the practice for two respectable merchants to gratify themselves with a social glass of good Hollands, for which purpose they regularly adjourned at a certain hour, to a neighboring gin-shop. It happened one morning that something prevented one of them from calling on his neighbor at the usual time. Many a wistful and longing look was cast for the friend so unaccourtably absent, but he came not. His disappointed companion would not go to the dram-shop alone; but ne afterwards acknowledged that the want of his accustomed cordial rendered him uneasy the whole day. However, this feeling induced him to reflect on the bad habit he was acquiring, and the consequences which were likely to follow. He therefore resolved to discontinue dram-drinking entirely, but found it difficult to put his resolution into practice, until, after some deliberation, he hit upon the following expedient:—Filling a bottle with excellent Hollands, he lodged it in his back-shop, and the first morning taking his dram, he replaced it with simple water. Next morning he took a second dram, replacing it with water; and in this manner he went on, replacing the fluid subtracted from the bottle with water, till at last the mixture became insipid and ultimately nauseous, which had such an effect upon his palate, that he was completely cured of his bad habit, and continued to live in exemplary soberness till his death, which happened in extreme old age.

Dr Kain, an American physician, recommends tartar emetic for the cure of habitual drunkenness. 'Possessing,' he observes, 'no positive taste itself, it communicates a disgusting quality to those fluids in which it is dissolved. I have often seen persons who, from taking a medicine in the form of antimonial wine, could never afterwards drink wine. Nothing, therefore, seems better calculated to form our indication of breaking up the association, in the patient's feelings, between his disease and the relief to be obtained from stimulating liquors. These liquors, with the addition of a very small quantity of emetic tartar, instead of relieving, increase the sensation of loathing of food, and quickly produce in the patient an indomitable repugnance to the vehicle of its administration.' 'My method of prescribing it, has varied accordingly to the habits, age, and constitution of the patient. I give it only in alterative slightly nauseating doses. A convenient preparation of the medicine is eight grains dissolved in four ounces of boiling water—half an ounce of the solution to be put into half-pint, pint, or quart of the patient's favorite liquor, and to be taken daily in divided portions. If severe vomiting and purging ensue, I should direct laudanum to allay the irritation, and diminish the dose. In every patient it should be varied

according to its effects. In one instance, in a patient who lived ten miles from me, severe vomiting was produced, more, I think, from excessive drinking, than the use of the remedy. He recovered from it, however, without any bad effects. In some cases, the change suddenly produced in the patient's habits, has brought on considerable lassitude and debility, which were of but short duration. In a majority of cases, no other effect has been perceptible than slight nausea, some diarrhœa, and a gradual, but very uniform, distaste to the menstruum.'*

Having tried tartar emetic in several instances, I can bear testimony to its good effects in habitual drunkenness. The active ingredient in Chambers's celebrated nostrum for the cure of ebriety, was this medicine. Tartar emetic, however, must always be used with caution, and never except under the eye of a medical man, as the worst consequences might ensue from the indiscreet employment of so active an agent.

It seems probable that, in plethoric subjects the habit of drunkenness might be attacked with some success by the application of leeches, cold applications and blisters to the head, accompanied by purgatives and nauseating doses of tartar emetic. Dr Caldwell of Lexington, conceives drunkenness to be entirely a disease of the brain, especially of the animal compartments of this viscus, and more especially of that portion called by phenologists the organ of *alimentiveness*, on which the appetite for food and drink is supposed mainly to depend. Should his views be correct, the above treatment seems eligible, at least in drunkards of a full habit of body, and in such cases it is certainly worthy of a full trial. I refer the reader to Dr Caldwell's Essay, in which both the above doctrine and the practice founded upon it are very ably discussed. It is, indeed, one of the ablest papers which has hitherto appeared upon the subject of drunkenness.†

It very often happens, after a long course of dissipation, and that the stomach loses its tone, and rejects almost every thing that is swallowed. The remedy, in this case, is opium, which should be given in the solid form in preference to any other. Small quantities of negus are also beneficial; and the carbonate of ammonia, combined with some aromatic, is frequently attended with the best effects. When there is much prostration of strength, wine should always be given. In such a case, the entire removal of the long-accustomed stimulus would be attended with the worst effects. This must be done gradually.

Enervated drunkards will reap much benefit by removing to the country, if their usual residence is in town. The free air and exercise renovate their enfeebled frames; new scenes are presented to occupy their attention; and, the mind being withdrawn from former scenes, the chain of past associations is broken in two.

Warm and cold bathing will occasionally be useful, according to circumstances. Bitters are not to be recommended, especially if employed under the medium of spirits. When there is much debility, chalybeates will prove serviceable. A visit to places where there are mineral springs is of use, not only from the waters, but from the agreeable society to be met with at such quarters. The great art of breaking the habit consists in managing the drunkard with kindness and address. This managment must, of course, be modified by the events which present themselves, and which will vary in different cases.

Persons residing in tropical climates ought, more than others, to avoid intoxicating liquors. It is too much the practice in the West Indies to allay thirst by copious draughts of rum punch. In the East Indies, the natives, with great propriety, principally use rice-

* American Journal of the Medical Sciences, No. IV.
† See Transylvinia Journal of Medicine and the Associate Sciences, for July, August, and September, 1832.

water, (congee;) while the Europeans residing there, are in the habit of indulging in Champagne, Madeira, and other rich wines, which may in a great measure account for the mortality prevailing among them in that region. A fearful demoralization, as well as loss of life, is occasioned among the British troops in the East and West Indies, from the cheapness of spiritous liquors, which enables them to indulge in them to excess. 'Since the institution of the recorder's and supreme courts at Madras,' says Sir Thomas Hislop, 'no less than thirty-four British soldiers have forfeited their lives for murder, and most of them were committed in their intoxicated moments.' Dr Rollo relates, that the 45th regiment, while stationed in Grenada, lost within a very few weeks, twenty-six men out of ninety-six; at a time, too, when the island was remarkably healthy. On inquiry, it was found that the common breakfast of the men was raw spirits and pork. It is remarked by Desgennetts, in his medical history of the French army in Egypt, that, ' daily experience demonstrates that almost all the soldiers who indulge in intemperate habits, and are attacked with fevers, never recover.' In countries where the solar influence is felt with such force, we cannot be too temperate. The food should be chiefly vegetable, and the drink as unirritating as possible. It may be laid down as an axiom, that in these regions, wine and ardent spirits are invariably hurtful; not only in immediately heating the body, but in exposing it to the influence of other diseases.* A great portion of the deaths which occur among Europeans in the tropics, are brought on by excess. Instead of suiting their regimen to the climate, they persist in the habits of their own country, without reflecting that what is comparatively harmless in one region, is most destructive in another. There cannot be a stronger proof of this than the French troops in the West Indies having almost always suffered less in proportion to their numbers than the British, who are unquestionably more addicted to intemperance. 'I aver, from my own knowledge and custom,' observes Dr Mosely, 'as from the custom and observation of others, that those who drink *nothing but water*, are but little affected by the climate, and can undergo the greatest fatigue without inconvenience.'†

It is a common practice in the west of Scotland to send persons who are excessively addicted to drunkenness, to rusticate and learn sobriety on the islands of Loch Lomond. There are, I believe, two islands appropriated for the purpose, where the convicts meet with due attention, and whatever indulgences their friends choose to extend towards them. Whether such a proceeding is consistent with law, and well adapted to answer the end in view, may be reasonably doubted; but of its severity, as a punishment, there can be no question. It is indeed impossible to inflict any penalty upon drunkards so great as that of absolutely debarring them from indulging in liquor.

In the next chapter, I shall consider the method of curing and preventing drunkenness by means of temperance societies.

CHAPTER XV.

TEMPERANCE SOCIETIES.

Much has been said and written of late concerning temperance societies. They have been represented by their friends as powerful engines for effecting a total

reformation from drunkenness, and improving the whole face of society, by introducing a purer morality, and banishing the hundred-headed monster, intemperance, and all its accompanying vices, from the world. By their opponents, they have been ridiculed as visionary and impracticable—as, at best, but temporary in their influence—as erroneous in many of their leading views —as tyrannical, unsocial, and hypocritical. Their members are represented as enthusiasts and fanatics; and the more active portion of them,—those who lecture on the subject, and go about founding societies,— traduced as fools or impostors. Such are the various views entertained by different minds of temperance societies; but, leaving it to others to argue the point, for or against, according to their inclinations, I shall simply state what I think myself of these institutions—how far they do good or harm—and under what circumstances they ought to be thought favourable of, or the reverse. Truth generally lies *in mediis rebus*, and I suspect these will not form an exception to the rule.

Temperance societies proceed upon the belief that ardent spirits are, *under all circumstances*, injurious to people in health, and that, therefore, they ought to be altogether abandoned. I am anxious to think favourably of any plan which has for its object the eradication of drunkenness; and shall therefore simply express my belief that those societies have done good, and ought therefore to be regarded with a favourable eye. That they have succeeded, or ever will succeed, in reclaiming any considerable number of drunkards, I have great doubts; but that they may have the effect of preventing many individuals from becoming drunkards, is exceedingly probable. If this can be proved,—which I think it may without much difficulty,—it follows that they are beneficial in their nature, and, consequently, deserving of encouragement. That they are wrong in supposing ardent spirits *invariably* hurtful in health, and they are also in error in advocating the instant abandonment, *in all cases*, of intoxicating liquors, I have little doubt; but that they are correct in their great leading views of the pernicious effects of spirits to mankind in general, and that their principles, if carried into effect, will produce good, is self-evident. Spirits when used in moderation, cannot be looked upon as pernicious; nay, in certain cases, even in health, they are beneficial and necessary. In countries subject to intermittents, it is very well known that those who indulge moderately in spirits are much less subject to these diseases than the strictly abstinent. 'At Walcheren it was remarked that those officers and soldiers who took schnaps, *alias* drams, in the morning, and smoked, escaped the fever which was so destructive to the British troops; and the natives generally insisted upon doing so before going out in the morning.'* The following anecdote is equally in point. 'It took place on the Niagara frontier of Upper Canada, in the year 1813. A British regiment, from some accident, was prevented from receiving the usual supply of spirits, and in a very short time, more than two-thirds of the men were on the sick list from ague or dysentery; while, the very next day, on the same ground, and in almost every respect under the same circumstances, except that the men had their usual allowance of spirits, the sickness was extremely trifling. Every person acquainted with the circumstances believed that the diminution of the sick, during the latter period, was attributable to the men having received the quantity of spirits to which they had been habituated.'† Indeed, I am persuaded that while, in the tropics, stimulating liquors are highly prejudicial, and often occasion, while they never prevent, disease, they are frequently of great service in accomplishing the latter object in damp foggy countries, especially when fatigue, poor diet, agues, dysenteries, and other diseases of debility are to be contended against. It

---

* In warm countries, the acqueous part of the blood loses itself greatly by perspiration; it must therefore be supplied by a like liquid. Water is there of admirable use; strong liquors would coagulate the globules of blood that remain after the transuding of the acqueous humour.—*Montesquieu, Book* xiv. *Chap.* x.
†,† Tropical Diseases.

* Glasgow Medical Journal, No. XV.
† Ibid.

has been stated, and, I believe with much truth, that the dystentery which has prevailed so much of late among the poorer classes in this country, has been in many cases occasioned, and in others aggravated, in consequence of the want of spirits, which, from the depressed state of trade, the working classes are unable to procure; and should this assertion turn out to be correct, it follows, that temperance societies, by the rigid abstinence urged upon their members, have contributed to increase the evil. The system is fortified against this disorder, as well as various others, by a proper use of stimuli; while excess in the indulgence of these agents exposes it to the attack of every disease, and invariably aggravates the danger. Water is unquestionably the natural drink of man, but in the existing condition of things, we are no longer in a state of nature, and cases consequently often occur wherein we must depart from her original principles. There are many persons who find a moderate use of spirits necessary to the enjoyment of health. In these cases it would be idle to abandon them. They ought only to be given up when their use is not required by the system. That such is the case in a great majority of instances, must be fully admitted; and it is to these that the principles of temperance societies can be applied with advantage. Considering the matter in this light, the conclusion we must come to is simply that ardent spirits sometimes do good, but much oftener mischief. By abandoning them altogether, we escape the mischief and lose the good. Such is the inevitable effect, supposing temperance societies to come into general operation. It remains, therefore, with people themselves to determine whether they are capable of using spirits only when they are beneficial, and then with a due regard to moderation. If they have so little self-command, the sooner they connect themselves with temperance societies the better. I believe that by a moderate indulgence in spirits no man can be injured, and that many will often be benefited. It is their abuse which renders them a curse rather than a blessing to mankind; and it is with this abuse alone I find fault, in the same way as I would object to excess in eating, or any other excess. People, therefore, would do well to draw a distinction between the proper use and the abuse of these stimulants, and regulate themselves accordingly.

Temperance societies, however, though erroneous in some of their principles, and injurious as applied to particular cases, may be of great use towards society in general. Proceeding upon the well-known fact that ardent spirits are peculiarly apt to be abused, and habitual drunkenness to ensue, they place these agents under the ban of total interdiction, and thus arrest the march of that baneful evil occasioned by their excessive use. So far, therefore, as the individual members of these institutions are concerned, a great good is effected at the sacrifice of comparatively little. On such grounds, I fully admit their beneficial effects, and wish them all success. At the same time, many sober persons would not wish to connect themselves with them, for the plain reason—that having never felt any bad effects from the small quantity of ardent spirits they are in the habit of taking, but, on the contrary, sometimes been the better for it—they would feel averse to come under any obligation to abstain from these liquors altogether. Such, I confess, are my own feelings on this subject; and in stating them I am fully aware that the advocates of the societies will answer—that a man's private inclinations should be sacrificed to public good, and that, for the sake of a general example, he should abandon that which, though harmless to him, in the limited extent to which he indulges in it, is pernicious to the mass of mankind. This argument is not without point, and upon many will tell with good effect, though, I believe, people in general will either not acknowledge its force, or, at least, refuse to act up to it.

T

Temperance societies have had one effect: they have lessened the consumption of spiritous liquors to a vast extent, and have left that of wines and malt liquors undiminished, or rather increased it; for although the more strict members avoid even them, their use is not interdicted by the rules of the societies. By thus diminishing the consumption of spirits, they have been the means of shutting up many small public houses; of keeping numerous tradesmen and laborers from the tavern; of encouraging such persons to sober habits, by recommending coffee instead of strong liquor; and, generally speaking, of promoting industry and temperance.

If a person were disposed to be very censorious, he might object to some other things connected with them, such as the inconsistency of allowing their members to drink wine and malt liquors, while they debar them from ardent spirits. They do this on the ground that on the two first a man is much less likely to become a drunkard than upon spirits—a fact which may be fairly admitted, but which, I believe, arises, in some measure, from its requiring more money to get drunk upon malt liquors and wine than upon spirits. In abandoning the latter, however, and having recourse to the others, it is proper to state, that the person often practices a delusion upon himself; for in drinking wine, such at least as it is procured in this country, he in reality consumes a large proportion of pure spirits; and malt liquors contain not only the alcoholic principle of intoxication, but are often sophisticated, as we have already seen, with narcotics. I believe that, though not in the majority of cases, yet in some, spirits in moderation are better for the system than malt liquors; this is especially the case in plethoric and dyspeptic subjects. Independently of this, it is much more difficult to get rid of the effects of the latter. Much exercise is required for this purpose; and if such is neglected, and the person is of full habit of body, it would have been better if he had stuck by his toddy than run the risk of getting overloaded with fat, and dropping down in a fit of apoplexy.

I know several members of the temperance society who are practising upon themselves the delusion in question. They shun spirits, but indulge largely in porter—to the extent perhaps of a bottle a-day. Nobody can deny that by this practice they will suffer a great deal more than if they took a tumbler or so of toddy daily; and the consequences are the more pernicious, because, while indulging in these libations, they imagine themselves to be all the while paragons of sobriety. Rather than have permitted such a license to their members, temperance societies should have proscribed malt liquors as they have done spirits. As it is, a person may be a member, and follow the rules of the societies, while he is all the time habituating himself to drunkenness. These facts, with all my respect for temperance societies, and firm belief in their utility, I am compelled to mention; and I do so the more readily, as there is a large balance of good in their favour, to overweigh whatever bad may be brought against them.

But notwithstanding this, the fact that a habit of drunkenness is far more likely to be caused by indulging habitually in spirits than in any thing else, is undeniable; and temperance societies, in lessening the consumption of spirits, have accomplished a certain good, in so far as they have thus been the means of diminishing, to a considerable extent, the vice of drunkenness, of reclaiming a few topers, and preventing many from becoming so who would certainly have fallen into the snare, had they not been timely checked by their influence and example.

In conclusion, I have to repeat that I do not agree with the societies in considering ardent spirits always hurtful in health, or in recommending the instant disuse of liquor in all cases of drunkenness. The reasons for entertaining my own opinions on these points are given in the work, and they are satisfactory to myself, whatever they may be to others. At the same time, I fully admit that these institutions may often prove eminently useful, and that the cases wherein they may be injurious to those connected with them, are not many, compared to the mass of good which they are capable of effecting. The man, therefore, who feels the appetite for liquor stealing upon him, cannot adopt a wiser plan than to connect himself with a body, the members of which will keep him in countenance in sobriety, and, by their example, perhaps wean him away from the bottle, and thus arrest him on the road to ruin.*

* The following account of temperance societies is by Professor Edgar, one of their most enthusiastic advocates:—
' Temperance societies direct their chief exertions against the use of distilled spirits, conceiving them to be the great bane of the community ; but they do not exclude these to introduce other intoxicating liquors in their room. Their object is to disabuse the public mind respecting the erroneous opinions and evil practices which produce and perpetuate intemperance ; and though they do not hold it to be sinful to drink wine, yet they are cheerfully willing to accord with the sentiment of inspiration,—' It is good neither to drink wine nor any thing whereby thy brother stumbleth, or is offended, or is made weak.' Were the wine spoken of in Scripture alone used in these countries, they do not believe that there would be a necessity for temperance societies ; yet even from such wine, so different from that commonly in use, the Scriptures gave them the fullest liberty to refrain. Avoiding, however, all appearance of rigorous abstinence, they leave to every man's judgment and conscience, how far he shall feel himself warranted in the use of fermented liquors, and only insist, as their fundamental principle, on an abstinence from distilled spirits, and a discountenancing of the causes and practices of intemperance. Their regulations respect persons in health alone ; with the prescriptions of physicians they do not interfere. Even the moderate use of distilled spirits they consider to be injurious ; and they call upon their brethren for their own sake, to renounce it. The great mass of excellences attributed to intoxicating liquors, they believe to be fictitious ; and though all the virtues attributed to them were real, they are cheerfully willing to sacrifice them, while they have the remotest hope of thus cutting off even one of the sources of drunkenness, or arresting one friend or neighbor on the road to ruin. They do not look on the use of intoxicating liquors as necessary either to their health or happiness ; they do not love them, and therefore, they do not wish to represent an abstinence from them as, on their part, a great sacrifice ; and they trust that they only require to be convinced that the good of their brother demands it, to induce them to do much more than they have yet done. They know that the only prospect of reformation for the intemperate is immediate and complete abstinence, and they joyfully contribute their influence and example to save him. They know that the present customs and practices of the temperate, are now preparing a generation for occupying the room of those who shall soon sleep in drunkards' graves, and it is their earnest wish to exercise such a redeeming influence on the public mind, that should the present race of drunkards refuse to be saved, there may be none to fill their place when they are no more. The abstinence of the temperate, they are convinced, will accomplish this, and that abstinence it is their business to promote by those means with which the God of truth has furnished them. They believe that such abstinence, instead of being productive of any injury to the community, will greatly benefit it ; and already there are the fairest prospects of the great objects of such voluntary abstinence being effected, by associations sustaining one another in new habits, to make them reputable and common. They require no oaths, no vows ; their bond of obligation is a sense of duty, and subscription to their fundamental principle, is merely an expression of present conviction and determination. The law of temperance societies, like the Gospel is the law of liberty—the law which binds to do that which is considered a delight and a privilege. They look forward to the time as not far distant, when the temperate, having withdrawn their support from the trade in ardent spirits, it shall be deserted by all respectable men, and shall gradually die away, as premature death thins the ranks of drunkards ; they trust that the falsehoods by which temperate men have been cheated into the ordinary use of ardent spirits, will soon be completely exposed ; and that full information and proper feeling being extended, respecting the nature and effects of intoxicating liquors they will occupy their proper place, and the unnumbered blessings of temperance on individuals and families, and the whole community, will universally prevail. Not only will temperance societies cut off the resources of drunkenness, but to the reformed drunkard, they will open a refuge from the tyranny of evil customs, and they will support and encourage him in his new habits. To promote these invaluable objects, they call for the united efforts of all temperate men ; they earnestly solicit the assistance of physicians, of clergymen, of the conductors of public journals, of all men possessing authority and influence ; and by every thing sacred and good, they beseech drunkards to turn from the wickedness of their ways and live.'

CHAPTER XVI.

ADVICE TO INVETERATE DRUNKARDS.

If a man is resolved to continue a drunkard, it may here be proper to mention in what manner he can do so with least risk to himself. One of the principal rules to be observed, not only by him, but by habitually sober people, is never to take any inebriating liquor, especially spirits, upon an empty stomach. There is no habit more common or more destructive than this : it not only intoxicates readier than when food has been previously taken, but it has a much greater tendency to impair the functions of the digestive organs. In addition, drunkards should shun raw spirits, which more rapidly bring on disease of the stomach, than when used in a diluted state. These fluids are safe in proportion to the state of their dilution ; but to this general rule there is one exception, viz. punch. This, though the most diluted form in which they are used, is, I suspect, nearly the very worst—not from the weakness of the mixture, but from the acid which is combined with it. This acid, although for the time being, it braces the stomach, and enables it to withstand a greater portion of liquor than it would otherwise do, has ultimately the most pernicious effect upon this organ—giving rise to thickening of its coats, heartburn, and all the usual distressing phenomena of indigestion. Other organs, such as the kidneys, also suffer, and gravelly complaints are apt to be induced. A common belief prevails that punch is more salubrious than any other spirituous compound, but this is grounded on erroneous premises. When people sit down to drink punch they are not so apt—owing to the great length of time which elapses ere such a weak fluid produces intoxication—to be betrayed into excess as when indulging in toddy. In this point of view it may be said to be less injurious ; but let the same quantity of spirits be taken in the form of punch, as in that of grog or toddy, and there can be no doubt that in the long run the consequences will be far more fatal to the constitution. If we commit a debauch on punch, the bad consequences cling much longer to the system than those proceeding from a similar debauch upon any other combination of ardent spirits. In my opinion, the safest way of using those liquids is in the shape of grog.* Cold toddy, or a mixture of spirits, cold water and sugar, ranks next in the scale of safety ; then warm toddy ; then cold punch—and raw spirit is the most pernicious of all.

The malt-liquor drunkard should, as a generla rule, prefer porter to strong ale. Herb ale and purl are very pernicious, but the lighter varities, such as small beer and home-brewed, are not only harmless but even useful. The person who indulges in malt liquor should take much exercise. If he neglects this, and yields to the indolence apt to be induced by these fluids, he becomes fat and stupid, and has a stong tendency to apoplexy, and other diseases of plethora.

As to the wine-bibber, no directions can be given which will prove very satisfactory. The varities of wines are so numerous, that any complete estimate of their respective powers is here impossible. It may, however, be laid down as a general rule, that those which are most diuretic, and excite least headach and fever are the safest for the constitution. The light dry wines, such as Hock, Claret, Burgundy, Bucellas, Rhenish, and Hermitage, are, generally speaking, more salubrious than the stronger varieties, such as Port, Sherry, or Madeira. Claret, in particular, is the

* The origin of the term 'grog' is curious. Before the time of Admiral Vernon, rum was given in its raw state to the seamen ; but he ordered it to be diluted, previous to delivery, with a certain quantity of water. So incensed were the tars at this watering of their favourite liquor, that they nicknamed the Admiral Old grog, in allusion to a grogram coat which he was in habit of wearing : hence the name.

most wholesome wine that is known. Tokay,* Frontignac, Malmsey, Vino Tinto, Montifiascone, Canary, and other sweet wines, are apt, in consequence of their imperfect fermentation, to produce acid upon weak stomachs; but in other cases they are delightful drinks; and when there is no tendency to acidity in the system, they may be taken with comparative safety to a considerable extent. Whenever there is disease, attention must be paid to the wines best adapted to its particular nature. For instance, in gout, the acescent wines, such as Hock and Claret, must be avoided, and Sherry, or Madeira substituted in their room; and should even this run into the acetous fermentation, it must be laid aside, and replaced by weak brandy and water. Champagne, except in cases of weak digestion, is one of the safest wines that can be drunk. Its intoxicating effects are rapid, but exceedingly transient, and depend partly upon the carbonic acid which is evolved from it, and partly upon the alcohol which is suspended in this gas, being applied rapidly and extensively to a large surface of the stomach.

Drunkards will do well to follow the maxim of the facetious Morgan Odoherty, and never mix their wines. Whatever wine they commence with, to that let them adhere throughout the evening. If there be any case where this rule may be transgressed with safety, it is perhaps in favour of Claret, a moderate quantity of which is both pleasant and refreshing after a course of Port or Madeira. Nor is the advice of the same eccentric authority with regard to malt liquors, less just or less worthy of observance —the toper being recommended to abstain scrupulously from such fluids when he means beforehand to 'make an evening of it,' and sit long at the bottle. The mixture, unquestionably, not only disorders the stomach, but effectually weakens the ability of the person to withstand the forthcoming debauch.

CHAPTER XVII.

EFFECTS OF INTOXICATING AGENTS ON NURSES AND CHILDREN.

Women, especially in a low station, who act as nurses, are strongly addicted to the practice of drinking porter and ales, for the purpose of augmenting their milk. This very common custom cannot be sufficiently deprecated. It is often pernicious to both parties, and may lay the foundation of a multitude of diseases in the infant. The milk, which ought to be bland and unirritating, acquires certain heating qualities, and becomes deteriorated to a degree of which those unaccustomed to investigate such matters have little conception. The child nursed by a drunkard is hardly ever healthy. It is, in a particular manner, subject to derangements of the digestive organs, or convulsive affections. With regard to the latter, Dr North† remarks, that he has seen them almost instantly removed by the child being transferred to a temperate woman. I have observed the same thing, not only in convulsive cases, but many others. Nor are liquors the only agents whose properties are communicable to the nursling. It is the same with regard to opium, tobacco, and other narcotics. Purgatives transmit their powers in a similar manner, so much so, that nothing is more common than for the child suckled by a woman who has taken physic, to be affected with bowel complaint. No woman is qualified to be a nurse, unless strictly sober; and though stout children are sometimes reared by persons who indulge to a considerable extent in

* Catherine I. of Russia was intemperately addicted to the use of Tokay. She died of dropsy, which complaint was probably brought on by such indulgence.
† Practical Observations on the Convulsions of Infants.

liquor, there can be no doubt that they are thereby exposed to risk, and that they would have had a much better chance of doing well, if the same quantity of milk had been furnished by natural means. If a woman cannot afford the necessary supply without these indulgences, she should give over the infant to some one who can, and drop nursing altogether. The only cases in which a moderate portion of malt liquor is justifiable, are when the milk is deficient, and the nurse averse or unable to put another in her place. Here, of two evils, we choose the least; and rather give the infant milk of an inferior quality, than endanger its health, by weaning it prematurely, or stinting it of its accustomed nourishment.

Connected with this subject is the practice of administering stimulating liquors to children. This habit is so common in some parts of Scotland, that infants of a few days old are often forced to swallow raw whiskey. In like manner, great injury is often inflicted upon children by the frequent administration of laudanum, paregoric, Godfrey's cordial, and other preparations of opium. The child in a short time becomes pallid, emaciated, and fretful, and is subject to convulsive attacks, and every variety of disorder in the stomach and bowels. Vomiting, diarrhœa, and other affections of the digestive system ensue, and atrophy, followed by death, is too often the consequence.

An experiment made by Dr Hunter upon two of his children, illustrates in a striking manner the pernicious effects of even a small portion of intoxicating liquors, in persons of that tender age. To one of the children he gave, every day after dinner, a full glass of Sherry: the child was five years of age, and unaccustomed to the use of wine. To the other child, of nearly the same age, and equally unused to wine, he gave an orange. In the course of a week, a very marked difference was perceptible in the pulse, urine, and evacuations from the bowels of the two children. The pulse of the first child was raised, the urine high coloured, and the evacuations destitute of their usual quantity of bile. In the other child, no change whatever was produced. He then reversed the experiment, giving to the first the orange, and to the second the wine, and the results corresponded: the child who had the orange continued well, and the system of the other got straightway into disorder, as in the first experiment. Parents should therefore be careful not to allow their youthful offspring stimulating liquors of any kind, except in cases of disease, and then only under the guidance of a medical attendant. The earlier persons are initiated in the use of liquor, the more completely does it gain dominion over them, and the more difficult is the passion for it to be eradicated. Children naturally dislike liquors—a pretty convincing proof that in early life they are totally uncalled for, and that they only become agreeable by habit. It is, in general, long before the palate is reconciled to malt liquors; and most young persons prefer the sweet home-made wines of their own country, to the richer varieties imported from abroad. This shows that the love of such stimulants is in a great measure acquired, and also points out the necessity of guarding youth as much as possible from the acquisition of so unnatural a taste.

CHAPTER XVIII.

LIQUORS NOT ALWAYS HURTFUL.

Though drunkenness is always injurious, it does not follow that a moderate and proper use of those agents which produce it is so. These facts have been so fully illustratated that it is unnecessary to dwell longer upon them; and I only allude to them at present for the purpose of showing more fully a few circumstances in which all kinds of liquors may be indulged in, not only without injury, but with absolute benefit. It is impossible to deny that in particular situations, as in those of hard-wrought sailors and soldiers, a moderate allowance is proper. The body, in such cases, would often sink under the accumulation of fatigue and cold, if not recruited by some artificial excitement. In both the naval and mercantile service the men are allowed a certain quantity of grog, experience having shown the necessity of this stimulus in such situations. When Captain Bligh and his unfortunate companions were exposed to those dreadful privations consequent to their being set adrift, in an open boat, by the mutineers of the Bounty, the few drops of rum which were occasionally doled out to each individual, proved of such incalculable service, that, without this providential aid, every one must have perished of absolute cold and exhaustion.* The utility of spirits in enabling the frame to resist severe cold, I can still farther illustrate by a circumstance personal to myself; and there can be no doubt that the experience of every one must have furnished him with similar examples. I was travelling on the top of the Caledonian coach, during an intensely cold day, towards the end of November, 1821. We left Inverness at five in the morning, when it was nearly pitch dark, and when the thermometer probably stood at 18° of Fahr. I was disappointed of an inside seat, and was obliged to take one on the top, where there were nine outside passengers besides myself, mostly sportsmen returning from their campaigns in the moors. From being obliged to get up so early, and without having taken any refreshment, the cold was truly dreadful, and set fear-noughts, fur-caps, and hosiery, alike at defiance. So situated, and whirling along at the rate of nearly nine miles an hour, with a keen east wind blowing upon us from the snow-covered hills, I do not exaggerate when I say, that some of us at least owed our lives to ardent spirits. The cold was so insufferable, that, on arriving at the first stage, we were nearly frozen to death. Our feet were perfectly benumbed, and our hands, fortified as they were with warm gloves, little better. Under such circumstances, we all instinctively called for spirits, and took a glass each of raw whiskey, and a little bread. The effect was perfectly magical: heat diffused itself over the system, and we continued comparatively warm and comfortable till our arrival at Aviemore Inn, where we breakfasted. This practice was repeated several times during the journey, and always with the same good effect. When at any time the cold became excessive, we had recourse to our dram, which insured us warmth and comfort for the next twelve or fourteen miles, without, on any occasion, producing the slightest feeling of intoxication. Nor had the spirits which we took any bad effects either upon the other passengers or myself. On the contrary, we were all, so far as I could learn, much the better of it; nor can there be a doubt, that without spirits, or some other stimulating liquor, the consequences of such severe weather would have been highly prejudicial to most of us. Some persons deny that spirits possess the property of enabling the body to resist cold, but, in the face of such evidence, I can never agree with them. That, under these circumstances, they steel the system, at least for a considerable time, against the effects of a low temperature, I am perfectly satisfied. Analogy is in favour of this assertion, and the experience of every man must prove

* ' At day-break,' says Captain Bligh, ' I served to every person a tea-spoonful of rum, our limbs being so much cramped that we could scarcely move them.'
' Being unusually wet and cold, I served to the people a tea-spoonful of rum each, to enable them to bear with their distressing situation.'
' Our situation was miserable : always wet, and suffering extreme cold in the night, without the least shelter from the weather. The little rum we had was of the *greatest service*—when our nights were particularly distressing, I generally served a tea-spoonful or two to each person, and it was always joyful tidings when they heard of my intention.'—*Family Library*, vol. xxv. *Mutiny of the Bounty.*

its accuracy. At the same time, I do not mean to deny that wine or ale might have done the same thing equally well, and perhaps with less risk of ulterior consequences. We had no opportunity of trying their efficacy in these respects, and were compelled, in self-defence, to have recourse to what, in common cases ought to be shunned, viz. raw spirits. The case was an extreme one, and required an extreme remedy; such, however, as I would advise no one to have recourse to without a similar plea of strong necessity to go upon.

It follows, then, that if spirits are often perverted to the worst purposes, and capable of producing the greatest calamities, they are also, on particular occasions, of unquestionable benefit. In many affections, both they and wine are of more use than any medicine the physician can administer. Wine is indicated in various diseases of debility. Whenever there is a deficiency of the vital powers, as in the low stages of typhus fever, in gangrene, putrid sore throat, and generally speaking, whenever weakness, unaccompanied by acute inflammation, prevails, it is capable of rendering the most important services. Used in moderation, it enables the system to resist the attack of malignant and intermittent fevers. It is a promoter of digestion, but sometimes produces acidity, in which case, spirits are preferable. To assist the digestive process in weak stomachs, I sometimes prescribe a tumbler of negus or toddy to be taken after dinner, especially if the person be of a studious habit, or otherwise employed in a sedentary occupation. Such individuals are often benefited by the stimulus communicated to the frame by these cordials. In diarrhœa, dysentery, cholera, cramps, tremors, and many other diseases, both spirits and wine often tell with admirable effect, while they are contra-indicated in all inflammatory affections. Malt liquors also, when used in moderation, are often beneficial. Though the drunkenness produced by their excessive use is of the most stupifying and disgusting kind, yet, when under temperate management, and accompanied by sufficient exercise, they are more wholesome than either spirits or wine. They abound in nourishment, and are well adapted to the laboring man, whose food is usually not of a very nutritive character. The only regret is, that they are much adulterated by narcotics. This renders them peculiarly improper for persons of a plethoric habit, and also prevents them from being employed in other cases where they might be useful. Persons of a spare habit of body, are those likely to derive most benefit from malt liquors. I often recommend them to delicate youths and young girls who are just shooting into maturity, and often with the best effect. Lusty, full-bodied, plethoric people, should abstain from them, at least from porter and strong ale, which are much too fattening and nutritious for persons of this description. They are also, generally speaking, injurious to indigestion and bowel complaints, owing to their tendency to produce flatulence. In such cases, they yield the palm to wine and spirits. It is to be regretted that the system of making home-brewed ale, common among the English, has made so little progress in Scotland. This excellent beverage is free from those dangerous combinations employed by the brewers, and to the laboring classes in particular, is a most nourishing and salubrious drink. I fully agree with Sir John Sinclair in thinking, that in no respect is the alteration in diet more injurious than in substituting ardent spirits for ale—the ancient drink of the common people. Though an occasional and moderate allowance of spirits will often benefit a working man, still the tendency of people to drink these fluids to excess renders even their moderate indulgence often hazardous; and hence, in one respect, the superiority possessed over them by malt liquors.

In higher circles, where there is good living and

little, work, liquors of any kind are far less necessary, and, till a man gets into the decline of life, they are, except under such circumstances as have been detailed, absolutely useless. When he attains that age, he will be the better of a moderate allowance to recruit the vigor which approaching years steal from the frame. For young and middle-aged men, in good circumstances and vigorous health, water is the best drink ; the food they eat being sufficiently nutritious and stimulating without any assistance from liquor. For young people, in particular, liquors of all kinds are, under common circumstances, not only nnnecessary in health, but exceedingly pernicious, even in what the world denominate *moderate* quantities. This is especially the case when the habit is daily indulged in. One of the first physicians in Ireland has published his conviction on the result of twenty years' observation—'That were ten young men on their twenty-first birth day, to begin to drink one glass (equal to two ounces) of ardent spirits, or a pint of Port wine or Sherry, and were they to drink this *supposed moderate quantity* of strong liquor daily, the lives of eight out of the ten would be abridged by twelve or fifteen years.' 'An American clergyman,' says Professor Edgar, 'lately told me that one of his parishoners was in the habit of sending to his son at school a daily allowance of brandy and water, before the boy was twelve years of age. The consequence was, that his son, before the age of seventeen, was a confirmed drunkard, and he is now confined in a public hospital.' The force of this anecdote must come home to every one, Nothing is more common, even in the best society, than the practice of administering wine, punch, &c., even to children—thus not only injuring their health, and predisposing them to disease, but laying the foundation for intemperance in their maturer years.

Having stated thus much, it is not to be inferred that I advocate the banishment of liquors of any kind from society. Though I believe mankind would be benefited upon the whole, were stimulants to be utterly proscribed, yet, in the present state of things, and knowing the fruitlessness of any such recommendation, I do not go the length of urging their total disuse. I only would wish to inculcate moderation, and that in its proper meaning, and not in the sense too often applied

to it ; for, in the practice of many, moderation, (so called) is intemperance, and perhaps of the most dangerous species, in so far as it becomes a daily practice, and insinuates itself under a false character, into the habits of life. Men thus indulge habitually, day by day, not perhaps to the extent of producing any evident effect either upon the body or mind at the time, and fancy themselves all the while strictly temperate, while they are, in reality, undermining their constitution by slow degrees—killing themselves by inches, and shortening their existence several years. The quantity such persons take at a time, is perhaps moderate and beneficial, if only occasionally indulged in, but, being habitually taken, it injures the health, and thus amounts to actual intemperance. ' It is,' says Dr Beecher, and I fully concur with him, ' a matter of unwonted certainty, that habitual tippling is worse than periodical drunkenness. The poor Indian who once a-month drinks himself *dead*, all but simple breathing, will outlive for years the man who drinks little and often, and is not perhaps suspected of intemperance. The use of ardent spirits *daily* as ministering to cheerfulness or bodily vigour, ought to be regarded as intemperance. No person probably ever did or ever will receive ardents spirits into his system once a-day and fortify his constitution against its deleterious effects, or excroise such discretion and self-government, as that the quantity will not be increased, and bodily infirmities and mental imbecility be the result ; and, in more than half the instances, inebriation. Nature may hold out long against this sapping and mining of the constitution which daily tippling is carrying on, but, first, or last, this foe of life will bring to the assault enemies of its own formation, before whose power the feeble and the mighty will be alike unable to stand.

Let those, therefore, who will not abandon liquors, use them in moderation, and not *habitually* or *day by day*, unless the health should require it, for cases of this kind we sometimes do meet with, though by no means so often as many would believe. Abstractly considered, liquors are not injurious. It is their abuse that makes them so, in the same manner as the most wholesome food becomes pernicious when taken to an improper oxcess.

APPENDIX.

Excerpt from Paris' Pharmacologia.

' The characteristic ingredient of all wines is alcohol, and the quantity of this, and the condition or state of combination in which it exists, are the circumstances that include all the interesting and disputed points of medical inquiry. Daily experience convinces us that the same quantity of alcohol, applied to the stomach under the form of natural wine, and in a state of mixture with water, will produce very different effects upon the body, and to an extent which it *is* difficult to comprehend : it has, for instance, been demonstrated that Port, Madeira, and Sherry, contain from one-fourth to one-fifth of their bulk of alcohol, so that a person who takes a bottle of either of them, will thus take nearly half a pint of alcohol, or almost a pint of pure brandy ! and moreover, that different wines, although of the same specific gravity, and consequently containing the same absolute proportion of spirit, will be found to vary very considerably in their intoxicating powers ; no won-

der, then, that such results should stagger the philosopher, who is naturally unwilling to accept any tests of difference from the nervous system, which elude the ordinary resources of analytical chemistry ; the conclusion was therefore drawn, that alcohol must necessarily exist in wine, in a far different condition from that in which we know it in a separate state, or, in other words, that its elements only could exist in the vinous liquor, and that their union was determined, and, consequently, alcohol produced by the action of distillation. That it was the *product* and not the *educt* of distillation, was an opinion which originated with Rouelle, who asserted that alcohol was not completely formed until the temperature was raised to the point of distillation : more lately, the same doctrine was revived and promulgated by Fabbronni, in the memoirs of the Florentine Academy. Gay-Lussac has, however, silenced the clamorous partisans of this theory, by separating the alcohol by distillation at the temperature of 66o Fah., and by the aid of a vacuum, it has since been effected at 56°; besides, it has been shown that by precipitating the colouring matter, and some of the other elements of the wine, by *sub-acetate* of *lead*, and then saturating the clear liquor with *sub-carbonate* of *potass*, the alcohol may be completely separated without any elevation of temperature ; and this ingenious expédient, Mr Brande has been enabled to construct a table, exhibiting the proportions of combined alcohol which exist in the several kinds of wine : no doubt, therefore, can remain upon this subject, and the fact of the difference of effect, produced by the same bulk of alcohol, when presented to the stomach in different states of combination, adds another striking and instructive illustration to those already enumerated in the course of this work, of the extraordinary powers of chemical combination in modifying the activity of substances upon the living system. In the present instance, the alcohol is so combined with the extractive matter of the wine, that it is probably incapable of exerting its full specific effects upon the stomach, before it becomes altered in its properties, or, in other words, *digested ;* and this view of the subject may be fairly urged in explanation of the reason why the intoxicating effects of the same wine are so liable to vary, in degree, in the same individual, from the peculiar state of his digestive organs at the time of his potation. Hitherto we have only spoken of pure wine, but it is essential to state, that the stronger wines of Spain, Portugal, and Sicily, are rendered remarkable in this country by the addition of brandy, and must consequently contain *uncombined* alcohol, the proportion of which, however, will not necessarily bear a ratio to the quantity added, because, at the period of its admixture, a renewed fermentation is produced by the scientific vintner, which will assimilate and combine a certain portion of the foreign spirit with the wine : this manipulation, in technical language, is called *fretting-in.* The free alcohol may, according to the experiments of Fabbroni, be immediately separated by saturating the vinous fluid with *sub-carbonate* of *potass,* while the combined portion will remain undisturbed: in ascertaining the fabrication and salubrity of a wine, this circumstance ought always to constitute a leading feature in the inquiry ; and the tables of Mr Brande would have been greatly enhanced in practical value, had the relative proportions of *uncombined* spirit been appreciated in his experiments, since it is to this, and not to the *combined* alcohol, that the injurious effects of wine are to be attributed. 'It is well known,' observes Dr Macculloch, ' that diseases of the liver are the most common, and the most formidable of those produced by the use of *ardent* spirits ; it is equally certain that no such disorders follow the intemperate use of *pure* wine, however long indulged in : to the concealed and unwitting consumption of spirit, therefore, as contained in the wines commonly drunk in this country, is to be attributed the excessive prevalence of those hepatic affections, which are comparatively little known to our continental neighbors.' Thus much is certain, that their ordinary wines contain no alcohol but what is disarmed of its virulence by the prophylactic energies of combination.'

THE END.

CONTENTS OF THE ANATOMY OF DRUNKENNESS.

CPSIA information can be obtained
at www.ICGtesting.com
Printed in the USA
BVHW080421231118
533756BV00029B/1095/P